NOTE .

SAID KEN
INSISTED ON
COVER PIC BEING
"WRONG WAY AROUND"
IE LEFT HAND
IS ACTUAL RIGHT
HAND PROFILE OF
CAR. CARB
INTAKE BOULGE

MANAGING A
LEGEND

By the same author:

ARCHIE AND THE LISTERS
ORIGINAL ASTON MARTIN

As part of our ongoing market research, we are always pleased to receive comments about our books, suggestions for new titles, or requests for catalogues. Please write to: The Editorial Director, G T Foulis & Co., Sparkford, near Yeovil, Somerset, BA22 7JJ.

MANAGING A LEGEND

STIRLING MOSS, KEN GREGORY AND THE BRITISH RACING PARTNERSHIP

ROBERT EDWARDS

First published in 1997

British Library Cataloguing-in-Publication Data: A Catalogue record for this book is available from the British Library

ISBN 0-85429-988-2

Library of Congress catalog card no. 97-72863

G T Foulis & Company is an imprint of Haynes Publishing, Sparkford, near Yeovil, Somerset, BA22 7JJ
Tel: 01963 440635 Fax: 01963 440001
Int. tel: +44 1963 440635 Fax: +44 1963 440001
E-mail: sales@haynes-manuals.co.uk
Web site: http://www.haynes.com

Haynes North America Inc, 861 Lawrence Drive, Newbury Park, California 91320, USA.

Book design, Christopher Gregory
Albion, 41 Eastcheap, London EC3M 1AS

Jacket design, Christopher Gregory and Richard Peacock

Jacket photography, Susan Bradley LBIPP, LMPA

Set in Stone Serif

Printed and Bound in Great Britain by
Creative Print and Design (Wales), Ebbw Vale

Contents

FOR RACHAEL AND ISABEL

Acknowledgements

A large number of people have cheerfully contributed to the writing of this book. Given that I have no direct experience of the events contained herein, I have relied, heavily, upon a host of recollections. I am pleased to report that while there have emerged differences of emphasis and detail, the comparisons between those recollections have been pleasingly consistent.

Obviously, Ken Gregory, Tony Robinson and Stirling Moss have all been extraordinarily helpful, particularly Ken and Tony, whose insistence upon accuracy has been exemplary; the contributions of both fact and anecdote, not to mention photographs, have played a very important role in fleshing out the tale. Gregory could teach history.

Elsewhere, I am grateful to Martin Brundle, Valerie Pirie, Bruce McIntosh, Rod Gueran, Brian Lister, Tony Brooks, Bruce Halford, Raymond Baxter, Doug Nye, Ross Finlay, Tony Dron, Paul Sheldon, Keith Mathieson, Fabian and Jeremy Samengo-Turner, Cyril Kieft, Rob Walker, Jack Sears, Peter Jopp, David Haynes, Les Leston and Rivers Fletcher, not to mention Susie Moss and Julie Gregory. Julie tolerated the revisiting of times past, not always happy times, either, with marvellous insouciance.

Further, I would like to thank Patrick Stephens, Darryl Reach, Alison Roelich, Harry Calton, Michelle Miller, David Strecker, Simon Banham and John Hardaker. Invaluable (and I mean invaluable) technical help was given by Christopher Gregory, who also designed the cover, and further technical support was given by Alistair Tomkins and Paul Kennedy.

The encouragement and support which I encountered

everywhere was extraordinary; the story of the British Racing Partnership is one which still captures the imagination, and more than one person I encountered still recalls the sense of disappointment they felt when the team finally closed; when they learn the reason, indignation often replaces it.

The Daimler-Benz Museum, the Indianapolis Raceway and the Royal Automobile Club have proved themselves to be utterly splendid institutions; their willingness to take up this subject and offer help with statistics, photographs, contacts and suggestions has transcended mere co-operation.

Support and encouragement are hard to quantify when you are a scribbler; we all know that there is only one way to do it, and that is the right way. Getting there is something else entirely. For all his comments, corrections, hints, suggestions and general professorial input, as well as the odd glass, I would particularly like to single out Dottore Mike Lawrence. For her perseverance, patience, commitment to my doing 'a proper job', as well as putting up with the invasion of her house by the memories of people she had never even heard of, let alone known, I must thank and applaud my wife, Sarah.

List of Illustrations

Foreword

'The more things change, the more they stay the same.' I've often heard that saying and without doubt it applies to Formula One motor racing. However, the similarities are as startling as the differences between the post war era and today.

I very much enjoyed reading the text for this book because it served again to remind me of the incredible risk and sacrifice of the post war drivers, indeed well into the 1970's. What motivated them to squeeze the throttle harder against such appalling odds of death or injury? The quotes, facts and feelings portrayed in these pages make it clear that these were revolutionary, gladiatorial and exciting times in motor racing when camaraderie and respect amongst the drivers was clearly a driving force and a key factor. It is different now, and the haphazard way in which drivers, teams, formulae, races and even championships emerged in those days was somewhat strange too.

The similarities are equally striking. The early quest for sponsorship to create a more competitive team through larger budgets, keeping the other teams behind the game, to then immediately look back over the shoulder as they politically regroup to redress the balance of power. With a few more zeros Ken Gregory could be talking about the 90's. With hindsight it is obvious that racing cars and drivers would become an advertising medium, but back in the 50's it must have been great foresight.

I remember a well known hot shoe team mate of mine giving a journalist a very hard time. I asked him why he was so tough on the guy and he expressed a strong belief that the likes of Carraciola did not need sponsors, press or PR so why should he? He constantly read books relating to previous eras, and he may not have been as thankful for those early commercial initiatives as most of today's wealthy owners and drivers, not to mention designers, engineers and mechanics certainly are.

In 1981 I was team mate to Stirling Moss in the works Audis. I will always vividly remember his drive in the rain at Brands Hatch. I looked up to him then, and even more so now that I know more of the ingredients of the Pa Moss, Stirling Moss, Ken Gregory relationship, and the many colourful characters who contributed along the way.

Martin Brundle
Norfolk, England.
20 June 1997

Author's Note

This is a book about an activity which started out as a sport and became a business – the business of motor racing. It starts nearly 50 years ago and portrays aspects of the development of motor sport into a financial, as well as a sporting, endeavour. Many of the names will be familiar, even to those who know next to nothing of motor sport – names like Stirling Moss, Juan Manuel Fangio, Graham Hill, Jim Clark. There are a host of others, though, who played their part in transforming what was previously an activity for the merely leisured into the unparalleled global business that it is today.

The man who is central to my story, Ken Gregory, was once a racing driver, an official of the sport, most famously the business manager of Stirling Moss, an airline operator and an entrepreneur. There is one thing for which Gregory, and indeed Moss, have never received the recognition (or blame, depending upon your point of view) which they clearly deserve, and that is their role in turning motor racing into something like the creature it is today. To use Moss's words: 'A great occasion, but not a sport.' Charles Jarrott had, of course, expressed similar sentiments before this in his classic *Ten Years of Motor Racing*. In 1906.

It was Ken Gregory's association with Alfred Moss, Stirling's father, which provided the mainspring for modern Formula 1 as a business. Colin Chapman, with his famous deal with John Player's tobacco merely imitated what the Moss/Gregory company, the British Racing Partnership, had already accomplished seven years earlier with their sponsorship arrangements – first, with Yeoman Credit and, later, with UDT Laystall – to operate what became the first

Formula 1 enterprise funded entirely by someone else's money. It is probably fair to say that Chapman took a lot more out, pound for pound, than either Ken Gregory or Alfred Moss would have dreamed of; but by then he could do it—the inflation had started.

Ken Gregory, in many ways the antecedent of Bernie Ecclestone, for a while virtually dictated the direction which a section of the sport was to take; first with the British Racing and Sports Car Club and then with his unique management of Stirling Moss. It was his faith in Moss's abilities, not always shared by their exponent, which by 1959 brought him to a position where he started to set the price of motor racing.

In this book there are many heroes, a few villains and several clowns; there is genius and venality, heroism and mere placemanship, engineering (and sporting) brilliance and ruthless cynicism. The financial details may seem unnecessarily prurient—they are included only because some sort of benchmark is required. The staggering amounts of money paid today by sponsors and to drivers (and the only relatively high costs of the sport then) should be put into some perspective. To some of the people you will read about here, money was vital; to others it was a thing to be despised, whether they had it or not; but to all of them, some sort of survival, with the exception of possibly one or two, was paramount. Many were disappointed.

I have to confess that I have never driven a competition car in anger; I have never known the sickening little slide of despair which must be felt when the engine lets go, or the transmission breaks, or a wheel falls off, or the resolve simply goes away, never to return. I wish that I had; it would enable me to understand more comprehensively what it was that drove a man like Stirling Moss to do what he did for a living. I have read almost every word written by or about him in preparation for this book, and, of course, I have also met him. He redefines, even at a distance of 35 years since his last race, the word 'competitive'. In writing this, I hope that I have come a little closer to comprehending, and passing on, something of both the age which produced him and the sport in which he was supreme. Moss's career is a matter of public record and this is no place to harp on about it; it is mentioned as it affects the relationship between the two men, or as it affected the development of the sport.

For it was a sport. Just as flat-racing had always been costly, post-war motor racing was destined to become so; from the early efforts of Charlie and John Cooper, Colin Chapman, Geoffrey Taylor and many others, opposed tooth and nail by the established players in Italy, with both sides truly appalled by the majesty of the German effort, the activity of motor racing evolved into, first, a national conflict, and then, as memories of the war receded, purely a technical one. It has further evolved into a financial one, and yet, happily, many of the extraordinary personal qualities which I have discovered while researching this book can still be found. The business of motor racing, however much money is thrown at it, remains unchanged at heart—it is about winning.

Preface

In late 1958, over an extremely expensive, unexpected and pleasant lunch, a young man was offered an extraordinary deal by a firm of financiers. It was simple. They would buy and equip a team of Formula 1 racing cars, and he would manage that team. The cars would be known not by the manufacturer's, nor the team manager's name, but by the owners', who would, significantly, keep all the trophies. This is what happened ...

Robert Edwards, Ditchling, E. Sussex, 1997

Prologue

LONDON 1949

To the rather undernourished young man in the singularly ill-fitting demob suit, the imposing premises at 83 Pall Mall, London SW1, must have seemed a singularly improbable place to be. He was awaiting an interview with Colonel Stanley Barnes, the Competitions Manager of the Royal Automobile Club. Essentially, he was there to talk about a clerical job; he had never seen a motor race, and despite the fact that he had been an army engineering apprentice, his most recent military activity had been that of glider pilot, an activity seldom even touched by the internal combustion engine, save to haul his massive unpowered Horsa military glider into the air. He was 22 years old, badly dressed, apprehensive and functionally broke. His name was Ken Gregory.

Life so far had not been easy for Gregory. He was born in Ashton-under-Lyne on 29 July 1926, the most significant historical event of that year, in May, having been the General Strike. He was not to know that a man, Alfred Moss, destined to play a part in loco parentis in his life had performed a modest function as a volunteer bus driver during that event. He lost his own father to tuberculosis at the age of five and, after an unseemly squabble over custody between his two sets of grandparents, he had been packed off as a boarder, at the age of seven, to the Bluecoat School in Oldham, Lancashire. Whatever family wealth there had been had not survived either the stock market crash or the great depression, and his mother had had to learn a profession in order to survive. She had chosen nursing, and after training for four years, while her son endured the

Dickensian conditions of the Bluecoat, she qualified as a nurse from St Mary's Hospital in Manchester.

TB not only claimed Ken's father, it almost carried Ken off as well. Medical opinion was that the city life was not for him, but for economic reasons a neat and expensive clinic in the mountain fastness of Switzerland was not a realistic option. So he was shunted out of the Bluecoat and off to Blackpool for a healthy dose of what seaside landladies called ozone. It worked, but he was not to be properly reunited with his mother until she secured a job, more than a year later, in the Lake District as a Nurse to the Patterdale District Nursing Association. They settled, with Ken's brother John, in the village of Glenridding at the southern end of Lake Ullswater.

It was a simple, Doctor Finlayish kind of life. Mrs Gregory had the use of a car – the inevitable Austin Seven Ruby – and most of her work was to do with midwifery. It was an important job in those slightly prudish days before pregnancy really became a medical matter.

By the time he was 14, Ken's formal education was over, which was hardly uncommon and not merely because the war had started. Those whose financial standing had taken such a brutal knock in the depression were not in a position to afford full-time secondary or higher education, even if they were minded to. The obstacles posed by school certificate, let alone University entrance, were as much economic as they were intellectual, and while Ken's education was as comprehensive as was possible, there were gaps in it; a matter of which he was fully aware even at that tender age. The university of hard knocks would fill them.

The recuperative qualities of the Lake District air worked sufficiently well to repair his damaged lungs. After a brief spell at Hanson's garage in Penrith, he joined the Army as an apprentice in January 1942 and was sent to Arborfield in Berkshire to enrol in the Army Technical School, which made him into quite a decent engineer. The Army recouped their investment by sending him to Catterick, where he used his new-found skills to rebuild tank engines, among other things; but it was to the air that his enthusiasms were more and more directed. He volunteered for the Glider Pilot regiment and was accepted, after a rather more rigorous medical (set by the RAF) than he had had before. The fact that he passed it, and survived the subsequent training, says much about the judgement of those who recommended his treatment for TB.

The Glider Pilot regiment, a part of the Army Air Corps, had taken a truly dreadful hammering at Arnhem in the third week of September 1944. No less than 1,262 pilots, some 90 per cent of the strength of the entire unit, had been directly committed to the action; 58 per cent of them were killed in action, wounded, or taken prisoner. The regiment had already sustained heavy casualties in the Normandy landings in June; now it was left almost totally bereft of qualified pilots – so an urgent call went out for replacements.

Ken's training, although hurried, seemed to be effective. He learned to fly on the inevitable Tiger Moth, but not without incident – he nearly put down in the grounds of 'a large house by the Thames' when chronically short of fuel; it transpired that it was, actually, Windsor Castle. He qualified as a pilot, which instantly conferred upon him the rank of sergeant, the minimum rank that a pilot could be, and it was in that capacity that he had arrived at the offices of the Soldiers', Sailors', and Airmen's Families Association in Ecclestone Square, Victoria, and from thence to the Royal Automobile Club, Pall Mall.

Colonel Barnes, avuncular and tweedy, rather took to him. Gregory, sensibly still not quite out of soldier mode, seemed a level-headed fellow, properly respectful and prepared to work hard. To Barnes, who was tasked with managing what appeared to be an almost unseemly explosion of interest in motor racing – the governing body of which was the RAC – speed was not only the essence of the sport, but also the main imperative in handling the vast amount of enquiries, liaison, public relations, licence applications and logistics of a pastime which, up to now, had been almost purely the pursuit of the leisured and the moneyed.

The reason for the change was a Vauxhall dealer in Surbiton, Surrey, of all places. His name was Charles Cooper and he had restarted, post-war, an exhausted business by sawing up pre-war Baby Fiat Topolinos and welding the front ends together to produce complete push-me-pull-you chassis with independent springing on all four wheels. The addition of a JAP motorcycle engine and Berman gearbox (in the back, for Heaven's sake) and some minimalist contour-hugging bodywork, had produced a cheap, reliable and revolutionary competition car, which he had offered for series production from the beginning of 1948. He knew his stuff, Cooper, having been a racing mechanic to Kaye Don before the war.

Charles Cooper was not the first to do this, of course, but he was certainly the best and the most successful and was selling into an already fertile and enthusiastic market. The 500 Club had been set up in December 1945, within months of the end of the war, in Bristol. The awareness of motor cars and motoring had been confined, before the war, to those who could actually afford to do it. Now, it was different. A whole slice of society had had direct exposure to engineering, in some shape or form, during the recent conflict, and had found it, to coin a phrase, quite riveting. Many people had experienced speed (and fear) for the first time as a direct result of the war, whether in aircraft, military vehicles, tractors or motorcycles. Cooper, of course, cared little for the strain that this new craze put upon the limited resources of the RAC; the purpose of his venture was to get his business back on to a secure footing, ravaged as it had been by the war. Shortages of both cars and petrol (then still rationed and of dubious quality), and customers, few of whom either had motor cars or money, had made things very hard.

At 83 Pall Mall the atmosphere was one of somewhat bemused optimism. The application for a competition licence was a matter of filling in a form and sending in a £3 fee. There was no medical test, merely a declaration form. The whole process was a matter of trust. The volume, as a result of this, was high. Gregory was even asked to manage the organisation of the London to Brighton Veteran Car run, so thinly stretched was the operation.

Now that Ken Gregory had a proper job, he was able to address the issue of finding a place to live. After some looking, in competition with many who were better off than he was, he found an absolutely tiny flat in Kidderpore Avenue, off Finchley Road in West Hampstead. It was pretty much as central as he could afford. The landlord was a Dr Philippe Bauwens, Professor of Physical Medicine at St Thomas's Hospital. He and Gregory had first met during the war, one of those random occasions which could easily not have happened, but did. It was later to have important consequences for motor racing.

In West Sussex, not far from Chichester, an ex-fighter base at Westhampnett aerodrome, located on property owned by the Duke of Richmond and Gordon but repossessed by him from the RAF after the war, opened its gates on 18 September 1948 – near enough Battle of Britain Sunday. It was motor racing – essentially pre-war style, as there was no other – around the perimeter track. Since the demise of Brooklands as a viable circuit, through its having been taken over by Vickers during the war and, as a result comprehensively wrecked, the Duke, a keen motorist, was making a tentative bid to keep motor racing as part of the English social season. It was to work very well as a strategy, despite the rather basic facilities, until the power of the vehicles involved outstripped the ability of the circuit to contain them, but the inaugural event put on to the stage a young man who was, after a series of successful hill-climbs and sprints, undertaking his first competitive circuit event – a three-lapper which he won going away at just a shade under 73 mph. Some observers felt that he was trying rather too hard – why, it almost seemed that he had practised! Very impressive and all that, but really!

The boy was but a teenager, still living at home. His support team consisted of his father, mother and a German ex-POW, Donatus Müller, who was little more than an enthusiastic farm labourer. The boy was to become arguably the most well-known figure ever in motor racing history. His name was Stirling Craufurd Moss and he would meet Ken Gregory quite soon.

It went like this ...

Chapter 1

MOSS

'People will not look forward to posterity, who
never look backward to their ancestors.'
EDMUND BURKE

Stirling Moss not only came from a prosperous background, which Gregory did not, but also one which had a definite link with the sport, which Gregory's did not. The Gregory family, in common with many in those days, had never owned a car. Stirling's father Alfred had been a racer pre-war, competing both at Brooklands and, unusual then, Indianapolis in 1924 and 1925. He had fought a modest rearguard action against Stirling's ambition to race, claiming that if he couldn't make a living at it, then how could his son? He would find out soon enough.

Stirling's mother, Aileen, nee Craufurd, who actually wanted to call her son Hamish, lost the argument over names, and thus unwittingly deprived Scotland, as opposed to a wider Britain, of a claim to her son's later greatness. He was, in fact, named after her home City. Aileen had also been a successful competitor before the war in rallies, driving a Marendaz Special. An ancestor of hers had been General Sir Robert 'Black Bob' Craufurd, who had commanded the Light Division during the Peninsular War in Spain and sat in Parliament for East Retford, a pocket borough in the gift of his sister-in-law, the Dowager Duchess of Newcastle. He had been the man who had held together a large part of Sir John Moore's army during its awful retreat to Coruña during the savage Spanish winter of 1808-09. A brilliant but hard soldier, he thought nothing of halting the retreat in order to supervise the administration of 100 lashes to the more recalcitrant of his division. He died – deeply mourned by all who knew him, even the victims of his ferocious discipline – in 1812, after grievous wounds received at the siege of Cuidad Rodrigo, one of the final battles of the savage Peninsular War.

Alfred Moss was a dental surgeon – a good one, too, and something of a businessman as well as being good with his hands. He hailed originally from Golders Green in North London. His dental practice extended to no less than 17 surgeries and a dental workshop, from Bond Street to the Mile End Road – he was, as it were, almost a wholesaler in teeth, and he had qualified as a dentist in America. Alfred was to develop painless dentistry, not on the Doc Holliday pattern, but on the basis of using such alternative techniques as hypnotherapy. He had several other interests, including a farm, and the young Stirling had been encouraged into the field of hotel management after leaving public school. He tried it but it palled; at that stage he was an ambitious but diffident young man, ill at ease in dealing with the public. In a racing car one could communicate with the public without having to deal with them face to face, making statements rather more profound, perhaps, than the polite enquiry to guests as to the happiness of their stay. No Uriah Heep, this; but chronically shy.

Alfred was something of an inventor. His most useful contribution to the war effort was to design the Morrison shelter. Whereas the Anderson shelter was a confection of corrugated iron and sandbags, the Morrison version was more substantial and designed to fit over a bed or a table – the idea came from the cradles used to protect the limbs of patients in hospital. It was of course named after Herbert Morrison, the Minister of Supply, rather than its inventor, who preferred to sleep through air raids rather than be inconvenienced by them. One other of Alfred's inventions was a rocket system to be attached to barrage balloons – as the enemy aircraft snagged the cable of the balloon, the rocket would finish it off. This was, perhaps wisely, dropped.

Ken Gregory and Stirling Moss had a nodding acquaintance via the RAC which was cemented in the autumn of 1949, after Gregory had been appointed assistant to the secretary of the 500 Club at the salary of £1 a week. It was something of a boost, this moonlighting, as it upped his income by exactly 20 per cent. One of Gregory's first tasks was to organise the Club's first end-of-season dinner dance at the Rubens Hotel, Victoria, where he found himself, no doubt deliberately, sharing a table with Moss and Peter John Collins, an affable young sprig from Kidderminster. All three were firm friends from that day on, particularly Moss and Gregory. A small deceit had allowed Moss to stay, ostensibly, at Gregory's tiny flat – more of a garret, really – instead of going home with his parents. The reason was, unsurprisingly, a girl. Plenty of them had been brought to the dinner by both Collins and his apparently shy friend.

The man who would become arguably Britain's greatest racing driver was born on 29 September 1929 at Queen Charlotte's Maternity Hospital in West London. As well as being a dental practitioner and businessman in London, Alfred Moss owned a farm near Maidenhead, and later another at Tring where, totally at odds with his cultural inheritance, he bred pedigree pigs. After prep. school, he sent Stirling to Haileybury, which had in the past specialised in providing talent for the East India Company as well as the British Army in India. (The British military presence in India had been, up to and including the Mutiny of 1858, entirely the bailiwick of 'John Company'). This tradition, despite its rather chequered track record, combined with the fact that Stirling's education was also a wartime one, would rather mould his character. His disappointment at being unable to undertake National Service in the RAF, or anywhere else for that matter, because of a recurring kidney complaint, was vast. Given that the air service was to provide many of the brightest talents of the post-war racing scene – Abecassis, Protheroe, Anthony Crook, 'Lofty' England, Brian Lister, John Tojeiro and many more, he was spurred on to be an immediately competitive man. His kidney problems also made him usefully teetotal; he was thus often to find himself at a distinct advantage on the grid against some of his more raffish opponents.

A whole generation of children, reared in wartime and destined to be spectators at, and often orphaned by, the great events which saved Europe, were, in the immediate post-war years, keen to prove that they were the spiritual successors to the heroes which the conflict had produced. Given that the war was no longer available as a stage upon which to show mettle, the opportunities offered by the efforts of Charles Cooper and his son John came a very close second. The names would become celebrated – Hawthorn, Collins, Brooks, Salvadori, Lewis-Evans, Scott Brown and, the best-known of all, Moss himself.

Ken Gregory was pitched right into the midst of this organisational nightmare. There was a logical fit between his activities at the RAC and his role as an organiser, and later secretary, of the 500 Club, but it was not one which Colonel Barnes always understood. Barnes tended to view it more as a conflict of interest than a particular convenience, given that the RAC was less profit-oriented and already more established than the 500 Club. Gregory's relations with Barnes and the RAC were to survive a little longer, sometimes shakily, but there is no doubt that Ken Gregory was well and truly smitten by this new movement, which was to be the direct precursor of the Grand Prix industry of today.

Stirling had put down a deposit on another 500 machine, a Marwyn, before settling on a Cooper; but Alfred took one look at it and vetoed the idea, citing the fact that Stirling was a minor, being under 21, and neatly voiding the contract. He took the view that there was no point in being experimental about this. If his son was going to race, he would at least have the best equipment that money could buy. It was probably just as well; the Marwyn marque never made it into the archives – at least, not that this writer can discover – and Alfred had cut his own teeth at Indianapolis on Frontenac Fords designed by the immortal Louis Chevrolet, so he knew of what he spoke.

Chapter 2

STARTING

*'If you can fill the unforgiving minute
With sixty seconds' worth of distance run,
Yours is the Earth and everything that's in it,
And – which is more, you'll be a man, my son!'*
RUDYARD KIPLING, 1910

There were few armchair critics of motor sport in its early post-war days; it was exclusively a live event with little or no television or newsreel coverage, and those who were present at Goodwood on 18 September 1948 were certainly not unanimous that the young Moss was touched with greatness. Some considered him an erratic young plunger who would overdo it one day and probably not live to regret it. Such an initial opinion in the sport is neither rare nor always wrong, but in this case it was grossly misplaced. Anyone who had read the competition Press over the previous six months would have known that this prodigy had won seven out of the last 10 events which he had entered – all hill-climbs and sprints up to now – so clearly this was no flash in the pan. Doubtless, there was more than a hint of green about – not British racing green, but the other kind. This lad had qualified for the elite – he had already been admitted to the British Racing Drivers' Club, which included hill-climbs in its qualifying events in those days.

Others, Ken Gregory included, who did not see Moss race until a year less a day later, on 17 September 1949, differed in their view. Actually, had he looked carefully, he would have noticed Moss winning the 500cc race at the British Grand Prix meeting at Silverstone on 14 May, but he was busy diving about in the control tower, which served as the race control office, so he didn't. Gregory saw in Moss, when he did eventually watch one of his races, not some curly-headed youngster 'having a go', but rather a person who seemed to find the very act of driving an expression of something else entirely. Of course, in his role in the 500 Club, Gregory heard little else but news of Stirling Moss, so immediate was the boy's impact on the sport.

Another spectator at that September Goodwood race was one Alfons Kovaleski; he had started work for John Heath and George Abecassis at around the same time as Ken Gregory had started working for Colonel Barnes – he was in the process of becoming a naturalised British citizen after war service in the Polish Brigade. His adoptive name would become almost as well known as Stirling's, in motor racing circles at least – Alf Francis.

It was not the first time that he had seen his future employer race; that had been on Easter Monday at the same circuit and, as he disarmingly stated in his memoirs: 'I must admit that at this time I saw Moss as a rather thrusting driver who tended to push his car and himself just a little too near the limit. How wrong I was.' And, later: 'Most of us, drivers and mechanics, held the same views about the young man. We were sure that sooner or later he would overdo things and that once would be enough. Then he would slow down and we would not hear much more about him. That was the general opinion.'

Kovaleski/Francis was to revise his opinion within months, as were many others. HWM (Hersham & Walton Motors), his employers at Walton-on-Thames, not far from Surbiton, were contemplating a team of sports cars based on the HW Alta with which they had campaigned in 1949. By December 1949 they were offering Moss a test drive in the new car at Odiham airfield in Hampshire. One reason for this apparent turnaround was that George Abecassis, a partner at HWM, had written off his own Cooper attempting to match Moss's practice times around the Manx Cup circuit on the Isle of Man.

The test went well, despite the HWM ripping its sump off on a landing light, and Moss was signed up for 1950. It was clear to all who witnessed the test that the earlier view of Moss was almost certainly wrong; despite his youth, here was a boy who could, almost completely by instinct, drive very fast indeed.

What sets motor racing totally apart from other sports is, of course, its inherent danger; the demands of concentration which it therefore imposes upon its participants are unmatched by any other game, and the price of losing that focus is commensurately higher. Any doubts which Stirling had about his own ability, and there were very few, were steamrollered by Alfred who was, effectively, his manager at that stage. He pushed his son hard, always encouraging, always looking for that extra something which marks out the truly great in any occupation, but particularly that of motor racing, the most competitive sport the world has ever known, even at this relatively junior level.

It worked. We, the public, often suspect that those characteristics which make you a nice person often act against you in a competitive situation, and some fall into the trap of assuming that the converse of that statement must be true. There is a universe of sportsmen, particularly in non-risk sports, specifically some of the stick and ball games, whose conduct would bear out both statements, and this makes all successful sportsmen seem somehow unapproachable. This is why we are often wary of them and why the yellow press constantly offers up examples of why such genius must be flawed, because many people find that thought pleasing or, at least, reassuring.

The competitors in motor racing in the late 1940s and early 1950s were, as they had been pre-war, almost exclusively amateur – in the post-war world there were few bright spots to lighten the view into a dreadful gloom. Rationing, particularly of fuel, was still under the control of the Ministry of Supply, and the allowances were meagre. There were areas of hyperinflation; particularly of cars, which could not be produced because of steel rationing, and the prices of even mundane vehicles of pre-war origin were rammed northward by the motor trade, some of whom had honed their skills in the black market during the war years. Many of them also raced; and some of them, on the starting grid, would have failed a breathalyser test, if such a thing had been invented then.

Moss was different. Still legally a minor, his outlook may well have been moulded by Haileybury; a wartime education while being steeped in the values and imperatives of Empire had given him an inner confidence of the kind so often resented by those who have come up against the English public schoolboy at his most competitive.

Outwardly, Moss was painfully shy. The enforced regimentation of someone who later would be revealed as something of an individualist has its downside, too. The most telling result of Stirling's education, though, was a patriotism bordering on the chauvinistic which was unable to find expression for some years. In its stead, a sober, tightly wound mien, which found its best outlet on the circuit, rather tended to define Moss to that growing group of people who were getting to know him.

One of those, of course, was Ken Gregory. The two had cemented their friendship in a variety of ways. That Gregory was an official of Moss's governing club actually had little to do with it – the relationship was essentially fraternal, with Gregory's almost pernickety attention to detail, honed in both the services and the RAC, balancing Moss's raw drive.

So, the 1949 season ended auspiciously for Moss, with a works drive in one of the few British contenders which were remotely competitive against European Formula 2 opposition. It was to be a relatively happy association, lasting two seasons.

Chapter 3

SEPARATE BUT PARALLEL PATHS

*'Friendship needs a certain parallelism of life,
a community of thought, a rivalry of aim.'*
HENRY BROOKS ADAMS, 1907

It was all very well for Ken Gregory to be working in the sport for both the RAC and the 500 Club, but he had never actually driven a racing car. It was a gap in his resumé which he was itching to fill. Currently carless, he had owned in his Army days a Riley 9 Monaco saloon car, hardly a roadburner, but was chafing at the competition bit somewhat. His opportunity to shine came one evening when working at his flat in Kidderpore Avenue, Hampstead, on the forthcoming 500 Club meeting at Brands Hatch in April 1950. It was to be the very first motor car race on the new one-mile circuit and required careful planning; the 'phone rang.

On the other end was a kitchenware manufacturer from Bridgend, South Wales, whose name was Cyril Kieft. He had built a Formula 3 car, but had yet to acquire either engine or driver. Could Gregory recommend either?

Well, certainly he could recommend a driver – Kieft was talking to him. A short pause. Fine. As for an engine; well, a Vincent would do nicely. A mistake, this, but Kieft, to whom one engine was very much like another, readily agreed and an entry was made for 16 April at Brands Hatch, with K. A. Gregory piloting his first racing car, a Kieft-Vincent.

Brands Hatch had been a motorcycle grass track, but it had come to the notice of the 500 Club that it had recently been resurfaced rather nicely with smooth tarmac. At a circuit distance of a mile, with excellent visibility for both drivers and spectators, it was ideal for small capacity cars, particularly single-seaters, and the track ran anticlockwise, which was unusual. The entry list, Gregory knew, was huge, with plenty of drivers attempting their debuts; so he was in good company, even if he was in the wrong car.

The best way to learn is to watch, so Gregory accompanied Moss to Chichester for Stirling's debut with the HWM at Goodwood, where he came a creditable second in the handicap race behind the late Duncan Hamilton in a Maserati. The HWM was the most powerful car that Stirling had handled up to now and – while the meeting was overall a disappointment for HWM, with poor weather and niggling mechanical troubles – he acquitted himself well. The prophets of doom from the previous year were slowly coming to terms with the fact that Moss really was someone different, with an attitude that redefined 'competitive'.

There was another reason why Gregory had to go – Stirling had been naughty in his Morris Minor and had had a driving ban imposed for driving without due care and attention. It had been nothing of the sort, actually – he had merely squealed the tyres at a junction in Maidenhead, which to the rotter who reported him must have seemed appalling. The specific charge was ironic, of course, since Moss never did, indeed never does, anything much without total care and attention, as he was to prove quite soon. A driver without a road licence, though, may not ordinarily hold a competition one, but this rule may be circumvented, particularly if one's best mate is rising fast in the Competitions department of the RAC. The issue was brushed under the carpet as a mere technicality; to scratch a marque debut under such trivial circumstances was clearly quite unthinkable. Friends at court.

Gregory and Moss were fast becoming inseparable. Moss, now that he was legally an adult, had started to lead a fairly blistering social life, and Gregory was at times rather pushed to keep up. The pair, despite their similarities, had rather different constitutions; Moss stayed up late and rose late, whereas Gregory had a proper job to do and kept more conventional hours. These differences became all too obvious a little later on when the pair decided to share a flat together. To some observers, the pair seemed joined at the hip; but the reality was a little different.

Gregory's own racing debut was, to say the least, inauspicious. Not only was the Kieft rather hastily thought out – one dare not say naïvely built – it had the wrong engine, (actually Gregory's choice) unusual suspension and thus rather odd handling. The Vincent engine in 1000cc V twin form, as designed by Phil Irving, later of Repco, was a thing of great beauty and terrific power; but its 500cc antecedent was somewhat less inspiring and was considerably inferior to the opposition. It was no accident that there were relatively few 500cc Vincent-engined racers.

In contrast, the J.A. Prestwich 500cc speedway unit – fuelled by methanol, gas-flowed, balanced and running a fearsome 14:1 compression ratio – was the usual choice of the cognoscenti, including Coopers themselves. Certainly, Moss used one in his car, although Peter Collins favoured a Norton.

The other point, of course, was that Gregory wasn't actually a particularly experienced driver. At Brands Hatch he came nowhere, as the unsuitable engine seized, but nor did Stirling, who also broke down.

The meeting itself, though, was a success, and started for Gregory a long association with Brands Hatch. It also started a long association with Cyril Kieft, who was cheerily unconcerned at the car's modest performance. In fact, Kieft was to accomplish much as a manufacturer, and making cars was a pleasant change from pots and pans. Gregory, displaying an emerging acuity which would eventually become something of a trademark, neatly trousered a pair of directorships for himself and Stirling in Kieft's company. The purpose was mainly promotional; for, quite soon, the new prototype Kieft car would be made not in Bridgend, but in a mews behind Victoria station, which was far more convenient for Ken and Stirling, even if it wasn't for Cyril. Moss used the opportunity offered to drop in on Ray Martin, whose garage it was, and learn all he could about engineering. He learned to weld, to panel beat, to overhaul; he became, in a relatively short time, extremely well-informed about any aspect of the art of car building which he thought would be useful to him, although he never exhibited any great interest in cars except as things to race.

This effective annexation of the Kieft project, to be redesigned with Norton power under the eye of Ray Martin, John A. Cooper, sports editor of the *Autocar,* and Dean Delamont of the RAC competition department, gave a new focus to the Moss/Gregory alliance. For Gregory, never a man to risk vertigo by looking back downward, his progress had been remarkable. Less than two years after first clapping eyes on a racing car, he was rising fast in the RAC, playing a pivotal role in the 500 Club, and was a company director, drifting into an alliance with some of the prominenti of the racing world. If this made him feel heady, he did not show it particularly, but resolved to stick at racing for a while, for he was on the verge of virtual addiction.

So, although Cyril Kieft's first effort wasn't much of a goer, Gregory persisted with it, and 1950 was to be a whirl of chaotic activity, with forays to the Continent as well as

UK circuits. Moss, despite his role as a director of Kieft, preferred to let his friend Gregory drive the little Welsh car, while he kept his Cooper-JAP to fill in between engagements for HWM.

The HWM-Alta was built under conditions which could only be described as noisome. The team, led by Alf Francis, struggled with old equipment more suitable for basic repair than construction, in premises which resembled an oil-filled coal mine. Money was perpetually tight and the hours would have had any trade unionist apoplectic with outrage. The set-up was semi-feudal and no benchmark for an industrial relations strategy, but for Francis, no self-sacrifice was too much – he had made a decision that his adopted country would have an all-British winning car, even if it killed him. The former diesel fitter and clockmaker from Grudziadz, Poland, would find a way. He was to succeed, but not at HWM.

The HWM was, of course, as history has told us, a very good car indeed. It really had absolutely no right to be, given the crude circumstances under which it was put together, just as much home-made as hand-built, but the effort put in by the men who worked upon it ensured that it was stable, reliable and as safe as it could be.

It was, of course, the Edwardian public schoolboy dream; John Heath, aristocratic languid toff, and Squadron Leader George Abecassis DFC, ex-bomber pilot, joining forces to thrash the impudent cabbage-chewing foreigners once again. It was a scenario straight from the Junior Common Room at Haileybury, and Moss was all for it. He spent much of his time oscillating between Ray Martin's mews workshop and the HWM garage in Walton, getting to know his colleagues and helping in the workshop while the cars were painstakingly assembled.

The engines were built by Geoffrey Taylor, another unsung hero of the time. He ran his business from nearby Kingston-upon-Thames, and Alf Francis came to more or less worship the man for his attention to detail, his professionalism and, most important to Francis, his capacity for sheer bloody hard work – a characteristic both men enjoyed, or possibly suffered from. Taylor's core design, a four-in-line 1500cc unit with hemispheric combustion chambers and two camshafts, dated back to 1936. In its final incarnation, as the 2½-litre Connaught Grand Prix engine, it powered Tony Brooks and Archie Scott Brown to victory in their respective Formula 1 debuts in the 1955 and 1956 seasons and deserves its place alongside the Offenhauser, Jaguar XK, Coventry Climax and Miller as a twin-cam great.

But this was 1950; there were three firms building racers in Surrey – Connaught in Send, Coopers in Surbiton and HWM in Walton. All used the Alta engine at some time or another, with varying degrees of success, and Moss was to drive all three marques. As the M4 corridor is now the capital of Formula 1, the A3 corridor played a similar role then, albeit on a more modest scale. East Anglia, with Lola, Lotus, Lister and Tojeiro, was to host the birth of the second generation, the success of which would, with the addition of Vanwall and – eventually, after a painful wait – BRM, form the basis of one of Britain's best kept secrets; total, uncompromising dominance in Formula 1, 2, 3, and Indycar racing. Those who continually bemoan the loss of a motor industry in Britain, by which they probably mean the Riley Nine or the Crossbeam Turbot, really should concentrate harder.

And the drivers were the test pilots. Despite the care and attention lavished upon them by the likes of Alf Francis, the cars were only as safe as they could make them, and, sadly, they were not always safe. Lightness was all, and the drivers who drove these insubstantial vehicles were totally unprotected. Fuel tanks were rigid, as were chassis, and fireproof clothing, eventually introduced by racing driver Les Leston, was a thing of the future. There was no Kevlar, carbon fibre, GRP or light alloy honeycomb. Drivers' helmets were invariably modified polo hats from the Herbert Johnson company in Bond street. They were entirely organic, made from strips of layered linen which had been marinaded in hot shellac and a solution of ammonia. They resembled nothing so much as solar topis and served only to protect the wearer from flying grit, giving no protection to the temples. Drivers eschewed seatbelts as being unsafe rather than wimpish; and they were probably correct in their assumption that being thrown out of a car was safer than being trapped in it as the Elektron magnesium body invariably ignited like a distress flare and the driver burned to death, screaming, trying to beat out the flames with nothing more fire-resistant than string-backed driving gloves. There were some circuit safety measures, and even a measure of streamlined communication – ex-army field telephones were often employed, for example – but fire-fighting facilities were generally sketchy, and fire was the nightmare. This was something which Moss was acutely aware of. One of his own heroes had been Richard Seaman, who had driven with tremendous élan for Mercedes before the war. Seaman had crashed at Spa-Francorchamps in Belgium on 25 June 1939. The beautiful car had burst into flames and Seaman, as a result, had died, slowly.

Circuit safety was minimal. Oil drums filled with concrete and inflammable straw bales marked out the course, and spectators were held back merely by ropes. Medical facilities were usually provided by a co-opted GP who liked the sport. The footage of marshals and St John Ambulance men trying to pull poor Mike Keen out of his inverted and blazing Lotus at the 1955 Goodwood 9-Hours race is nightmarishly horrifying, particularly for the overwhelming sense of impotence which they clearly feel.

The wretched straw bales themselves, of course, were a particular liability. It takes little imagining to visualise the effect of a racing car brushing one at 140 mph. The knock-off wheel spinner winds itself into the tightly packed straw, gouging its way inwards, flipping the car end-over-end as the weight of the bale acts as a fulcrum. St John Horsfall died like this and many others nearly followed.

So, racing in those far-off days was as dangerous as it could be. The cars were themselves the culmination of contemporary technology, as were the tyres, the brakes and the engines. The drivers and mechanics worked as hard as they could, but perhaps the main thing which was lacking was imagination; the imagination to work out what could go wrong if one was not very very careful. This would be pointed out cruelly within a few years.

MANAGING A LEGEND

Chapter 4

ON THE BLOCKS: THE 1950 SEASON

*'... amateur sport, which is the best
and soundest thing in England.'*
SIR ARTHUR CONAN DOYLE,
THE RETURN OF SHERLOCK HOLMES

Until the 10 April 1950 Goodwood meeting, about the only car which Moss had driven competitively was a Cooper, either with a 497cc or 996cc JAP engine. Simple, light and cheap, it resembled, conceptually at least, nothing less than a tiny pre-war Auto-Union Grand Prix car. In a sense, the front-engined Maseratis, Ferraris, Connaughts, Vanwalls and BRMs that were to come marked something of a bottleneck in racing car development, given what was to follow later. But the impetus to develop Grand Prix cars as front-engined projectiles was predominantly a function of what road cars looked like – for most people, Tatras and Volkswagens were too obscure to be taken seriously.

The HWM was of the 'two bloody great tubes' school of chassis design. More man-hours went into its construction than can ever be calculated, but as a result, it was ridiculously well made. No careless blobs of random weld scattered about here, no hastily patched and filled de Dion tubes, no hotch-potch of other people's proprietary parts shoved together in a mish-mash of unattributable jigsaw; it was a proper piece of work. This may well have been down to Francis because it could well have been different; he recollects in his memoir that Heath had thought that a chassis from a Triumph Mayflower might have worked. Certainly, there were enough around, the ghastly Mayflower having been a well-deserved flop – characteristically so because, like so many Triumph cars, it was actually a Disaster. It is rumoured that the massive marketing effort launched in the Far East by Sir John Black, Chairman of Standard Triumph, who by all accounts did not acquire his knighthood through charm, failed because the car resembled, at first glance, a Chinese coffin; and simple superstition, rather than the Korean War, killed it – allegedly.

Whatever, the HWM had a hand-built chassis. The rear chassis member, roughly tricorne in shape, which carried the final drive, was actually made from 67 separate pieces of sheet steel, all cut on a hand-operated guillotine and, at least in retrospect by those who recalled performing the task, lovingly welded together. Like many such projects, however speculative it was in nature, the imperative behind its construction was not merely price-driven and nor was it mere artisan vanity – it was in reality the only way to make such a thing.

Ken Gregory knew little of this as he was starting to bustle around the 500 circuit. An amusing diversion, though, was that despite the fact that the 500 Club was a thing of itself and well-established, it also shared the same appellation as a theatrical boozing and philosophising circle in Albermarle Street, Piccadilly – a sort of precursor of the Groucho. There were, apparently, protests at the constant appearance of distinctly un-thespian punters – loud, check-shirted and sweaty – turning up on the doorstep, with brake dust rather than greasepaint on their faces, Herbert Johnsons in hand, demanding and receiving copious quantities of drink. Richard Attenborough and John Mills, whose brainchild the happy band of clubmen was, took a rather dim view of this storming of the bastions of luvviedom, and said so by letter – thus the '500' Club hastily became the

Half-Litre Club. Half-litre of precisely what was never made clear; we can assume displacement, but further cultural mismatch was neatly avoided, possibly to the disappointment of some. A circular was sent, pointing out that the recreational facilities in Albermarle Street were not in fact open to members; that was what the Steering Wheel club in nearby Brick Street was for, if they cared to take out a modest subscription.

Gregory was also doing more racing, and with some success, but it was hard work, mainly due to a combination of repeated mechanical failures rather than sloppy driving, and he was learning. At Mons, in Belgium it nearly all ended when he parked his Kieft right in the doorway of the house being used as a circuit first-aid post after he fell off the track.

Gregory's racing career was short but not undistinguished; he actually won a race, pleasingly at Brands Hatch, which is more than can be said for most who have dipped their toes into this most compulsive of sports. Ironically, he did it in a Cooper-JAP rather than a Kieft, borrowed from a chum, Jack Leary. The Kieft, or rather its engine, gave up the unequal struggle and was scratched from the race. Gregory had a taste of what Moss felt, and savoured it.

To an extent, an itch had been scratched, but he persisted with racing and hill-climbing until the end of 1951, when, for obvious reasons, he gave it up to concentrate on business, but not before finishing third to Alan Brown and Les Leston in the prestigious 100 mile Duke of York Trophy Race at Silverstone. He was driving Stirling's Kieft-Norton.

Another hint of what might have been came at Great Auclum, when, throughout the day, he and Stuart Lewis-Evans, of whom much more later, took turns to smash the outright record. They were sharing an 1100cc works Cooper JAP. This ding-dong competition might have lasted longer save for an oiled-up spark plug on Gregory's final run.

There can be little doubt, then, that it was not a lack of ability which prevented Gregory taking his racing further, but more critically, a lack of money. By the time he had the money–and he would–his horizons had moved on. Despite the efforts of the Coopers et al, motor racing was still a costly hobby. That it was becoming democratised was clear, but it has never been cheap to do. Despite this financial handicap, Ken Gregory qualified as a member of the British Racing Drivers' Club at the end of his last season.

All this 500 activity proved to be something of a magnet. Leslie Johnson was the current owner of the ERA concern, and also a works Jaguar driver, turning out as an amateur for the Coventry team. Johnson was the very image of the 1950s English driver; lantern-jawed car designer and, by profession, cabinet maker–confident, opinionated and very skilful. He had raced pre-war and had re-emerged relatively quickly, partnering Jock St John Horsfall in the 1949 Spa 24 hour race, which they won in an Aston Martin. His firm may well have been the one which actually built Ken's plywood Horsa glider, in fact, as the furniture trade was deeply involved in the construction of such things. What makes a Mosquito fighter bomber so precious is that many of them were built by Gillow's in Lancaster, and most collectors of English furniture would give their eye teeth to possess anything made by that firm.

Actually, Leslie Johnson was rather frailer than he looked. His bullish appearance, enhanced by cavalry twills and Tattersalls check, was rather more through him having suffered from acromegaly, a cruel pituitary disorder, when young. This had the effect of uncontrollably accelerating bone growth in the hands and face and, in fact, the poor chap died when relatively young. He had contacted Ken

Gregory and Stirling Moss with a view to resurrecting the ERA marque as a Formula 3 effort.

English Racing Automobiles had been the brainchild of Raymond Mays before the war; a British attempt to develop a car which was competitive against European opposition. It was a struggle which Mays never abandoned. ERA evolved into BRM, more or less, but the ERA which Johnson owned – the rump of it – was but a pale shadow of those extraordinary cars driven by Raymond Mays himself and, more famously, Prince Birabongse Bhanutej Bhanubandh, the nephew of the King of Siam, sculptor, writer, racing driver and agreeable old Etonian grandee, who sensibly entered the lists as simply B. Bira.

Johnson had in mind yet another 500cc car, to be called an ERA F type. It was all to come to nothing, being both slow and hideous, but while discussing the matter over dinner, Gregory casually mentioned Moss's ambition to raise his game a little. Would Johnson pull a few strings at Brown's Lane, Coventry to help Stirling up the ladder into a works Jaguar drive in the up-coming TT race at Dundrod on 16 September? They were entering three, after all, and the boy was good, very good.

Moss had already written to just about every manufacturer, including Jaguar, to take part in this race. It was a blue riband event, difficult to win because of the often dodgy weather and a fundamentally unsound circuit, and the chance to enter, particularly in a proper car, would be one to be treasured. The Jaguar response was predictable. Lack of experience, et cetera, et cetera … no, thank you very much. Johnson's reply to Gregory's request was very much in the same tone, if not more negative.

Absolutely not, came the answer, under no circumstances. The vehemence of this response startled Gregory somewhat. It is possible that Johnson treasured his role as a works driver and would brook no opposition, but from what we know of him, he was a gentleman, generous with praise and as tolerant of rivals as any serious racing driver could be. It seems that he was clearly in the doubter's camp from the point of view of Stirling's relative lack of experience, an argument which was already threadbare anyway, and which certainly cut no ice with Gregory, given that Johnson was trying to recruit the boy. The issue ruined a perfectly good dinner.

There was another avenue; the private one. It so happened that the motoring correspondent of *The Daily Herald*, Tommy Wisdom, was an enthusiastic driver and the happy owner of an XK120, prepared for light competition and selfish road use by the works. It was only one of six in the country. He also ran an example of that most underrated of cars, the Jowett Jupiter and, quite out of the blue offered the Jaguar for Stirling to drive, splitting the start money and winnings 50:50, while he would drive the Jowett. It was a huge leap of faith for Wisdom, but it was justified by events, for Stirling won, handsomely. Wisdom's daughter Anne, later to marry Peter Riley, was a good friend of Stirling's sister Pat. The two women would later cut a swathe together through the sport of rallying.

F.R.W. England, the Jaguar racing manager, who had turned Stirling down originally, was watching: 'He'd never even driven this thing before he got to Ireland ... he won in the wet and walked the race. So, of course, we took him on.'

It would be agreeable to think that Lofty England had somehow played a part, even a minor one, in discovering Moss, but it wasn't so. If anyone did, after Ken Gregory, it was Tommy Wisdom. England, or rather William Lyons, had to see his own works effort comprehensively trashed by this infant prodigy before he acted, but once he had decided, he didn't hesitate. England knew his stuff, too, having worked for Whitney Straight before the war, but it is possible that he was over-influenced by the likes of Johnson, never having actually seen Stirling race before.

Moss had yet to attain his majority, as his twenty-first birthday was not until the next day, but he had won one of the most important races on the calendar and, more significantly, secured for himself a works drive in sports car events, which, at that stage in Britain, were more popular than the still emerging (and essentially rather foreign) Formula 1.

There was little negotiating with England; the price was the price and that was that. Jaguar were beset by applications for works drives and it was something of a buyer's market. England had little time for 'comedians' demanding vast sums of money and, later, even less for their managers; he had to justify every penny to the ever-careful William Lyons, who held on to the purse-strings with a grip every bit as intense as rigor mortis. Building competition cars was expensive; racing them needn't be.

It was not purely a matter of money for Stirling, although he was starting to think that he could make a living at this; there was the important matter that every drive for which he was paid became an important morale-booster, and the Jaguar deal, however modest the amount of money involved, would lead to great things – a works drive in a class at which he would come to dominate the world – sports cars.

Chapter 5

1951 · RUMBLINGS

*'Know ye not that they which run in a race run
all, but one receiveth the prize?'*
1 CORINTHIANS 9:24

It was fairly clear to anyone who watched that this boy
Moss was something out of the ordinary, for what he lacked
in experience he clearly made up for in preparation, study
and concentration. In this, he had a soul-mate in Alf Francis
who had – by the time the 1951 season was under way at
the March Goodwood meeting, where Moss won the Lavant
cup – converted to being one of Moss's biggest fans. In a
1959 *This Is Your Life* broadcast, the presenter, Eamonn
Andrews, asked Francis a simple question: 'What do you
think of Stirling's ability, Alf?' Francis shuffled, looked coyly
at the camera, clearly shy: 'I think, dat he is de best, (pause)
alive.'

Not everyone agreed with him in the early days, at least
domestically, but they were not necessarily concentrating as
hard as Francis was. Much of Stirling's progress was being
made in Europe, most significantly at two races which he
entered in Italy in May 1951, the first being the Monza
Formula 2 Grand Prix on 13 May, the second at Genoa a
week later, during which he shone brightly against the
short-odds contenders from Ferrari. He came third at Monza
but his engine blew up at Genoa. This performance, unexpected as it was, attracted further attention, which he further encouraged by setting a new lap record in a C-type
Jaguar at Le Mans on 24 June.

Within a week of that, Enzo Ferrari had contacted the

BRDC secretary, Desmond Scannell. He sent a telegram offering Moss two drives, the first in a scant three days' time at Reims in the French Grand Prix on 4 July, the second at Silverstone a fortnight later. The car offered was the 4½ -litre Ferrari 375 Grand Prix machine, admittedly a year-old one, but of the same type as raced by the great Alberto Ascari the year before, probably even the same car.

The logistics of the HWM operation were less than perfect; all Gregory knew was that Moss was in Berlin; he knew not where, but he contacted Reuters to ask them to find out. They were well up to the task and tracked Moss down to his hotel and telexed Gregory to tell him where, complete with telephone number. Eagerly Gregory called him to tell his chum the news.

Stirling was, as luck would have it, booked to race in the Formula 2 event at the Avusring on the same day, 4 July, turning out for HWM as usual. He was, however, free for the Silverstone race and would be delighted to accept Mr Ferrari's kind offer. The prospect of even entering his home Grand Prix at the age of 22 so soon after starting his career was a compelling one and he leapt at the chance. A telegram to this effect was duly sent to Modena.

Enzo Ferrari unsurprisingly saw it rather differently. The offer had been not for either the French or the British events, but for both of them – or none of them. Take it or leave it. It is, of course probable, if not certain, that the HWM team would have released Moss to take up this extraordinary offer, but he did not even mention it to them. Ferrari insisted that the offer would be for both events, and, sadly, that was that. Ferrari would make another approach later in the season, with famous results, but meanwhile, he signed up Froilan Gonzalez for his Ferrari debut at Reims. The Argentinian rewarded Ferrari by coming third. At

Silverstone, though, he won by over a minute from Fangio in an Alfa Romeo. Stirling won the 500cc Formula 3 supporting race, which was small consolation. Few knew of the offer from Ferrari at the time, but despite the Commendatore's intransigence over the terms, it reveals that Gregory's optimism for his friend was shared at a high level in Formula 1 as early as 1951. Moss would not actually drive a works Formula 1 car for another three years. It would not be a Ferrari, either; it would never be a Ferrari.

Enzo Ferrari took a similar view to many manufacturers about drivers, but could quite simply get away with expressing it in a manner which others would dare not. In his choice of both drivers and the people with whom he surrounded himself he insisted upon total subservience to the objective of glorifying the name of the marque. His name. He was as unsentimental about his cars as a farmer was about his crop and would leave few avenues unexplored in order to deal upon his own terms. He once called himself 'an agitator of men' – it seems accurate.

The year 1951 was to be a good one for Stirling's replacement, Gonzalez. He came third in the Championship, to be topped by second in 1954, which was to be a year of personal tragedy for him, triggering his early retirement. The contribution to the sport made by Gonzalez is too easily forgotten now, as he has rather been eclipsed by the memory of Fangio, Ascari, Farina and, of course, Moss.

So, Stirling's 1951 season, although successful, was a rather lower-octane one than it could have been; Formula 3, Formula 2 and sports cars. A good one, though, but tiring, involving endless travelling to obscure parts of Europe where racing is rare now, but where a motor race was the highlight of the calendar. Genoa, Rouen, Mettet in Belgium, Erlen, Freibourg. A pleasant life, even idyllic, but an unfocused one. Stirling, though, disliked travelling. He clearly agreed with the then King, George VI, that 'abroad is bloody'. His Majesty had clearly read Nancy Mitford on the subject: 'Frogs are slightly better than Huns or Wops, but abroad is unutterably bloody and foreigners are fiends.'

It was not a rare sentiment in Britain at the time, as the war, which had more or less bankrupted the country, was still the single most formative influence over the lives of more or less the entire population; and political correctness was, of course, still far in the future.

The solidity of hearth and home, and the sense of security and well-being which it gave Stirling is one of the strongest motivations in his life, so it was with a slight sense of reluctance that he set off, with Alfred, in pursuit of a better drive when Ferrari made another approach in August. It was to have terminal consequences, which both Moss and the Commendatore would come to regret. The occasion was to be a Formula 2 race at Bari on 2 September, so Alfred and Stirling drove all the way down to Southern Italy, relieved that the episode over the French and British Grands Prix had apparently been forgotten, and looking forward to starting again. As Moss put it: 'When you're asked to drive for Ferrari; boy, you cross yourself and face Modena.'

The mystique which had grown up around the Italian marque since May 1947, when the modest 125 sports car had made its debut, was extraordinary, even then, largely because of the efforts of Luigi Chinetti in America and those of Gonzalez and Ascari on the track. After the Dundrod triumph, and a good showing elsewhere, here would be a way into the first rank.

Well, there was no car – or, rather, there was, but it was to be driven after all by the veteran Piero Taruffi. No explanation was given, no expenses offered or paid and, of course, no apology. Whether or not this was Ferrari's elaborate and scheming way of repaying, with interest, what he might have considered to be a slight over the Formula 1 issue, we cannot be sure, but it was the sort of rude put-down frequently used by him, and one which a whole series of drivers would have to become accustomed to if they were to drive the scarlet cars. A privateer who witnessed the episode offered Stirling a drive in his own Ferrari, but the brakes went out. Moss, père et fils, departed back to England to prepare for the event at the Curragh barely a week later. Moss's attitude was hardened by the treatment he had received in Italy, and he vowed, crudely and with great sincerity, never to have anything to do with Ferrari again. He certainly never drove a Ferrari works car, despite the high regard he had for the make. Wouldn't a British car be nice?

A slight emollient was his second victory at the TT race at Dundrod the next month, where Jaguar also won the team prize, Stirling's colleagues being Leslie Johnson and Peter Walker. Ken Gregory went with him, and the two started to discuss the idea of a professional relationship which might reflect the closeness of their personal one. Basically, Moss disliked travelling alone and wanted company. So, without consciously having a theme, their talks started to centre around the idea of Gregory being the details man, leaving Stirling the chance to concentrate on driving.

He knew he could trust Gregory completely, and given that Ken had already made great (and successful) efforts to promote the interests of his chum from within both the RAC and the 500 Club, it seemed logical to put the non-personal aspects of their relationship on, to use one of Stirling's favourite expressions, a 'commercial basis'.

This was not to be entirely a bipartisan arrangement, as

Alfred Moss, with his formidable common sense and acumen was always lurking in the background, keeping a fatherly eye on the possibilities of youthful excess. He was inordinately fond of Gregory; the two of them had almost developed a father/son relationship, which Stirling minded about not at all, given the fraternal nature of his friendship with Ken. In effect, the Moss family had grown by one. Moss more or less lived in Gregory's tiny apartment, which conveniently overlooked a ladies' college of London University, and Gregory was spending almost every weekend at the White Cloud Farm at Tring, at the family's insistence, so that they could at least monitor his food intake.

The Moss family lived in some style. The White Cloud Farm was, originally, the home farm of the nearby Rothschild estate, and Alfred had bought it from a merchant banker just after the war. It was an Edwardian structure, large and spacious, and the outbuildings were beautifully constructed and finished – they would be doubly useful later on. But, as a working farm, which it was, there was little to touch it in terms of design. The dairies were a work of art in themselves, cooled by fountains, marble-floored and airy. The quadruped accommodations – perfect for the horses which Pat Moss, Stirling's sister, was becoming eminent at riding – were just as luxurious. Stirling had cut his teeth on an Austin 7, roaring round the orchards, and had also shone as an equestrian. Brother and sister had dominated local gymkhanas for some time before Stirling had discovered motor racing. Pat, too, would later compete with unparalleled success on four wheels, having been introduced to rallying, with her friend Anne Wisdom, by one Ken Gregory.

It may seem all very intense to modern eyes, replete with half-remembered 'blood brother' ceremonies – more the type of thing that 13-year-olds might indulge in now – but these were the days before the invention of the pains of adolescence and hormonal agonies of young manhood. The formative influence on both men, apart from boarding school, had been the war, their observation of which had left Stirling, at least, with perhaps a slightly *Boy's Own* view of the world which the presence of the slightly older Gregory, who only just missed out on active service, may well have helped to balance. It was a symbiosis born of friendship which was later to become a highly efficient business machine. At this stage, though, Stirling might well have been leaping, not into an HWM to do battle with the foe, but rather a Hurricane or, to be fairer to Hawker's, at least a Gloster Gladiator.

The first thing Gregory had to do under this new arrangement, of course, was to resign from the RAC. The news was greeted with a slight sniff from Colonel Barnes – what on earth does a manager do? It seemed little short of commercial travelling. Gregory wasn't actually very sure – he rather had to find his way and write his own job description. Of one thing he was totally certain, though; it was obviously going to be a lot of fun. How wrong he was to be in that judgement, at least in the short term, as he would discover quite soon.

Alf Francis was deeply unhappy at HWM. Always a man rather more convinced of his own talents than certain others were, he had fallen out with John Heath over the vital issue of whether to develop the existing car and coax more power from the engine or to start again from scratch. Not unsurprisingly, he viewed the prospect of a total redesign with horror; a blank sheet of paper is a frightening prospect for most people, but particularly so if you take the view, as Francis did, that there was nothing really wrong with the old design. He resigned and exiled himself to Berwick-on-Tweed as a garage foreman, which was just awful for him – a whisky-fuelled hell. Geoffrey Taylor rescued him by helping him to get a job with Peter Whitehead, a skilled privateer, as his personal racing mechanic, which, if it did not satisfy his every ambition, at least kept him in the sport – another forgotten service for which we should give Taylor a standing ovation.

Moss rather shared Francis' view and declined to sign up for the whole of the 1952 season with HWM. Although he would drive some races for them, he was replaced by his friend Peter Collins as the main star of the team. Now he had his own manager, a Jaguar works drive and a developing role in a rapidly-developing field, he and Gregory had every reason to look forward with confidence to the sunlit uplands; which just goes to show.

There was one event at the end of the 1951 season, after the Spanish Grand Prix at Pedralbes, which was to affect the whole of the sport. This was the withdrawal of Alfa Romeo from competition. Fangio had won the Championship for them, albeit narrowly, from Ascari and Gonzalez, both in Ferraris. Farina, who came fourth in another Alfa 159, replaced Gonzalez at Ferrari for the next season, so the Modena team, minus Fangio who took a sabbatical, was composed of Ascari, Farina, Taruffi and Villoresi. With the unreliability of the BRM, which was the only small capacity supercharged car, the field was left entirely open to the Ferrari team. It would have been a total whitewash and, consequently, poor sport. Ferrari's cars also dominated the 2-litre class and, even better, he now had an all Italian team, with the exception of André Simon, the French driver late of Gordini, as a back-up.

Another British driver was also considering his options

for 1952. Through the previous year, he and his father had campaigned a pair of pre-war Rileys in minor club events with relative success, and the 22-year-old was making a modest name for himself. They were trading up to a 2-litre, which would now be eligible for the championship, but very late in the day, and only when a friend offered to buy a new Cooper-Bristol for them to enter. The driver was Mike Hawthorn, and his rise to prominence was to be nothing less than meteoric.

Chapter 6

TWO LEAN YEARS

*'There is a friend that sticketh
closer than a brother.'*
PROVERBS 18:24

Well, most plans seldom survive their first contact with reality, and this was no exception to that dismal truism. The pair decided not to stint themselves on travel. Not for them the prospect of sleeping under the trailer in some damp orchard, being pursued by irate foreign farmers. No, they would do it properly, and they bought and equipped a caravan to be towed behind Stirling's Jaguar. In many ways this was the precursor of the famous house in Shepherd Street, and reflected Moss's mild obsession with gadgetry and gizmos, which has never really left him. As we would expect from the first man in England to own an electric trouser press, the conveyance was the closest thing to the Orient Express which £800 could provide. Style et Luxe incarnate, the poor thing was written off early in its Continental career – loaded with food, it was comprehensively smashed when the Jaguar towing the caravan parted company with it on a long downhill slope in Belgium. Stirling's pride and joy performed two complete somersaults and ended up blocking the traffic in both directions. Afterwards, its interior apparently resembled the insides of an undercooked Spanish omelette. Philosophically, the insurance money went toward hotel bills from then on.

Not an auspicious start, and possibly an omen. The 1952 season was, if not disastrous, certainly very hard work, with still no sign of a Formula 1 drive. The Jaguar works drive, now in the peerless C-type derivative of the XK120, offered a consistent lift to the otherwise interminable round of Formula 2 and 3 races, none of which was a particular challenge. Naturally, the Formula 3 races were, more often than not, a walkover, thanks not just to skill but also a much better Kieft now that Ray Martin had basically redesigned it. But this was jobbing stuff, workaday and less than inspiring. The elusive Formula 1 seat was coming no closer and he had basically stopped learning – a state which, in a profession driven by innovation, is the Black Spot.

Many people have the sense of being under-utilised, and it is also the case that many of them are a serious pain. Not so Moss. He put in all the time he could, and Gregory reciprocated, digging up the most unlikely and trivial drives to keep his client busy. The most potentially challenging of these was the 1½-litre supercharged BRM in the Ulster Trophy at Dundrod. Sadly, the BRM, the previous season's Formula 1 candidate as driven by Parnell and Walker, proved to be as unreliable in Formule Libre as it had been in Grands Prix. Moss retired after three laps, and later labelled it 'the worst car I ever drove', a statement which does not seem unreasonable.

The BRM – expensive flop that it was – had been a long time coming, and its disappointing performance, coupled with the withdrawal of the works Alfa Romeo team from competition, had made the FIA reconsider its options for the 1952 season. The approach of the 2-litre Formula 1 for 1954 had already been announced, but that was two years away; the sport was going to be very dull indeed if it was merely going to be a Ferrari benefit. So, in a wonderfully star-chamber manner, the rules were changed. For the immediate future, the Grands Prix would be run to Formula 2. It was, in fact, a Ferrari benefit anyway, with Farina and

Ascari more or less doing as they pleased, but the move did at least open up the possibilities a little.

But not for Moss. Leslie Johnson reappeared in the spring with grand plans for the ERA G-type, the 'spiritual successor', so the sales puff ran, to the immortal pre-war ... et cetera, et cetera. It was to be a Formula 2 device, eligible for Grands Prix now and depressingly unoriginal. Would Stirling care to drive it?

Now, Stirling Moss, as he is the first to admit, has driven some fairly ropy machinery in his time. For a race driver, he is a poor judge of cars, or so it is said, but on a scale of 1 to 10 for sheer awfulness, the ERA G-type was a perfect 11. It was as unlike the pre-war ERAs – the creations of that clever but flawed man, Raymond Mays† – as was possible. It was an ugly, slow, overheated 'Bitsa' which handled hardly at all. It was on all fronts a complete lemon, out of which little frustration could be squeezed. It was the Trabant of racing cars, a real clunker; but it was British, powered by a Bristol engine, and it was green and bore a famous name, so Moss gave it the benefit of the doubt. Any concerns he may have felt about the total integrity of the package were well supported by the fact that it retired on lap one of its first outing at the European Grand Prix at Spa-Francorchamps on 22 June. Coming as it did after a retirement from Le Mans, through overheating, the previous weekend, while in one of the perhaps ill-advised long-nosed C-type Jaguars, the experience rather summed up the season for Moss.

To be sure, there was great success in Formula 3, sports and saloon cars, but much of this he had enjoyed already.

---

†Mays was instrumental in the design of the BRM V16. By way of balancing the record, the later BRM P25 was in Moss's opinion the best-handling front-engined car he ever drove, albeit only after the whole concept had been redesigned by Tony Rudd. (See Chapter 13).

✗ LONG NOSED ON S. MOSS RECOMMENDATION !
"NEED MORE SPEED"

There was little progress, and for the man who had turned down a Ferrari Formula 1 drive so early in his career, this was lowering, but not particularly a matter for great regret, as he knew full well that there was no going back, not even for a split second.

At the 2-litre single-seater level, the star was clearly Mike Hawthorn. On occasion he was outpacing by significant margins the 4½-litre Ferrari entrants – by now relegated to Formule Libre – most famously at Boreham in August. Within a month of that he had been snapped up by Ferrari for 1953, becoming the first British driver since Richard Seaman to work for a proper Continental team; an honour which could have gone to Moss had he chosen to let down the HWM team in 1950. Ferrari, ever pragmatic, took the view that if this driver could threaten his huge 4-litre Grand Prix cars in a low-budget special – which is how he would view all British cars until the Vanwall – then he deserved a proper vehicle. Ferrari was quite right. No-one has ever accused Enzo Ferrari of being a poor judge of drivers. It was just that he found it extremely difficult and totally unnecessary, in a buyer's market, to treat them nicely. In that particular, Grand Prix racing at the top level is a remarkably consistent sport.

Hawthorn's sudden elevation into the first rank served well to illustrate Stirling Moss's relative lack of progress as the 1952 season moved past half way. It was to be years before Hawthorn won the Championship, but he caught the imagination of the British public in a way which few drivers had, before or since. Not only was he hugely skilled, if a little inconsistent, he had the great advantage, so far as the media were concerned, of looking the part as well. Tall, blond and easy on the eye. He was also extremely ill for much of the time, afflicted by a kidney ailment much more

65A. *Edna Gregory, Ken's mother, in her Nurse's uniform, c. 1938. (Ken Gregory).*
65B. *Ken Gregory, aged 6, with his grandmother, Gertrude Howarth, c. 1932. (Ken Gregory).*
65C. *Ken Gregory's grandfather Sam, standing in front of the family's Dorman Ricardo-engined Daimler charabanc. The family butcher's shop is in the background. The little boy sitting next to the driver is Ken's father, Cecil, aged 10. This picture dates from about 1918. (Ken Gregory).*

66A. Ken Gregory, aged 15, as a boy soldier, 1942. (Ken Gregory).

66B. Gregory as a qualified sergeant pilot, Glider Pilot Regiment, 1945. (Ken Gregory).

66C. Gregory's last Army job was as transport sergeant at the school of Combined Operations, Fremington, North Devon. The trucks are an assortment; Bedford, Chevrolet, Austin. (Ken Gregory).

67A. *First victory. Gregory after winning the Junior championship 500 race, Brands Hatch, September 1950. Frank Bacon, a pioneer 500 driver, who is acting as steward, chats with him. (Ken Gregory).*
67B. *Castle Combe, 1950. Gregory driving a Kieft Mark II, having overtaken, rather untidily, Peter Braid in a Cooper. (Guy Griffiths)*

68A. *Ken Gregory and Stirling Moss at the Chelsea Arts Club Ball, 1950. Further comment is probably unnecessary… (Sports and General Press).*
68B. *Gregory in the prototype Cooper T12 at Brands hatch, 1950. (Ken Gregory).*

MANAGING A LEGEND

69A. Tony Robinson push-starting the Ray Martin Cooper-ALTA at Silverstone. Alf Francis is just visible next to him. An ALTA engineer has refuelled the car. (Autocar).

69B. Alf Francis and Tony Robinson overhauling Stirling's Maserati 250F at Barlby Road, W. London, courtesy of Rootes Group. The Commer transporter is also receiving well-deserved attention. (H.R.Clayton).

70A. *Tony Robinson preparing Stirling's Maserati at the White Cloud farm, Tring. Note that the car has received disc brakes and Dunlop wheels. These were fitted by Jaguar's at Coventry, which dates this picture to 1955. (Ken Gregory).*
70B. *Harry Schell, chatting with Stirling at Pescara, 1954.*

71A. Stirling, Gregory and Alfred Moss at Hockenheim for the Mercedes-Benz test, December 1954 (Bert Hardy, Daimler-Benz Classic Archive).
71B. Peter Collins in the 300SLR, Targa Florio, 1955. The car was to end up even more battered that this, but it won… (Daimler-Benz Classic Archive).
71C. The Monaco Grand Prix, 1955. The opening lap. Stirling (6) was the only Mercedes home, albeit in ninth place. Fangio (2) and André Simon (4), both retired. (Daimler-Benz Classic Archive).

72A. *Stirling, Mike Hawthorn, Tony Robinson, Alf Francis and Rob Walker, with the Maserati at Crystal Palace, 1955. (Charles Dunn).*
72B. *Alf Francis closes the filler cap on Stirling's Maserati. Goodwood, 1955. (G.D.McKechnie).*

severe than that from which Stirling suffered, and this may be the reason for his inconsistency. He hid it well, though, at least to those outside his immediate circle.

Stirling Moss soldiered on. He ran into Alf Francis at Goodwood at the end of the season, and the two compared notes. Francis was bored stiff, basically. His re-entry into the sport through working for Peter Whitehead had been, in his words, 'interesting, but not much fun'. Stirling made the rather Delphic remark that he had a project under way and would like Francis to be involved with it?

Basically, Moss, Gregory and John 'Autocar' Cooper were going to re-invent the approach which had led to the Ray Martin Kieft, but as a Grand Prix car. They would use a Cooper chassis and put a hairy 2-litre engine in it. Gregory wrote to Maserati to see if they would provide an engine and transmission; the doughty Gonzalez had quite frightened the Ferraris at Monza with his new A6GCS car, the light alloy engine being the precursor of the planned 2½-litre Formula 1 power plant, and the trio were optimistic about buying one. Their hopes were predictably dashed when the canny Omer Orsi wrote a cheery note back offering to sell them an entire car but no bits. Gregory then tried Jaguar – perhaps the XK100 four-cylinder twin-cam would be available? Sadly, they were not producing it, so that was that. It would probably have been too heavy anyway.

The natural choice of most special builders was, of course, a Bristol unit, if they could afford it, but Cooper's were already producing such a vehicle. It would have been rather bad form to effectively copy the Surbiton car. There was, however, an alternative.

Francis, who clearly believed that Geoffrey Taylor was the greatest living Englishman, thought that Taylor's faithful Alta design would do very well indeed. Better still,

Francis knew the unit well from his HWM days and was keen to carry on developing it – the issue over which he had fallen out with Abecassis and Heath just a year before. Accordingly, a dry-sumped racing unit was bought from the Kingston works, and Francis started to tune it. He joined Ray Martin Motors as works manager, and the effort began.

Martin and Francis came to roundly detest each other after quite a short while, and the resulting car was predictably iffy – just as the camel is said to be a horse put together by committee, so the Martin Cooper-Alta was the result of compromise borne out of mutual dislike. On the one hand, Alf Francis, touchy, perfectionist and argumentative; on the other, Ray Martin, the boss, whose name the car was to bear, brooking no interference. It was a marriage made in hell, and it showed in the car. Technically, it was not a Cooper at all; they merely provided the tubes for Francis and his staff to weld together.

One of the staff was Tony Robinson, who has a much bigger role later in this story, and the pair of them worked ridiculously hard – 16 hours a day in the most frightful conditions – on the Martin car, which had ended up as complicated as was possible. While not building the chassis, Francis was tweaking Taylor's engine over at Tolworth. He was a man in a hurry, having accepted the challenge of building the car in time for the Easter Monday meeting at Goodwood, then traditionally the season's opener in Britain. He was, unsurprisingly, the only one who thought this possible. When Keith Challen, the *News of the World* motoring correspondent, expressed his polite but real doubts as to the viability of the enterprise, Francis, perhaps excusably, rudely told Challen to 'fuck off and leave him alone.'

Poor Francis – a total perfectionist, deadly serious and

very quick to take offence – set himself the most appalling tasks and drove himself and others with no quarter to achieve them. Like many foreigners, he found Anglo-Saxon invective easy to learn, and he fell victim to the age-old trick of being taught it before proper English by mischievous Brits, to everyone's amusement save the astonished person being addressed.

Well, it all came together in time but showed itself to be, in the jargon of the sport, 'underdeveloped' – motor racing shorthand for total lemon. Francis was, of course, not deterred, but Ray Martin was, and rather high-handedly sacked him.

Gregory and Moss were naturally outraged and immediately asked a lowered but relieved Alf to their flat in Challoner Mansions. They hired him, and Robinson too, to carry on developing the car. The pair set to, borrowing space in the Cooper Car Company's tiny works in Surbiton. It never really worked out, though, and the project was finally abandoned, despite Gregory having entered it for the German Grand Prix in August.

Obviously, Moss needed another car. Francis and Robinson built one – in 11 days – from scratch, using a chassis from Coopers, off the shelf more or less, with the engine from the Martin car and a preselector transmission, all covered in a skimpy body. It was an extraordinary achievement, the more so because Moss came sixth, beating three Ferraris. He scored no points for it, the lowest scoring position then being fifth, but it was, to say the least, encouraging. It was a better car than the Martin one, on all fronts, which doubly pleased Francis.

This seemed an omen, reinforced by Stirling winning the TT at Dundrod for the third time, but despite the relative success of the Cooper-Alta, the 1954 season still loomed dark and empty. It was to be a 2½-litre Championship contest, and Equipe Moss had no 2½-litre car. There was a chance that the Alta would go to that capacity, a route which Connaught were taking, but there was always some doubt about stretching an engine too far, as Connaught were to find out. Besides, there were several brand new cars on the blocks with much more up-to-date mechanical specifications. That this was so was plain to see; the racing press was drooling over the new Italian offerings in every issue and speculating about the Mercedes which had already been announced. The team turned its thoughts toward getting a drive for Stirling.

Stirling had a very nasty crash at Castle Combe in the late summer, and was thrown out of an 1100cc Cooper JAP, breaking his shoulder. The plaster cast put on at Chippenham hospital was less than comfortable, so Gregory called upon the pair's ex-landlord, Philippe Bauwens, who fixed the problem very neatly, without the use of plaster at all. It was the start of a very long association between St Thomas's and the motor racing fraternity; a relationship which was to keep Thomas's depressingly busy for a long time.

Chapter 7

FALSE STARTS

*'Ten thousand difficulties do not
make one doubt.'*
CARDINAL NEWMAN, 1864

The 1954 Championship season saw the reversion to
Formula 1 racing following the two-year spell of Formula 2.
The new engines of 2½-litres in normally aspirated form,
and 750cc supercharged, offered intriguing possibilities for
Moss, provided he could actually be got into a car. The
options were either to get a works drive, as there were no
private teams to speak of, or to take the more costly route of
becoming an owner-driver.

The FIA had given good warning that this new formula
would apply from 1954-1960, having announced it in 1952.
No-one was likely to attempt to loosen Enzo Ferrari's somewhat white-knuckled grip on the 2-litre formula, apart from
the awesome Gonzalez in a Maserati, but several manufacturers were showing interest in the new specification. The
prospect was sufficient to lure both Mercedes-Benz and
Lancia back into racing, each after a long interval away from
the sport, and Maserati were at work on their new customer
racing car. Alfa Romeo had already given up, of course, and
this had had the hidden benefit, for Maserati at least, of
releasing Gioacchino Colombo on to the market. Colombo
has been treated harshly by the revisionist historians, but at
the time he was a catch of major proportions. He would
head up the design and development of the new Maserati
Formula 1 car. Ferrari, his other ex-employer, was also going
to have to start from scratch. No-one very seriously enter-

tained the idea of a supercharged 750cc engine, so the contest was to be between engines of an entirely new generation – the formula did not really allow anything warmed-over to be entered in the lists, as Ferrari was ruefully to discover.

British offerings, unsurprisingly, were few and far between. Coventry Climax were in the throes of developing a V8 engine, while Connaught Engineering were building their B-type chassis to accept it. The V8, to be called 'Godiva', after Coventry's first and only equestrian nudist, was delayed, so Connaught were forced to use a development of the Alta engine which was already struggling a bit in 2-litre form, based as it was on a pre-war 1500cc design. BRM, after their major reliability problems in 1951, were not yet ready to contemplate competition, and Cooper were also waiting for the new Climax engine and still stuck in the mire with the 2-litre formula, with only long-stroke, tall, Bristol engines, or over-stressed Altas to use. Basically, they were fighting the previous war, not the next. Nothing new there.

The two Cooper-Altas which the Moss équipe had campaigned, although occasionally showing promise, were never in serious danger of competing with the European opposition, either in road-holding or sheer grunt, despite the Stakhanovite efforts of Alf Francis. He had experimented with exotic fuels as well as fuel injection, but the latter was very much a black art in those days – outside Germany, at least.

The stirrings at Stuttgart were clearly the most exciting of all these developments. They were not entirely unexpected, of course. The re-creation of the pre-war racing department under Neubauer, with cars designed by Rudolf Uhlenhaut, supervised by Fritz Nallinger, had not gone unnoticed. This took place while the Stuttgart factory still had holes in the roof, and the basically hand-made, but primitive, cars – built to pre-war plans – were steered down the production line in between piles of rubble. Some of the drivers were still around, too, but the most famous of them, Caracciola, was spending most of his time in Switzerland, attempting to recover the two W165 racing cars which had been hurriedly built for the 1939 Tripoli Grand Prix and later revised to produce 280 bhp. The Swiss government had annexed them in 1945. What the Swiss proposed to do with them was not immediately clear, but they were not made available on any basis until December 1950 when, unsurprisingly, they were offered for sale. Mercedes-Benz, smiling bravely through gritted teeth, bought them back, paying through the nose to ensure their bid was accepted and, muttering, they prepared to enter them in Formula 1 events.

Much had changed, though, or was perceived to have done. The Alfa Romeo/Ferrari rivalry, between engineers Colombo and Lampredi, had moved the benchmark for normally-aspirated engines out of the reach of the blown machines by more or less 100 bhp, or seemed to have done until the appearance of the new V16 BRM at the 1951 British Grand Prix at Silverstone, where the ludicrously complex machines, allegedly capable of 400bhp, showed well. The delays caused by Swiss greed, though, had stolen vital years of development time from Mercedes and, reluctantly, they decided not to reinvent the W165, preferring to put the cars into honourable retirement. Instead, they concentrated on the up-coming 2½-litre Formula 1. They spent the intervening time well, although it was perhaps ironic that the BRM proved unworkable and the Alfa team quit racing at the end of 1951, causing the interim Formula 2 phase of the Championship to apply. There is little doubt that the handling of the 165 would have impressed, particularly against that of the relatively crude Ferraris, but there would have been no time to improve the engine.

There was little doubt that Mercedes-Benz was to be a force to be reckoned with, particularly with the great Fangio at the wheel, so Ken Gregory took it upon himself to attempt to obtain a Mercedes works drive for his client. He did not actually tell Moss what he was doing, and flew to Stuttgart for a meeting with Rudolf Uhlenhaut, the Anglo-German chief engineer. Gregory sent him a telegram, saying he was arriving and would be staying at the Park Hotel – how about a drink? All rather unorthodox, and he had no idea whether Uhlenhaut would turn up; but he did. The charming Rudi was friendly, although he knew full well where his responsibilities lay. Easily the equal of many of the drivers of his day, and a skilled tester, he had little discretion in matters outside his immediate purview. After a drink at the Park Hotel he pointed Ken in the direction of Alfred Neubauer, the Mercedes racing manager, assuring him of an appointment, to be confirmed by telephone the next morning. He was as good as his word, and Gregory was offered an interview at 8.45 a.m. which allowed him 45 minutes to make it. This was not like dealing with the Coopers, Cyril Kieft or Lofty England. This was the man who had masterminded the Mercedes racing effort pre-war. With slight trepidation, Gregory scorched over to the works, which were now in full operation, in a taxi – a Mercedes, of course.

Neubauer was one of history's lucky men in the sense that circumstances allowed him to have two separate career peaks, 15 years apart, doing the same job. He achieved a hard-earned immortality as racing manager of one of the finest organisations ever to grace the starting grid in motor racing. Born in 1891, in what was then Imperial Germany, he was as old as the motor car itself. He had seen war service in the Kaiser's army, a legendary crucible of discipline, from which he had learned much, and he ran the Mercedes team the way a genial senior NCO might. He had learned his racing with Austro-Daimler and, in lighter days, had raced. His sense of humour, though, was entirely his own.

Often imitated, usually feebly, but never bettered as a manager and selector of drivers – as well as being keenly sympathetic to their needs and aspirations – he was the antithesis of many of his impersonators, having both a robust sense of humour and a nice line in self-parody. One thing had changed about him; he had become even heavier since masterminding the last Mercedes effort, and there was now no chance of him actually getting into one of his precious cars, despite his pre-war efforts. What he did do, though, was to set an example, and it became clear that all teams would ultimately have to be run this way if they were to survive. If Stirling Moss was the first professional racing driver, Alfred Neubauer was the first professional team manager, and no one has ever come close.

The colossal Neubauer, all 21 stone of him, one eye pointedly on his giant turnip watch – the accuracy of which more or less defined his life – politely but firmly said no to Gregory's request for Stirling to have a works drive. Moss was a good, even excellent sports car driver, he said, but clearly lacked the experience in Formula 1 which Stuttgart felt was necessary. He had Fangio and enough Germans on hand to relive the 1930s as it was. He was not quite yet prepared to put Moss in the same category as one of his favourites, Richard Seaman, despite his surprisingly detailed knowledge of Moss and clear appreciation of his abilities, which, he acknowledged, were the equal of several of the drivers who were already listed, with the possible exception of Fangio. The others were Kling, Herrmann and Lang, the latter a veteran of the original silver arrows team.

It was, he implied, a matter of preparation as much as anything else. While, before the war, Neubauer had presided over the Mercedes-Benz racing effort when partly funded by state money, now was an entirely different matter. The operation had to pay for itself, be efficient (a thing which it always was anyway, even if at huge cost) and justify its existence, which was to sell motor cars. It was and is rumoured that each Mercedes road car sold was 'loaded' with a little something for the putative racing department. Despite this and some creative budgeting, money was relatively tight and the cost of a racing programme was still a matter of debate, given that Mercedes were no longer part of a war economy. Few cars were available for practice, these being tuned road vehicles and hard-used at that, and only one Grand Prix car had actually been built, with the rest still under construction.

He advised Gregory to first take his client elsewhere, get him some experience (perhaps as a privateer), and the possibility of a works drive would be considered for the 1955 season. No advice from Alfred Neubauer could ever be considered patronising or evasive; he simply wasn't that sort of man.

Gregory trailed back to Britain and told Moss what had happened. At that stage Gregory simply hadn't thought that the plan would go awry, but had looked forward to a triumphant fait accompli; if not with Mercedes then with someone else. He was by now starting to share Moss's depression.

It had not actually been a snub; the door had been left ajar rather than slammed in his face. Gregory had merely taken it upon himself to make the attempt, and the attempt had, for the moment, failed. No discredit in that, but he knew full well that Stirling's confidence needed topping up, and so for that matter did his own since he had committed himself to managing Moss and his friend's morale was slipping fast. Moss, in fact, was pleased at Gregory's effort, even if downcast by the result.

In fact, given that Mercedes were clearly all sorted out for the 1954 season, at least as far as drivers were concerned (cars were clearly a different matter), it was an extremely encouraging meeting. It was only that there was no obvious team place for Moss anywhere else which made the whole thing seem to fall flat. After all, Neubauer was not well known as a 'promiser' and for him to be so well-informed about Stirling Moss, who had never scored any Championship points, was an encouraging sign, although Gregory and Moss seem to have missed it at the time. Perhaps some of Neubauer's attitude was lost in translation, for his prediction about a man he had never actually met proved accurate.

Mercedes-Benz felt that, Fangio aside, they should use Germans wherever possible. The return to racing was to be, to use a military analogy, not so much a blitzkrieg in the 1930s style, but more a surgical strike – in and out in two years, job accomplished. Budgets were, although sufficient and even generous, not particularly flexible, and deviation from the plan was unthinkable. The post-war German economic miracle, more correctly defined as Marshall Aid, was well under way, but was geared rather more to infrastructure projects than speculative ventures in motor racing, which even then was the costliest sport on the planet. The next year would be different, but for the moment Gregory had to look elsewhere.

Chapter 8

HOW NOT TO BUY A MASERATI

'Thou Paradise of exiles, Italy!'
PERCY BYSSHE SHELLEY

'When doing business in Italy, eat first.'
KENNETH ALBERT GREGORY

The only logical alternative to Germany was Italy, but Ferrari was out of the question, of course. Although, as Moss's manager, Gregory was able to act with total discretion, motor racing is a small world and he couldn't go to Modena, cap in hand, and risk further humiliation despite the danger that Stirling might well give up if things didn't improve, putting them both out of a job. British opportunities – the preferable option for several reasons, the main one being Stirling's patriotism keenly honed in a wartime childhood – were few and far between.

Happily, Ferrari was not the only manufacturer in Modena. Actually, the Commendatore was the upstart, at least as a 'Grand Constructor' manufacturer, when compared to Alfa Romeo, Lancia and Maserati.

The Maserati concern, a few minutes down the road from the town centre, had announced its intention of building a production run of 2½-litre Formula 1 cars for the 1954 season. It was to be called the Maserati 250F, and would be designed and built as a customer racer with selective works backing. Gioacchino Colombo, the mainspring behind the programme, had not stayed to see the project through, leaving in August 1953. He left behind him Valerio Colotti, who he had persuaded to leave Ferrari, to develop the transmission and finer points of the new car. Colotti thought sufficiently well enough of it that he was, in fact, to persist in its development long after it had ceased to be competitive.

Syd Greene, owner of the Gilby Engineering racing team, had ordered a Maserati 250F to go with the A6GCS sports car which he had bought in May 1953. Roy Salvadori was to drive the new Formula 1 car and it occurred to both Moss and Ken Gregory that he might order another one for Stirling to drive. Greene was reluctant – they were £5,000 apiece, after all, compounded by the fact that the Gilby team was supported by Esso, whereas équipe Moss, such as it was, was supported by Shell Mex & BP. Gilby were rather better supported, too; Esso were more or less paying for the Salvadori car, whereas Shell Mex & BP had given no indication that they would be prepared to stump up for a second car to be run in a team sponsored by Esso, and persuading Esso to 'double up' would be an even harder task, given that Moss was a BP-sponsored driver.

Drivers, as well as teams, were contracted to fuel companies – two drivers, sponsored by different organisations could not race in the same team. That this would produce conflicts of interest was obvious, although the potential pairing of Moss and Salvadori (a star in his own right) in the same Formula 1 team must have been a tempting one – but, as it turned out, not tempting enough. Greene persistently put off making a decision – quite possibly delayed by Esso.

This was a pity for équipe Moss, as doors were closing every day. Works drivers were being signed up by Connaught, Ferrari, Maserati and Lancia, as well as a host of other less notable players, and private cars were being laid down (and paid for) in readiness for the opening race in Argentina in January. Winter is a season for commerce rather than competition in motor racing, but time was fast slipping by and they were getting nowhere.

Greene had still not decided by the end-of-year BRDC dinner in London, and Alfred Moss and Ken Gregory rather belatedly decided to make their own approach to Modena, which, with the benefit of hindsight, was perhaps a little ill-prepared. Certainly it was to be expensive, as unavoidable choices often are. On being pressed during the evening, Greene had declined to take the matter forward, so it was agreed between Alfred and Ken that Ken should go to Italy the next day.

Stirling had flown to America to take part in the Great American Mountain Rally, driving for the Rootes competition department. Before departure he had said to Gregory: 'See if you can sign me up with Connaughts or someone ... I don't mind, as long as you fix up something.'

Gregory, taking Stirling at his word, and picking up rather more than an echo of quiet desperation in his friend's mien, resolved to dust off his pitch to Mercedes and simply flew to Modena, arriving at 7 p.m., and handed in his business card at the Maserati factory gate. Signor Omer Orsi was still there and agreed to see him immediately. Orsi was no clown; his family had effectively taken over Maserati in 1937, when the Maserati brothers' enthusiasm for racing had rather outstripped their business acumen and they had departed to Bologna to form the OSCA concern when their 10-year earn-out period had lapsed. It had been unfortunate for them that the war had neatly sectioned out so much of the potential. The Orsi family had built the Modena tram network, as well as being owners of steel mills and agricultural equipment factories. They had, with single-minded determination, developed Maserati into a full-blown engineering company. Their machine tool sales, mainly milling machines, to the Peron regime in Argentina – assisted by the occasional presence on their works team of not only Juan Manuel Fangio, but also Froilan Gonzalez (until 1953) and Onofre Marimon – were large and growing. Ken Gregory was 27, just under nine stone, no money, little experience with Italian business practice, even less time, and still lowered by apparent rejection from Mercedes. He had only one bargaining point in his arsenal; his absolute and unshakeable faith in the ability of Stirling Moss. It was not to be enough.

Maserati was almost an Argentinian team. They had committed to two or three works-supported cars, to be driven by Fangio, whose Mercedes contract would not come into effect until later in the 1954 season, and Onofre Marimon, the highly-rated Fangio protégé. Other drivers they had considered shortlisting were Roberto Mieres, also from Argentina, and Sergio Mantovani, as well as the two Luigis, Villoresi and Musso. There was the chance that Froilan Gonzalez, who always drove his heart out, might also return. It is not fair to say that Italy and Argentina were to be the sole source of drivers for Maserati, however it may look. In Italy it is the car that wins, not the driver. If the car wins, then that is to the maker's credit. If the car fails, then that is the driver's fault. The triangular fight between Maserati, Ferrari and Lancia was, over the next 18 months, to reach its grand operatic zenith.

The time spent waiting for a decision from Gilby Engineering had been totally wasted, so Gregory was not in a strong position – a condition which he worked hard to conceal. Orsi showed him into a small meeting room off the drawing office, together with Alfieri, the chief engineer, as interpreter. Gregory could see through to the factory floor and make out the alluring shape beneath the dustsheets of the racing cars under construction. Orsi, well-fleshed, relaxed and immaculately tailored, his suit a masterpiece in pigeon grey, politely enquired as to the purpose of the visit, and how he could be of assistance to Signor Moss or, indeed, even his representative? He knew quite well, of course. We do not know whether he had had conversations with Gilby Engineering about the possibility of their buying two cars, but it seems highly unlikely that the manoeuvre had not been discussed.

Just a little blusterish, and calling upon reserves of adrenalin he was unaware he possessed, Gregory plunged into his skimpily-rehearsed pitch. He pointed out that unless Maserati secured Moss's services now, possibly to replace Fangio when he moved to Mercedes, then he would be driving for someone else the next season … and how about that, hey? Orsi greeted this bombshell with a polite smile. There was, he knew, no shortage of drivers for this new formula, for which all had been waiting. Alberto Ascari, the current World Champion, for example, might even be persuaded from Lancia. Orsi knew perfectly well, for that was his business, that this late in the year (December) if Signor Moss wanted a Maserati, or anything else decent with five wheels and an engine for that matter, then he would have to buy one, probably at retail price, and it transpired, happily, that they had just one left. Was that not felicitous? Like everyone else in motor racing, he also knew about Enzo Ferrari's previous rudeness, for Stirling had not concealed it, as well as the state of play in all the other serious teams, Ferrari's in particular. He knew that Gregory was in between the proverbial rock and hard place. He was, though, first and foremost a gentleman, so he did not press the point – or didn't appear to.

But, after all, this was Maserati, founded in 1914. This

was Modena. This is where they didn't give birthday presents to little boys, they gave them a piece of tin and a hammer and watched proudly as they made their own. This was where the fabulously wealthy Whitney Straight had come to give substance to his own racing ambitions almost exactly 20 years before. That had been when the Maserati brothers had still been running it – they might as well have given their cars away for all the good it had done them. But really, what could have changed?

Now, clearly, a harder trader than Gregory was then might well have expressed sympathetic regret that the cars were selling so poorly; after all, the opening race of the season was barely a month away; the cars were untried; there could be difficulties with an import permit, as sundry jacks-in-office played a huge role in simple commerce then; the issue of fuel sponsorship could perhaps be circumvented; was it not regrettable that the only UK buyer of such a car was using a driver with an Italian name, and so on. But Gregory didn't. He didn't mention the fact that his boy had been offered a Formula 1 drive as long ago as 1950, which was precisely the point. He was under too much pressure to deliver a result so that Moss would not end up joining the myriad and growing ranks of Europe's jobbing drivers and wannabes – a fate which would surely handicap, or perhaps even destroy, both their careers.

Omer Orsi saw this, of course, but was a courteous man, solicitous and hospitable, and Gregory was offered cup after cup of espresso and cigarette after cigarette until his nerve ends were almost popping through his skin, but nary a scrap of food. So, there he sat, stomach and wallet rumbling as Orsi politely, almost confidentially, but with great finesse, leaned forward and proceeded to sell him a car. Gregory, of course, could not call Alfred Moss to get authorisation for what he was about to do, not unless he lost great face – never a smart move in Italy, and certainly not an option if you intend or even hope to do business there again – so he started manfully to haggle over the sixth machine. He spoke for no money, had no proper mandate, but neither did he have any real option.

It was rather like playing tennis against a wall. Finally, the specification and price were settled – the latter pretty much list, the former a cause of deep concern at the Maserati works. The men agreed a final form of words for the contract, it was drawn up there and then, both signed, and Orsi took Gregory out to dinner – at 1 a.m. It transpired that he had ordered the local restaurant kept open until it was needed. Gregory, fainting with hunger while hopped-up on nicotine and caffeine, realised, as the rest of the Orsi party strolled casually into the empty restaurant as if they owned the place (which, of course, they may well have done) that he had much to learn. When doing business in Italy, he reflected later, eat first. Food is important, vital even, but money provides the best nourishment of all.

Orsi was quietly thrilled, of course. Moss's performance in the Italian Grand Prix the previous September had given both Ferrari and Maserati something to think about; he had finished 13th in a car which had little business even being in the race, as it had all the appearance of having been cobbled together in a garage at a moment's notice (which it had) and, by way of mitigation, had had to endure no less than eight pit stops and had been running a comfortable fifth for part of the race. Only tyres, inferior handling and a huge fuel consumption had let him down – that is to say, everything. He had impressed deeply. If Orsi was surprised that Moss hadn't been snapped up already by a works team, he said nothing. Orsi had no idea who was to pay for the car, but work could not possibly start before a deposit was received. Whatever his delight, business was business.

One of Gregory's most important stipulations about the car, apart from the central issue that it should be green, was that it should have a pedal layout in the manner of a British racer; that is to say with the pedals laid out as for a normal road machine, which caused a politely disguised shudder to run through the entire factory. Back home, racing cars were always set up this way to allow the driver to 'heel and toe' while performing racing changes up through the gears, and, in the event that a driver used more than one type of car at a given meeting (almost guaranteed then), to avoid any confusion which could be dangerous or fatal. To Maserati and Ferrari, though, racing cars meant Italian racing cars – men's cars. Men drove with a centre throttle, always had, always would – one of the laws of nature, surely. Although Orsi and the chief mechanic, Bertocchi, eventually acquiesced to Gregory's strange and perverted request, the matter was to crop up again, even though it was already enshrined in the contract. Behind the scenes, grubby hands were thrown up in genuine horror.

The deal then, if we can call it that, was for one car and, more important, one engine. This may sound normal and logical, but racing cars are designed to win races, not for longevity. The risk is that the car will fall apart the instant it crosses the line, its purpose accomplished. The Micawberish truth was that, if a racing car lasted 300 miles to finish a Grand Prix – result, happiness; if it lasted 299 miles to expire just short of the finish line – result, misery. Not everyone had the means to rebuild the entire vehicle after every race like the works teams could, as the costs were prohibitive. Privateers, like Moss was unknowingly about to become, had to preserve their engines and transmissions –

even tyres – using fewer revolutions than the works machines. This was precisely the point. Maserati and Ferrari would both sell cars and in all probability win more races than their customers through their drivers' being able to risk wrecking the engine and, by default, the gearbox and axle. In Moss's case, this was to effectively limit his engine to around 7,200 rpm, as opposed to 7,600-8,000 available to the works cars – a critical difference of perhaps 10-15 mph in top gear. The only way to correct that was via a higher axle ratio, which would probably also mean changing carburation, and thus paying penalties in acceleration. Take it or leave it, but it would have to be driven relatively gently.

Gregory had no choice. He had gritted his teeth and gone ahead. He telephoned Alfred Moss at 3 a.m. local time and told him what he had done. Happily, Alfred did not repudiate the deal, knowing that Ken had done the best he could at short notice, and was pleased that the choice had been Maserati rather than Ferrari; the two agreed to sort out the details upon Gregory's return. For the moment it would be a secret from Stirling, who, so they both rightly thought, was in need of a boost.

He had done the only thing possible. Maserati was the sole concern offering a suitable car for the forthcoming season. Lancia was purely a works team and the Germans did not sell their cars to privateers (a strategy unchanged from that which prevailed before the war, as Whitney Straight had found out when he had tried to buy an Auto-Union) and a Maserati was infinitely preferable to a Ferrari, for reasons which were obvious. The main thing was that Stirling now had a car for the 1954 season, albeit as a private owner/driver – the costliest way of doing things.

Would Stirling Moss have been offered a works drive earlier in the year? Probably not by Maserati – their preference for Argentinian drivers, themselves sponsored by the Automobile Club of Argentina (a Peron quango) made them cheaper to use, as well as helping the sales effort, not only in Argentina but all over South America, where market share for machine tools and engineering products was easier to get than in Europe and North America. The simple reason for this was that the end of the Korean War had released a huge manufacturing capacity in the NATO countries, and competition was stepping up, particularly in the USA's back yard where the men in the Brooks Brothers' suits were laying siege to all the buyers and fighting off the Germans, who were armed with both large lumps of American money and a suspiciously competitive exchange rate.

After the South Americans, there were also plenty of skilled Italian drivers, many of them keen and wealthy enough to pay Maserati to drive. In many ways, this aspect of the sport has not changed much, as it still happens today, although not in the top echelons. A long-emerging Brit – Le Mans runner or not, touched with greatness or not – probably came fairly low in the potential pecking order, given the drive for sales with which Maserati were faced. That the firm were to reverse this opinion so soon speaks volumes for both the ability of Moss, which is now a matter of public record, and the preparedness of Maserati, or more particularly Orsi, to perform an elegant voltafaccia with such seamless flexibility. This latter rather suggests that he knew exactly what he was doing when he neatly inserted the unknowing Moss into one of his cars in the small hours of that December morning.

Orsi was not to know that Gregory had been quite prepared to go to Ferrari the very next day had no 250F been available, as he was quite prepared, with Alfred's support, to face Stirling's ire when presented with one of the products of the man who had dealt with him so badly. Happily for all concerned, it was not necessary to do so.

As it turned out, the choice of Maserati over Ferrari was a sound, even prescient, one – however randomly it had been arrived at. The Orsis were 'proper people' compared to Enzo Ferrari – they would not have dreamed of behaving so deviously to a potential top-line driver as Ferrari had. Furthermore, the Maserati racing programme was, like that of Neubauer, more or less sorted for the coming year, in broad sweep at least; whereas Ferrari was stomping about the place, hamming it up in his usual manner – on the one hand threatening to withdraw from Formula 1 altogether (a posture which no-one took awfully seriously, given that racing defined the man's life), and on the other rooting furiously through his great coffer of assorted engine capacities, bores, strokes and compression ratios, these the results of his terrorising of a pair of gifted engine designers who had come and gone since 1945. They were Gioacchino Colombo and Aurelio Lampredi, and Ferrari had ruthlessly played one off against the other until Colombo departed in 1953 to kick-start the Maserati 250 project. Lampredi had left a year later.

Ferrari's ill-disguised panic was justifiable; having seen the results that a properly-funded operation can have upon the competition in the 1930s – the last time that Mercedes had entered the fray – he had reason to be concerned. As the Patron of the Alfa Romeo racing team before the war, he had seen his prized Alfa P3s humbled before the might of Daimler-Benz and Auto-Union. He was nervous at the prospect of a rematch. Fair enough, though – it was both his passion and his business.

In the 1952 and 1953 seasons, when Grands Prix were run to Formula 2, Ferrari had won all but one of the World

Championship races (the odd one out being, ironically, the Italian Grand Prix) giving the championship to Alberto Ascari twice in succession. In 1954 Ferrari would win only two Championship events, the British and the Spanish, being beaten on every other occasion by either Maserati or Mercedes-Benz.

The reason was the car. The Type 553 'Squalo' (Shark) was a bulbous, understeering pig of a car, hurried into manufacture and as unlike its namesake that the hand of man could ensure. It was powered by an oversquare four-cylinder blaster which owed something to the 2-litre Formula 2 effort, which itself drew inspiration from the American Offenhauser design but lacked that unit's smoothness. Compared to its predecessor, the car was very hard work indeed. 'Balena' (whale) might have been a more suitable appellation. The car needed a driver of formidable strength and endurance; in Froilan Gonzalez, it got one.

Ferrari had experimented with several engine layouts (which he could do with ease because the firm had an in-house foundry), even a 2½-litre twin-cylinder unit which must have functioned rather like a rabid pogo stick, but they opted for simplicity and cheapness, as well as a proven formula – they were, unlike Mercedes, in a parlous financial state. What Stirling Moss would have made of the Squalo would have been interesting to see, but Ferrari was not given the chance to ask him. The Lampredi-designed V12 from the 4½-litre Grand Prix car would famously find its feet in years to come, but it was the Colombo V12 which would win immortality in the 250GTO, which enthusiasts define as the finest thing which any human being has ever put together – with the possible exception of any Daimler-Benz racing car, that is.

Fangio was to win the 1954 Championship with 20

points in hand over Ferrari's Froilan Gonzalez, which was not really a fair reflection upon the stupefying skills of 'Pepe the Pampas Bull', whose underdeveloped car was simply outclassed. While he was clearly possessed of the heart and gonads of the eponymous bovine, the Ferrari itself was not, at least when compared to the Stuttgart effort, which was not a warmed-over Formula 2 car but rather one designed purely to win the World Championship. The Squalo cars were competing in such company that only a driver of the calibre of a Gonzalez, a Hawthorn or a Moss could have managed them effectively – Gonzalez as much by strength and sheer heart as anything. Within the narrow confines of the sport the two tubby Argentinians – Fangio and Gonzalez – would for a while become the Tweedledum and Tweedledee of racing. Fangio would be draped in the mantle of immortality, while Gonzalez, stricken by grief at the sacrifices which the game demanded, would retire early by choice. When the two Argentinians raced each other, though, there was often very little in it.

Ferrari was later to pretend to regret, probably with some feeling, his rudeness to Moss, but it would take him a decade to attempt to make amends with an offer, by which time it was to be sadly too late for both of them.

Stirling was on the way back from the USA after a fairly fruitless spell of rallying, and knew nothing of this new toy when Gregory made an announcement to the Press that the deal had been struck. Upon his return to Southampton on the Queen Mary, Moss was swamped at the quayside by British reporters looking for a comment, which stretched his improvisational skills almost to the limit. Whatever he thought of the previous two seasons, and they had been singularly unfulfilling, Gregory had ensured that Moss was still a name to conjure with in Fleet Street.

The Moss family, displaying a solidarity seldom found anywhere, rallied round to raise the money, the sources for which even included Stirling's sister Pat's savings. It was a Moss family trait; nothing was for nothing, all for one and one for all. Stirling went straight to business, though, and was pleased that the Maserati would at least be green, with proper British pedals, even though he had never even clapped eyes on one.

Moss confesses readily now to a degree of nervousness. He had always relished the role of underdog, of the man trying his heart out in second, or even sixth place – that part of the race which the professionals watch – and this sudden propulsion into the big league gave him pause for thought. He was now in the perfect position to either justify the faith which the media, his family, Gregory and Alf Francis had in him, or make a total fool of himself – to make either a fair fist or a pig's ear of the whole thing.

The faithful Alf Francis appeared at Modena on 21 March 1954, complete with a supply of petrol and oil – even paint in Moss's favourite shade of green. Work on the car had not even been started. Stirling then became extremely edgy that the machine might not be ready for the non-championship race at Pau in April; a warm-up for the serious business to come. He was right to be so – it wasn't.

Chapter 9

FORMULA 1

'There is no such thing as inner peace.
There is only nervousness or death.'
FRAN LEBOWITZ

For Gregory, the fact that Moss was now sorted out for the coming season – or at least had a drive, albeit in his own car – was a source of great relief. His friend had been, instead of planning, indulging in displacement activities which threatened to drive Gregory completely to distraction. Every detail had to be analysed and every possibility explored, for there had been little to do until the matter of a drive was sorted – at which point Ken Gregory could carry on doing his job, as opposed to sharing it.

The green Maserati was delivered by Francis to the Moss farm and installed in one of the luxurious outhouses. There was a technical problem about paying the vast import duty on the car which was circumvented by using the good offices of Earl Howe, who suggested that Moss apply to keep the car on a temporary import carnet from the Customs and Excise which, provided he spent more than 183 days out of the country, would obviate the necessity of paying duty on it. This was not a problem, as the car would mainly be used in Europe, anyway, and would be frequently returned to the factory. It did mean, though, that the car could only be sold outside the country when the occasion arose. This would cause a little confusion later.

A few warm-up, non-championship races were common then, and were put in the category of 'International' events. The crowds would see Formula 1 cars at work, although the events would count for nothing in terms of the Championship itself, and were merely shakedowns.

The first Championship race which the Maserati was ready for after its two-month gestation was the Belgian Grand Prix in June, where Stirling came third, but only after some unforeseen unpleasantness.

Fangio, yet to depart for Mercedes, was the No. 1 works Maserati driver, with Marimon and Mantovani in support. On lap one Marimon over-revved his engine, after which it was off song and he retired after two more laps. Orsi sent Alfieri over to ask Francis whether he would consent to retiring Moss and letting Marimon use his car. The formidable Alf refused. Not to have done so would have been tantamount to admitting that Marimon was the better driver, and there had been no attempt to reallocate Mantovani's car, for example, let alone any of the other privateers. Certainly, no one would dare ask Prince Bira, who was also driving his own Maserati. Stirling, despite extreme discomfort from a nasty abscess under his arm, was lying third and running well, even though a pit stop was inevitable because of the vast amounts of oil which the engine was using.

If there was one core problem with the 250F it was lubrication. Save its startling beauty, which forgives many faults in retrospect, it was otherwise merely a sound car. The engine was perhaps rather showily constructed, with no significant use of main gaskets – as if to prove that decent engineering needed no such flabby inexactitudes – so that a tired or overheated engine would start blowing oil out through its aching joints relatively quickly. Francis had a fair idea of the oil consumption and had worked out that the car would need two gallons – 16 pints, mind you – on or about the 25th lap if it wasn't going to start blowing metal out of its exhaust and turn itself inside out.

Francis's blunt response to Alfieri, in fluent and dismissive Italian that 'even with a boil, Moss is as good as Marimon' annoyed Alfieri, even if he thought the remark true, and he withdrew the admittedly modest pit support forthwith. Francis ignored him anyway and called Stirling in so that Tony Robinson could heave the oil in. They had no pressurised container and he seemed to be taking a fair time about it, so a Maserati mechanic (redundant now that Marimon had retired, and who was now hopping about doing his best to help) tried to take away the can and slam the filler cap down, as he had failed to realise – probably couldn't imagine – that so much oil was needed. This burlesque of inefficiency carried on just a few seconds too long for Alf Francis who stepped up and thumped the man on the jaw, instantly rendering him both horizontal and tearful. Stares of disbelief accompanied Moss's departure back into the race. The poor mechanic, only a boy really, came to and retired to the back of the pit in something less than a state of grace.

To understand both the action and reaction of this baroque little episode, it is important to recall that for many Italians – particularly those marinated in the traditions of engineering, of which Emilia is justly proud – a motor race, not only in its preparation, but in its conduct and its result, is ahead even of opera and football in importance, which makes it the most significant human activity on the face of the planet next to sex. To participate at all in what might turn out to be a victory is a powerful stimulus, which in this case overrode any sense of discipline, for which the poor boy was humiliated.

Whether Francis really needed to actually hit the fellow is uncertain, but clearly he was angry at the Maserati team attitude, which was breathtakingly high-handed from his point of view. It is probable that he might have preferred to hit Alfieri, and even may have visualised doing so, to the misfortune of the mechanic who, when all is said and done, was only trying to help. With one blow, as it were, Francis established himself as a man not to be messed with; not that this would stop the Maserati team from doing so whenever they thought that they could get away with it. In this case, two Argentinians in the money would make better reading in Buenos Aires than one, hence the manoeuvre. It was just business, not the comic opera it appeared – not that Francis really gave a toss. He later consoled the poor chap and the episode went down as one of those occasions often put down to 'just motor racing'. He also took the trouble to explain to Orsi what had happened. He quite understood, and may even have secretly approved of such a macho statement.

Stirling's third place assured him of winning the Churchill Challenge Trophy, the prize for the highest placed British driver, before then in the hands of Mike Hawthorn, who had won it by coming eighth the previous year, which rather sums up the lowly position of Brits in the sport at that period.

Stirling was not the only one suffering skin eruptions. Gregory – sapped by the raw energy of his friend, client and flatmate, now that the season was under way – had a delayed reaction to the stress and suffered what he describes, with commendable insouciance, as a slight nervous breakdown – a little bit pregnant, as it were. Moss, always late to rise and late to bed, worked an entirely different schedule from that of his manager, and the friction between their lives tired Gregory. He retired for a fortnight to a clinic near Godalming, waking only to feed, answer calls of nature or to take sedation. Upon recovery he wisely found a flat of his own (a bare two streets away) and probably wondered more than once whether the dull routine at the RAC hadn't been such a bad idea after all.

Moss was contracted to Jaguar for the Reims 12 hour race, two weeks later, which effectively prevented the équipe from entering the Grand Prix which followed it, so the Maserati would not have a driver. Francis, who had gradually built up a good working relationship with the Maserati works, despite the fisticuffs at Spa, was asked if Moss would consent to lend the car to them so that Villoresi, borrowed from Lancia, could enter it in the race. Orsi naturally undertook to rebuild the car free of charge afterwards, incorporating several updates.

Stirling was initially iffy, but Francis persuaded him, and he agreed on condition that they used their own engine and drivetrain. In the event, they used his, which was perhaps cheeky of them, having made Moss pay through the nose for it in the first place, but they knew, because Francis had told them, that Moss never over-revved his car, as a rebuild would be so expensive. He was a man to be taken seriously, as the episode at Spa had shown, so they could be assured that the unit was therefore in good condition, if still using oil, (but it always did) and the car was entered as a works effort, hastily painted Maserati red and minus its Union Jack decals.

Villoresi started in 14th place but tried hard and came fifth, despite a persistent misfire. Orsi was as good as his word, and work started to totally rebuild the car in time for the British Grand Prix two weeks later. The car was fettled from stem to stern, given a more advanced cylinder head and totally overhauled suspension. The work naturally included a respray back to green. Francis had stayed in Modena to watch the rebuild, and as the car was finished he was summoned to engine designer Bellantani's presence, where an offer was made. If Moss would drive at a works level of revs, the works would agree to underwrite the cost of a wrecked engine, should it be necessary, or any other repairs which would be needed as a result of thrashing the car in order to win Moss's home Grand Prix which was next on the calendar.

Subtle, this. If Moss blew the engine up, he was a privateer; if he didn't, he was a works driver. No contract changed hands, but Maserati sat back to watch the fun. No less than 11 Maserati 250Fs were entered, and after a fierce practice, Moss was on the front row of the grid, in fourth place, but alongside Fangio in a Mercedes and Hawthorn and Gonzalez in Ferraris. For the first time, Moss had been able to drive to his potential, almost secure in the knowledge that Maserati would keep their word. Sadly, a silly fault in the final drive put him out after 80 laps while in third place, but the sensation of the race was Onofre Marimon, who came third after starting in 27th place – a record, I think, which because of grid size in modern races will probably stand for ever. More impressive at the time was that he beat Fangio. Gonzalez, driving almost purely with his arms as usual, wrestled his unresponsive Ferrari Squalo into first place from the start and led for the whole race to win by over a minute from his team-mate Hawthorn. It was a spectacular Ferrari success, but one of few that season. (In 1996, Gonzalez returned to Britain for the Goodwood Festival of Speed, in which he paraded a V16 BRM up the Hillclimb past Goodwood house. In the paddock, this dour, chubby, taciturn man, wearing his famous yellow helmet, was almost moved to tears by the response of the crowd, the backslapping and the endless requests for autographs. He could not believe that anyone still remembered him.)

A fortnight later was the Grand Prix of Europe, held at the Nürburgring. After Moss had again managed to win a place on the front row of the grid in early Friday practice, Maserati offered him a works drive. More correctly, works support, as the works team was a fluid thing, insecurely but imaginatively financed and rather prone to concertina in size as the mood changed. No matter that he was to drive his own car, it was to be absorbed into the factory effort. No mention was made of buying the car back, merely that from now on, prizes would be shared and expenses paid. The fact that Moss could now really afford to work the car to the limits for which it had been designed, on a consistent rather than piecemeal basis, was the main prize, though.

So, after a matter of a few months, and only two World Championship events, Maserati were prepared to perform a neat U-turn and offer Moss and Gregory what they had been after all along, to take the place of Fangio in the works team – after having forced them to buy a car, of course.

This news, fine though it was for équipe Moss, certainly unsettled Onofre Marimon. After his results at Silverstone and Castel Fusano, he had no real reason to feel insecure, but conversations which he had with Francis suggest that he was at least a little demoralised by this development. He envied Moss and Francis their rapport and intimate knowledge of the car, for example, and even went so far as to remark that he felt that, all things being equal, he could never hope to beat Moss; remarks which suggest that he was at best depressed and feeling desperately insecure. There is some supposition that he was becoming a victim of the hype to which the Argentinian drivers were being subjected in the light of the success being enjoyed by Fangio and, to a lesser extent, Gonzalez. With the departure of Fangio to Mercedes, it can be supposed that he had hoped for

105A. *Drivers' line-up, Targa Florio, 1955. L-R: John Fitch, Desmond Titterington, Peter Collins, Stirling Moss, Juan Manuel Fangio, Karl Kling. (Daimler-Benz Classic Archive).*

105B. *Fangio, the winner, congratulates Moss, second, at the Dutch Grand Prix, June 19, 1955. (Daimler-Benz Classic Archive).*

106A. Peter Collins. (Ken Gregory).
106B. Collins and Moss, competing
for 'the crumpet.' (Ken Gregory).
106C. Stirling's stag night.
Clockwise from left: Macdonald
Hobley, Stirling Moss, Godfrey
Smith, David Haynes, Lionel
Leonard, Alfred Moss, Denis Druit,
Basil Cardew, York Noble, Peter
Garnier, Peter Jopp. Ken Gregory
had 'flu. (Mark Harrison).

107A. Moss, Gregory and friends at the Stork club, E.53 St., New York. (Ken Gregory).

107B. Stirling window shops at 'The Beefburger', next to one of Alfred's surgeries, William IV St. (Ken Gregory).

107C. The redesigned swing-axle Kieft, Goodwood, 1952. (Graphic Photo Union).

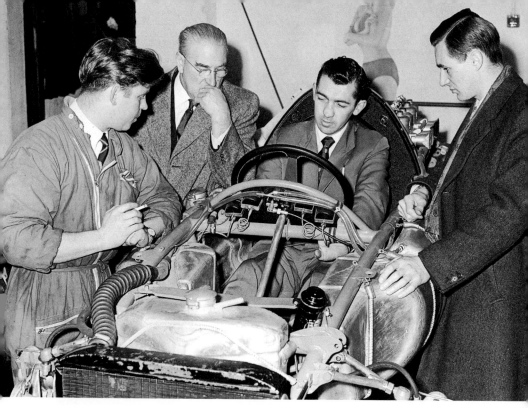

108A. *Tony Robinson, Alfred Moss, Stuart Lewis-Evans and Ken Gregory at the Cooper Car Co. works, Surbiton, fitting Lewis-Evans into the BRP Cooper-Climax, 1958. (Autocar).*

108B. *The finished product at Goodwood, complete with radio receiver, built by Ken's brother John. Lewis-Evans could hear nothing; the engine noise drowned out the messages. Ahead of its time, though. (Tony Robinson).*

109A. *The launch of the Yeoman Credit Racing Team, Lot's Road. 1958. In the car is Chris Bristow. L-R: Doug Armstrong (with moustache), Tony Robinson, Charles Cooper, John Cooper, Fabian Samengo-Turner, Paul Samengo-Turner, Bruce McIntosh, Don Haldenby, William Samengo-Turner, Stan Collier, Alfred Moss, unknown, Ken Gregory, Unknown, Rod Gueran , John Blunsden, Gregor Grant. (Maxwell Boyd).*
109B. *Cooper-Borgward leads Cooper-Climax. Ivor Bueb in the Yeoman Credit Cooper at Silverstone, 1958.*

110A. A close-up of the remarkable Borgward engine. The gearbox was made by Jack Knight. (Maxwell Boyd).
110B. The 1960 Cooper Climax under construction at Lot's road. Note the BRP trademark high fin on the rear deck of the car. (Maxwell Boyd).

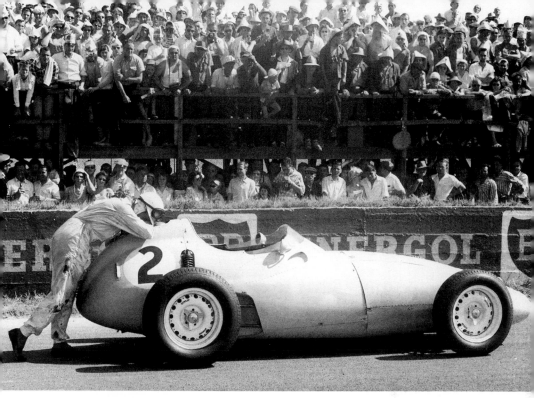

111A. Stirling, slumped exhausted over the tail of the BRP BRM at Reims, 1959.
(Bernard Cahier).
111B. Better luck in the BRM at Aintree; he came second. *(Ken Gregory).*

100. Hans Herrmann stares in disbelief as his BRP-BRM goes berserk at the AVUSring; German Grand Prix, 1959. He has simply fallen out as the car somersaults. (Ken Gregory).

advancement to an as yet ill-defined No. 1 slot. The immediate arrival of Moss in the team lowered him.

Francis chivvied him along; he had not yet acquired the experience of Moss, but would surely learn. Given that Marimon had already entered 11 Championship Grands Prix up to that point and finished 11th in the 1953 season, Francis's remarks were perhaps at best disingenuous and undiplomatic, but tact was never his strong suit and he was sincerely trying to help this affable but insecure young man. His remarks to Alfieri about Marimon at Spa may well have got back to their subject, but there is no reason to think so, as the two men dealt very well together and, anyway, there was never any suggestion that they were remarks meant in any way personally.

Marimon, from Cordoba, Buenos Aires, was 31 years old, and one of the three key Argentinian drivers of the era. He and his fellow countrymen, Fangio and Gonzalez, were close friends and they were more or less inseparable, sharing as they did the goodwill of the Peron regime and the support of the Automobile Club of Argentina. These South American three musketeers were ably supported by a singularly level-headed d'Artagnan in Roberto Mieres, from Mar del Plata, a courageous, skilled and, more important, reliable driver, but one with perhaps not quite the same fire in his belly as the other three. There could, or perhaps should, have been a fifth, Oscar Galvez, but he was not an officially sanctioned driver. It is not without significance that the circuit used for the Argentinian Grand Prix today is called l'Autrodromo Oscar Galvez, which suggests a local revisionism with reference to this highly politicised era of Argentina's motor racing. Perhaps non-Argentinians should be grateful that the full pool of talent was not trawled; few others might have had a look in.

Peron was following elements of the pre-war Hitler strategy of attempting to nationalise motor sport, but even the Argentinian dictator never went so far as appointing such a ridiculous figure as 'Rennabteilungfuhrer' Huhnlein, who had been effectively a political officer for the Mercedes team before the war, dressed in a thoroughly Ruritanian outfit, and more or less the bane of Neubauer's busy life.

The Saturday morning practice period, the last chance to shine before the main event, was brisk. No-one, with the possible exception of Moss and Marimon, was working as hard as Fangio and Herrmann were, as the Mercedes works team was making its first appearance on German soil since the halcyon days of 1939. After two laps trying, Marimon was provisionally eighth on the grid, next to Maurice Trintignant in a Ferrari, whereas Moss was third, on the first row. Marimon set off again but this time failed to return. There was some confusion, but it was just becoming clear that something was amiss when the news filtered through. He had crashed off the circuit at the Wehrseifen corner and was clearly dead when eventually discovered. Alf Francis, in his memoirs, put it this way: 'I wonder whether it was, in fact, pride that killed him?'

The Maserati team was naturally devastated; this was their first fatality since before the war and Marimon was a highly popular and gifted member of the team, whatever his own misgivings had been about his No. 1 status.

With cruel irony, Orsi was in Argentina when the tragedy happened. He was cabled with the news and replied that the works team were to withdraw from the race as a mark of respect, but not, significantly, without some manoeuvring. What actually happened was that Villoresi, still on loan from Lancia, withdrew – as he was driving the only other factory car – but Moss, Mantovani and Mieres – all of whom were, after all, driving cars not actually owned by the works – entered the race. The Owen organisation, entering a 250F for Ken Wharton, also cancelled their entry as a mark of respect for one of the sport's great 'nearly' men.

Whatever Fangio and Gonzalez wished to do, they entered the race. Gonzalez was almost maddened by grief at the death of his friend, and was quite possibly not really fit to drive at all, but he overcame this handicap to give of his best and come second to Fangio, who brought the W196 to victory in its home debut. The two friends were just able to store up their grief for later. Gonzalez in fact was to more or less retire from racing within the year.

Stirling, struggling manfully with another lubrication problem, ran a big end on the engine and retired on the second lap. The bottom end of the engine was a little suspect, anyway, as he had over-revved it in practice which, given the tall gearing used on the huge Nürburgring circuit, suggests that he was a little over-enthusiastic in finding its limits, but the starting money was a great compensation, and Maserati had undertaken to rebuild the engine. Although Moss had reverted to being a 'private' entrant to allow the works to express its grief in a proper manner, which they sincerely wished to do, their arrangement still stood. There was insufficient time to fix the Moss Maserati before the Oulton Park Gold Cup, so the works lent him Villoresi's car. He won with it.

Moss's career, despite the tragedy at the Nürburgring, was now gathering momentum. In less than 10 months he had gone from considering giving up, so much frustration and bad luck had he had, to being a works-supported front runner; indeed, as Marimon had suspected, the de facto Number One.

This development of a works drive was a godsend to

Gregory. The persistent worry of the cost of an engine rebuild, equivalent in price to no less than two new Jaguar XK120s, was a big one. With the Maserati offer, Moss had the flexibility of owning his own car, coupled with the benefit of effective works support should he wreck it by trying to win. This new situation transformed Gregory's job, and he now set about earning his pay in a rather different way.

There were few professional sportsmen in the 1950s; it wasn't really a British thing, and particularly so in motor racing. Almost all the drivers effectively had amateur status, treating the sport as a hobby. Many of them, such as Mike Hawthorn, Ivor Bueb and Roy Salvadori, had other sources of income, linked to the motor trade in some way, usually garages. Others, like Harry Schell or Masten Gregory, were affluent – or at least apparently so – and doing it for the fun of it. Still others, like the Marquis de Portago, Count 'Taffy' von Trips, the Baron de Graffenried or Count Carel de Beaufort, were rich toffs. The Marquis de Portago felt that success in racing might lead to a life in politics. He cherished an ambition to be the foreign minister of Spain, a post to which he was, at least by bloodline, eminently qualified.

To an extent, the 'toffs' were sought out by the affluent but, by and large, it was a surprisingly democratic environment; unlike the turf, for example, from which motor racing inherited so much of its characteristics and nomenclature and which has been the source of some of Britain's most unpleasant little sporting snobberies. Portago, like Marimon, held one record which will also be unchallenged but which went a little further – he was the only man to be placed around Aintree on horse and car in both the Grand National and the British Grand Prix. He was a sporting polymath.

Mechanics, though, in contrast to the dashing amateur

heroes, were often paid badly in randomly chosen bundles of assorted currencies, accumulated over extended European tours. Exchange control regulations, common then, were routinely broken – nothing wrong in that from our standpoint, as they were clearly stupid anyway, but it was a conspiracy in which all were forced to take part, ably assisted by the motor manufacturers themselves.

Professional sportsmen, then, were slightly frowned upon by the establishment figures who often ran the sport itself. There had been hardly any pros in the sport before the war, and those that had such a status were treated rather like jockeys, and many people were minded to keep it that way. Too much money, it was rationalised neatly, might ruin a perfectly good hobby. Some team managers actually expected drivers to buy rides, others preferred to pay them a pittance. Many of the more eminent ones knew that there was a bottomless pit of talent, some of it questionable, who would go to almost any lengths to secure a ride, spending vast amounts of their own, or someone else's money, to secure status with a manufacturer by buying that firm's road cars. This was particularly true of Ferrari, although it is fair to say that Ferrari's road cars paid for the racing, rather than that the racing promoted the road cars.

Many drivers, though, enjoyed some personal sponsorship or funding from fuel and oil companies, or makers of tyres, plugs and brakes, either in terms of cash or kind. Gregory had organised a deal with Shell Mex & BP to run for two years, and subsequently a 10-year deal was negotiated, which carried Moss through to his retirement. Such things, though, were comparatively rare, and most drivers paid their own way with fairly minimal assistance.

Moss looked at it all rather differently. He adopted a 'professional' attitude to the sport, in its widest sense, at a time when no such thing properly existed, so to an extent he wrote the rule book, becoming a benchmark for those who came later. This is not to say that he enjoyed racing any less than the playboy tendency, but he did one thing which set him apart from the gifted amateur so prized in English sporting mythology; he practised. He practised grid get-aways, he practised Le Mans starts. He also expected to get paid for what he did, in whatever field he did it. He was a businessman, whose product was value for money.

He was ably guided and assisted in this by Gregory. As early as 1952 Moss had been paid, albeit only £100, to endorse Craven A cigarettes, of which he smoked very few, but that was before Gregory was handling his business, and Gregory had an intuitive grasp of the endorsement game. He did not go overboard, being most careful not to devalue the brand name, which is what it was becoming, to the extent of associating it with questionable products – not yet anyway – but the first deal he did exploited the fact that Moss is more or less teetotal. The lucky company was Lucozade, which became a favourite after-race drink. Two crates a week were delivered to the offices, in fact.

The business of being Stirling Moss was becoming an active one. Gregory, in offices provided by Alfred Moss at William IV Street, near the Strand, was still running the Half-litre Car Club as well as Stirling Moss Ltd, which was in the process of formation and was obliged to start hiring extra help.

The Maserati 250F is the definitive production racer of the 1950s – possibly of all time. At a period when it was virtually impossible to buy a competitive car from a manufacturer, all of whom entered their own works teams, it found for itself a market which was a perfect niche. Not only did they sell well, total production being several dozen, but the customers updated them themselves, making design improvements and modifications from which the factory learned much. The customers often found weaknesses before the factory did, which was a cost-effective way of development testing which ordinarily the firm could not have afforded. Only in the field of sports car racing was there any parallel to the 250F, in the guise of the Jaguar C- and D-types and, later, the Lister-Jaguar and the Aston Martin DB4GT. Of course, both Maserati and Ferrari sold sports cars to well-heeled customers, and many of them were raced, but the other Modena firm had already become infamous for the breathtaking commercial eye-gouging of its road car clients in order to fund its own racing efforts; which was not a reputation which Maserati ever achieved, possibly because the manufacture of cars was an indulgence for the Orsi family. Ultimately, though, Ferrari survived as a racing concern while Maserati did not – one of those all too common outcomes which fall into the 'sad but true' category.

The Italian Grand Prix at Monza on 5 September 1954 saw a slight reversal of the situation which had obtained at Silverstone, in that the Maserati team seemed keener to promote Luigi Villoresi, the 44-year-old veteran, than their new team member Moss, which, if it did not upset Stirling, because he knew little of it, certainly annoyed Alf Francis, ever ready to confront issues on his employer's behalf.

After a late practice, in the cooler evening air, Francis was aghast to find the factory mechanics stripping down Stirling's engine and swapping his usefully-scrubbed in tyres over with the unmarked ones of Villoresi's car. A very loud conversation ensued between Chief Engineer Bertocchi and Francis – reminiscent of Spa, but falling short of its denouement – the result of which was that Francis stalked away.

Never a man to avoid a confrontation when he thought it would do any good, he decided not to tell Stirling what was going on and, after a quick break to decide strategy, returned to the pits to find the proper tyres back on the car and the strip-down halted. Bertocchi sheepishly acknowledged that they had been a little unfair about the tyres and that the strip-down was unnecessary. Francis worked all night to reassemble the engine and, in his tiredness, neglected to modify a section of pipe running from the dry sump to the engine, which he had previously marked as being too rigid and perhaps prone to breakage. Pleased that Bertocchi had backed down, and assuming that the issue was finished, he worked on the car all through the night and grabbed a few hours sleep before the 3 o'clock start.

On the day, Francis ran the Moss pit and Gregory kept the lap chart. The works pit was adjacent. If this separation of management seemed sinister, nothing was said until the race had lasted 40 laps and Villoresi seemed to be gaining on Moss, who was third behind Ascari and Fangio, biding his time. Suspicious, Francis asked Bertocchi why he was promoting a Maserati battle for third place. Bertocchi coolly replied that for the Italian Grand Prix, the works considered Villoresi the No. 1 driver, and they would like him to win. Francis's immediate reply, probably in his native Polish, is not on record, and probably just as well, but he declared his intention of running the race for Stirling's benefit, not that of the works. He may have understood the Maserati team's chauvinist strategy, but did not approve; he was only a quasi-works mechanic and owed his loyalty totally to Moss.

Gregory saw a new side to Moss as they sat chatting on the grid. Ken sat on the left rear wheel, passing the time of day, chatting about business housekeeping issues and minor details. The two-minute board went up, and Stirling started to pull on his gloves. Ken noticed that he had stopped replying and suddenly realised that, so far as Stirling was concerned, he was just not there any more. He left the grid to walk back to the pit, in the sure and certain knowledge that, had he remained on the wheel, Stirling would have just run over him.

The race started to go according to the Maserati schedule. Villoresi speeded up, overtook a surprised Stirling, and promptly wrecked the transmission on his car. Stirling pressed on, driving a consistent race, and the two leaders, Ascari and Fangio, started to flag, whereupon Moss took the lead, to the delight of the spectators and a rather embarrassed Bertocchi. Ascari fought back and retook the lead until he blew his engine on lap 48, after which Moss extended his lead over an exhausted Fangio.

Fate dictated that Omer Orsi should see for himself what was going on, Bertocchi being too embarrassed to ask, and he strolled over to where Gregory and Francis were chewing their fingernails. He pulled rank as diplomatically as he could, suggesting that Stirling should be slowed enough to merely hold his lead, and Francis and Gregory concurred. Correspondingly, the 'slow down' signal was hung out for the rest of the race until, on lap 68, a haze of oil from the Moss car was spotted. The pipe which had concerned Francis had cracked and despite three gallons of oil being dumped in, most of it came straight out again and the Maserati coasted to a stop, its engine totally ruined half a mile from the line. Moss hopped out and pushed the car round to the finish, where he waited, a very tired man indeed, 10 laps, for the eventual winner, Fangio to cross it.

Over in the Mercedes pit, Neubauer, as usual festooned in stopwatches, nodded to himself appreciatively. He walked over and gave a few quiet words of congratulation to the exhausted Moss, echoed by Fangio, who later gave Stirling the moral victory after he had pushed the wrecked Maserati over the line to finish tenth. With those few muttered words in German, Moss's future for the next season was almost certainly assured, although no-one, apart from Neubauer and perhaps Fangio, seemed to realise it at the time. But it was to be exactly – exactly – as Neubauer had said it might be.

So, the season was suddenly taking on an entirely different feel. Irritating gremlins aside, Moss had, with the Italian Grand Prix, pushed himself firmly into the front rank by virtue of all those skills which the sport still holds dear; courage, certainly, professionalism of a kind which would always mark him out, but above all the concentration and determination which to a team manager, is the greatest prize of all. Had Maserati not been so bashful at the failure of their half-hearted jingoism, they might have signed Moss up for the next season on the spot, to which he would have agreed (and stuck to it), instead of merely mentioning the possibility. Despite the fierce joy in the Moss camp, Maserati still felt that they had lost the Italian Grand Prix. Rosier's was the highest placed Maserati, in eighth place behind no less than four of the hated Ferraris. They had missed the point entirely that Moss, in his first 2½-litre Formula 1 season, had led the best of the best, in the most hotly-contested race on the calendar, for 20 laps. Neubauer hadn't missed it, though.

Despite the troubles Moss was to have with the Maserati, they can never be put down to anything but misfortune. From time to time the theory is expounded that Moss was a car breaker, but this is refuted by the evidence. The Maserati was inherently weak in many areas in its early forms, not only in the lubrication department, but also in terms of its final drive and rear suspension, before the bugs were more or less ironed out of it, by which time it was obsolete. Moss was certainly unlucky, but seldom careless – it was always his car, after all.

Chapter 10

MERCEDES-BENZ

'It is a wretched taste to be gratified with
mediocrity when the excellent lies before us.'
ISAAC D'ISRAELI, 1823

The Great American Mountain rally, despite the fact that he never won it, was clearly a good omen for Moss. He was taking part in it when Gregory bought the 250F, and he was packing up ready to take part again, when a telegram flopped on to the door mat. Neubauer had wasted no time. Worded with great economy, it asked, or rather said:

CABLE WHETHER STIRLING MOSS BOUND FOR 1955 STOP. OUR INQUIRY WITHOUT COMMIT-MENT. DAIMLER-BENZ.

'Tell them, sorry, nothing doing,' he said. 'I'm contracted to Shell' is the official version of his response. In reality Moss, fretting at the prospect of more overseas travel and literally minutes away from departure, was rather more brusque.

A hasty and odd reaction, one may think, particularly when the fuel sponsor problem was not an issue over Greene's putative Maserati deal, nor Connaught's; and one with which Gregory heartily disagreed. He saw the chance which Neubauer had hinted at being several degrees more promising than the Maserati drive, which had not been reconfirmed by Modena, but merely suggested. Unwilling to gainsay his client on his own, Gregory colluded with Alfred Moss to push for a positive response. He urged a visit to Stuttgart and an aggressive position on price, so that if

Neubauer baulked at it, there was no harm done and no face lost. Alfred agreed.

The Mercedes W196 cars themselves, spiritual successors to the famous pre-war Silver Arrows, were the finest racing cars which could be built at that time. It is unlikely that mere humans could build them now, in fact, so pernickety was the attention to detail. Castings were scraped and burnished on the inside, for example, as was every facet of all the gear components. No-one is quite sure how much they cost, as the budget was a company secret (rather like Neubauer's weight) and still is, but they marked the pinnacle of design within the constraints of the formula. Obviously, Daimler-Benz had learned much about engine building during the war, and some of that experience was put to work, together with some pre-war know-how as well. The engines were extraordinary. Of straight-eight layout, they employed dry sump lubrication for the roller-bearing crankshaft, used high-pressure direct fuel injection like an aero-engine and a novel system of desmodromic valve operation, which opens and shuts the valve gear mechanically using cams rather than just the traditional spring. This has the virtue of increasing the potential rpm without valve bounce. In theory, such an engine, friction considerations aside, would be capable of infinite rpm. In practice, the engines could rev much higher than anything else on the circuit, peak power coming in at around 9,000 rpm, and they proved themselves to be eerily reliable, Monaco excepted, apart from the Bosch fuel-injection pumps, not a Mercedes part, which had failed a few times in the 1954 season. When on song, though, the unit produced a reliable 100 bhp per litre, unsupercharged and running on Avgas, a similar power/displacement ratio to today's BMW-powered McLaren F1, and a holy grail in the 1950s.

*ROAD CAR!

Such outputs were not unheard-of. Several of the Formula 3 cars upon which Stirling had cut his teeth used power units which, although of only 500cc displacement, produced 50 bhp – notably the double-knocker Norton, though it ran on methanol and employed an even higher compression ratio than the JAP; some 18:1. The fact that it would only last 100 miles or so was clearly a function of this, as such compressions are more commonly found in diesel engines. It was the success of the Norton engine architecture which led G.A. Vandervell to use it as the basis of the cylinder head design of his own Formula 1 engine. To produce such performance with reliability was the target – it seemed that Mercedes-Benz were well on the way to achieving it.

The core design of the W196 was to provide both the 300 SLR sports/racer and the later streamlined Formula 1 car. It owed little to its pre-war antecedents in any way except in terms of the general approach to its manufacture. Its relationship to the road cars which Mercedes were selling was minor; even the great gullwing coupé used a production 3-litre straight-six engine, despite the obvious similarities in general appearance between the SLR and its road-going cousin.

On the flight to Stuttgart, Gregory was considering his position. He had, with Alfred, worked out a minimum figure which Stirling's services should be worth, as well as an idea of how high he might pitch them. He decided to play his cards as close to his chest as he could and respond to Neubauer rather than try to set the pace of what he assumed would be fairly hard negotiations.

In the event, Neubauer's opening gambit on price totally winded Gregory. He also had the distinct impression that it was non-negotiable. Literally, an offer he couldn't refuse.

Again, the startling thoroughness of Neubauer's knowledge floored Gregory; Mercedes had the Moss lap times for every race at which Mercedes had been present to time him as well as those of several other drivers, and estimates of the output and performance of their cars. All were entirely accurate. Neubauer flatly stated the offer in the terms of what Mercedes would do for Moss; the money, the benefits, the insurances, the medical support services, the travel and the supply of his Mercedes road car, free of charge and in his own choice of colour; but to be kept scrupulously clean, at Daimler-Benz's expense, of course.

Moss would be allowed to drive his Maserati in non-Championship Formula 1 races, of which there were plenty (unlike today), as well as being allowed a Union flag decal on the racing car. What he expected Moss to do for Mercedes was largely obvious – win races – but there was to be more to it than that, as Moss was to discover, elements of which, (including bed by 10 o'clock the night before a race) he would find restrictive. But it was worth it. At an exchange rate of 16 marks to the pound (!), the total package was worth in the region of £28,000 for the season, certainly unheard-of money for any team to pay up to then, and more than twice what Gregory and Alfred had considered 'competitive'. To put it into perspective, it was roughly five times the salary of a cabinet minister or the head of the Civil Service, but by the time the 1955 season was over it would not seem so very much at all. Neubauer's price was aggressive for two reasons. First, there was no point in playing about. The up-coming season was to be the last in Formula 1 for Mercedes-Benz and the cost of engaging Moss was a one-off, to be set against the purpose of the Mercedes-Benz Rennabteilung, which was, in the final analysis, to sell cars. Fangio had clearly been the star the previous season, or rather the Mercedes had, but the cars failed to dominate against the Ferraris. Second, Moss was clearly the best and both Fangio and Neubauer wanted him. His exhibition at Monza had seen to that, and there was no point in haggling, it was unseemly.

The lunch which Neubauer gave Gregory to celebrate the deal was memorable. Gregory, Neubauer and the faithful Frau Bauer, the interpreter, were driven out of Stuttgart to the tiny village of Stetten, where the great man was well-known. Neubauer took complete charge; 12 glasses of four different wines were produced and the trio proceeded to down them, whereupon Gregory was asked which one he had preferred. Good. That then would be the one that they would have with their lunch. Neither Gregory nor Neubauer did much more work that day.

There was one potential problem, though, which was Shell Mex & BP, from whom Moss was drawing a retainer, whereas Mercedes used Castrol lubricants, which offered conflict, but it transpired that Bryan Turle, the competitions manager, was almost as pleased as Moss and Gregory were at Neubauer's offer and resolutely refused to stand in Stirling's way or impede his career in any way, waiving Stirling's contract for the 1955 season, for which the pair were extremely grateful. Had the German team not used Shell fuels the situation might have been harder to sort out.

Gregory ruefully recalled his disappointment at Neubauer the previous year but rationalised that financially, as this was more than twice Gregory's highest putative price, Moss was still better off having taken the Maserati route, including having bought the car. Now he had to tell Stirling, who was still in America, that he had kept his own counsel, which may have given him a slight twinge, but then, of course, Stirling did not yet know the price.

Stirling, when Gregory tracked him down in New York, was predictably chilly, and broadly felt that his manager had completely overstepped his authority. He thawed immediately when the fee was mentioned and reduced his objections down to the potential difficulty with Turle. If that could be resolved, then he would agree to test the car as soon as was practically possible. Another persuasive element, specifically negotiated by Gregory to mollify Moss, rather than flatly offered, was that for the Le Mans race Moss would be paired with Fangio.

The all-important testing session – after which it was hoped, not assumed, that Moss would sign up – was arranged at Hockenheim on Saturday afternoon, 4 December 1954. The news was carefully leaked to *Picture Post* by Jerry Ames of Downtons, the publicity company for both Mercedes-Benz UK and Castrol. The magazine was sufficiently impressed by the news to send Trevor Philpott to report on it, and no less a giant than the late Bert Hardy to capture it on film. The PP crew were neatly side-tracked by Neubauer upon arrival at Frankfurt airport and driven off in the wrong direction by a Mercedes factory driver, who pretended no knowledge of English, so that the various parties could get on with their business uninterrupted. Neubauer clearly knew the value of Public Relations, but also needed to know that Mercedes would 'win the business' before allowing Grub Street in. To be turned down by Moss, even though the financial package was a closely guarded secret, would be the PR equivalent of an exploding cigar. Face was at stake.

The preparations made by Neubauer and Uhlenhaut redefined the meaning of the word painstaking. The seat of the Grand Prix car was modified and padded to Moss's exact measurements. This sounds routine now, of course, and

Mercedes had been doing this since the 1930s, but it was rather new to the Brits.

It put added pressure on Stirling, too. If every measurement of seat, wheel and pedal, every roll bar setting, tyre pressure and toe-in of the wheels was set to his exact satisfaction, how could he not shine? Very easily, actually, as the weather was filthy. Karl Kling had, but a few days before, set a new unofficial lap record for the circuit at 200 kph in the dry, a nice round number which hung there like a polite caveat. Kling, though, was no Moss.

Uhlenhaut was nervous, too. He was not as chauvinistic about the nationality of his drivers as some, and actually he was a rather better driver than many of those who he employed. Having an English mother (he had been brought up in Highgate, North London) made him keener than some to retain the services of Moss.

Stirling was enchanted by the sheer power of the race car, after trying a 220A saloon and a gullwing 300SL, but felt that the handling was questionable. Compared to the Maserati, it was light and unpredictable. He likened it to a thoroughbred horse, a subject on which he was well-informed, and he began to appreciate Fangio's tiredness at Monza. He readily acknowledged, though, that he could get used to it, and demonstrated his confidence by winding the car up to circulate at 201 kph – on a track which had not even completely dried after an earlier downpour. Happy nods all round.

Because Moss really was that good, the helpless disbelief which followed his progress in the right car, and more often in the wrong one, was a consistent feature of his career. He had never driven this Mercedes before, it had a five-speed transmission which initially confused him and he spoke no German. At Hockenheim he was among foreigners; the enemy, as it where. His bravura performance was quite shocking even to those who rated him. All had known of his skill, but they had not seen it at work this close up before. Gregory, of course, was thrilled, as were the Alfreds, Neubauer and Moss. Uhlenhaut's face was a picture of pleasure.

Other people, though, were particularly upset about Stirling joining Mercedes-Benz. One was Orsi, who had assumed that Moss would stay on for 1955, despite the cavalier way in which Maserati was occasionally prone to behave. Orsi felt that the loss of Fangio to Mercedes had cost Maserati the 1954 world title and he now felt that the defection of Moss would have the same effect in 1955. Maserati were to sign Jean Behra for the '55 season – he had been Neubauer's second choice after Moss, actually. Closer to home, though, the other malcontent was Alf Francis.

Francis had not been informed about the offer from Neubauer, nor about the proposed testing at Hockenheim, so when Gregory told him about the matter, and the likelihood of Stirling accepting it, he was stunned and not a little miffed. As a Pole, Francis loathed Germans with an intensity that only one of his countrymen could have grasped, and he made few exceptions. Despite Gregory's assurances that he would be needed to look after the Maserati just like last year, he did not look forward to 1955 with anything like the enthusiasm with which he had greeted the previous year. Despite the niggles about the car and the occasional shouting match with the Modenese, he had developed a profound respect for Orsi, Alfieri, Bertocchi and the team, even if he did occasionally thump one of them. He totally understood and shared their gloom. He particularly disliked the prospect of a series of what he viewed as jobbing rent-a-drivers (few of them anywhere near as skilled as Stirling) perhaps being foisted upon him and racing around in the car which he had worked so hard to prepare.

Having seen the Mercedes team in action, Francis was fully aware that the offer would be a hard one to refuse, on purely professional grounds, never mind the money, which he assumed, but never knew, was sure to be significant. He comforted himself with the thought that perhaps one of the British teams which were still coming to terms with the new Formula 1 would eventually hire him. He was to be proved right as it turned out, but his timing was off. Connaught, Cooper and Vanwall were still making heroic efforts to play catch-up, but the Coventry Climax engine was still not ready so they had to make do with more or less the same power units that they had in 1954, during which none of them had really come anywhere.

He made his views clear to Moss at the pre-Christmas BRDC dinner in London. Gregory had held out the possibility of a job with Mercedes in an interpreter and liaison role, an option to which Neubauer had readily agreed, but Francis already knew more German than he cared to and undertook only to struggle ahead with the now-private Maserati in a rather uncomfortable compromise role vis-à-vis the disgruntled Maserati works. He could co-operate with Italians, he said, but never Germans. That was that and he was never to change his mind.

* * *

Shell Mex & BP did not actually produce a single drop of fuel and oil. The company was a hybrid created purely for the purpose of marketing the physical products of Shell, British Petroleum and National Benzole. It was a purely British operation and the commercial hostility outside the UK was as fierce as it could be, at least within the cartelised world of oil production and selling. The racing track was an excellent way of promoting products in the fertile domestic market, and Shell Mex & BP existed in part to provide a 'lockout', as best it could, for foreign competition.

The fuel companies split their sponsorship between oil and fuel and teams and drivers, so that a BP-sponsored driver would find it quite difficult to drive for an Esso-sponsored team, for example, and a BP-sponsored team would find it very hard to hire an Esso-sponsored driver, unless the sponsorship deal could be broken and replaced for the same amount or more. The dissolution of Shell Mex & BP in 1960 was to have a dramatic effect on Stirling's subsequent career.

Moss did not actually sign the Mercedes contract until January, just before departure for the opening races in Argentina, but that does not suggest any reluctance on his part, there were merely some details to sort out. Mercedes were to enter no less than four of their W196 racers, and Maserati attempted to rise to the challenge and entered seven 250Fs, drafting in some gifted amateurs to beef up their new works team.

Gregory and Felix Nabarro, the solicitor, flew to Stuttgart to finalise all the details and see their boy on his way. The pair were impressed at the organisational elements of the Mercedes works, particularly the legal department, so that when they departed back to London, they were left in no doubt that Stirling was in good hands.

Commercially as well as professionally, the Mercedes contract lifted Moss out of the upper middle ranks. He had completed only one full Formula 1 season, after all, and while he was already making a relatively decent, albeit unreliable, living at racing, the simple scale of the Mercedes offer required a rethink of the way he did business. It was immediately decided to form Stirling Moss Ltd, a company to which Stirling would contract his exclusive services. In turn, all contracts to employ Stirling would be routed through that company so that he would, in effect, be employing himself. It was certainly tax-efficient, and the other two directors, Gregory and Alfred, were thus able to keep a commercial barrier between Stirling and his suitors. It was the formation of this commercial concern which had caused the delay in completing the contracts until just before the Argentinian race.

This was important. By contract, Stirling was not allowed to work for anyone apart from Stirling Moss Ltd, and all deals had to be ratified by the directors. Stirling was thus unable to negotiate terms on his own behalf, so his enthusiasm for a particular drive would not be permitted to lower the price which could be charged. It was inflationary, to be sure, and would cause some resentments, but it was a template for the future. Clearly, not everyone could afford to pay Mercedes-Benz prices, and indeed nor did they have to, but the inevitable rumours, few of them accurate, about the level of Moss's income became of rather more interest than his practice times as the season developed.

At Buenos Aires, the factory team carried out extensive testing, even down to fitting a brake servo to the Moss car which was sourced from a Chevrolet saloon. The Mercedes facilities in Buenos Aires were extensive already, for the sale and servicing of both cars and trucks. One of the local employees there, we assume unknown to anyone, was one Ricardo Klement, who was rather better known elsewhere by the name with which he had been born – Adolf Eichmann.

Unaware, we hope, of the presence of the former SS General, Uhlenhaut and Neubauer worked very hard indeed to keep the drivers happy – they were not overindulged, but their wishes were accommodated as far as possible. Uhlenhaut, having been a driver, understood the requirements of comfort and convenience perfectly, as well as comprehending the difference between a legitimate criticism and a red herring. Whilst Mercedes were perhaps not staffed by the most spontaneous and imaginative people, they clearly understood that a deal was a deal down to minute detail. Whereas the insistence upon a conventional pedal layout at Maserati had nearly spawned several arias, the request that Stirling had a three-spoked wheel on his car so that he could see the rev. counter more clearly caused not a ripple. They merely constructed it and put it on. While the cars were as alike as he could make them, each driver had his own preferences, which were obliged as a matter of course. It was part of the Mercedes-Benz philosophy, and it was to pay huge dividends that year.

As a debut, it actually had overtones of comic opera. The temperature and humidity were both very high and heat exhaustion was a bigger factor in the rankings than anything else. Moss pulled up with a vapour lock in his fuel system and, himself also overheated, he lay down on the grass. A zealous ambulance crew spotted him, scooped him up and whisked him off in the direction of Buenos Aires. He eventually persuaded them to return him to the Autodrome, where his absence had caused some concern and he was put into Herrmann's car and finished a tired and dehydrated fourth. Fangio, better acclimatised than most, won the race and set fastest lap at 80.9 mph. His countryman, Gonzalez, came second in a Ferrari 625.

Two weeks later, still in Argentina, Mercedes tried out a 3-litre version of their Grand Prix engine, for which they had sports car plans. The race was run to Formule Libre rules, with no capacity limits, in two heats. Stirling won the second. It was an engine of this type which Mercedes proposed to use in the 300 SLR sports car for that season. It obviously worked well. It wasn't merely a bored out 2½-litre, either. The crank throw was changed so that the engine was exactly 'square' at 78mm for both dimensions.

There were six events which the SLR would contest in 1955, from the Mille Miglia in April to the Targa Florio in October, by way of the Nürburgring, Le Mans, Sweden and the Tourist Trophy at Dundrod. Stirling would win three of these and come second in two. The other one, Le Mans, would also be notable for other, famously tragic reasons.

But before the European racing season started, there was Sebring, which Mercedes were not entering. In this, he would drive an Austin-Healey 100S with Lance Macklin. Gregory went, too, as team manager of the Austin-Healey effort. It was the start of a fruitful relationship with Healey, as Gregory was later to take up the PR role for the Healey works, as well as acting for Donald Healey himself, to add to his other portfolio of activities. The two reached Sebring via a holiday in Nassau, where Gregory was introduced to the delights of deep-sea fishing and waterskiing.

The Sebring event was, since the launch of the Austin-Healey 100/4, the main marketing tool available to the British maker. Success here – even finishing here – would give the sales effort for the subsequent year a substantial boost, if only to prove that the cars were tough. British sports cars had always been popular in America, but every race of the calibre of Sebring helped. In the event, Moss and Macklin came sixth, which, given the quality of the opposition – Ferraris and the like – was a creditable result.

Now that Moss was in the capable hands of Mercedes-Benz, Gregory had a small breathing space in which he could organise himself a little. He was doing quite well financially, being on a five per cent commission from Moss's earnings as well as a salary, and his other activities were building nicely, including the Healey assignment. Gregory received no salary for this, but rather was paid in kind; a new Healey 100M sports car and free office accommodation for his own activities, which he kept separate from those of Moss, in the North Audley Street, Mayfair offices of the Healey Motor company.

He threw himself into the PR fray on Healey's behalf with total enthusiasm. One of his creations, intended to publicise the arrival of the Austin-Healey 100/6, was a motor show model which boasted mink upholstery, ivory dash fittings and gold-plated accessories. It was not uncommon then for show models to be 'bulled up' to the nines, and this was also the era of the profoundly vulgar Lady Norah Docker, but here was a quite startling confection. More's the pity that the car, the limp precursor of the immortal 3000 model, was such a lemon. Actually slower than the car it replaced, it merely looked the part. Donald Healey was actually rather nervous of the cost, so Gregory neatly pre-sold it to the *Daily Express* as a competition prize. Needless to say, Healey made a profit.

The fact that Stirling was away so much actually gave him more time to further address the issue of generating revenue for Stirling Moss Ltd. A professional sportsman is lucky if he is able to amass enough money from his short working life on which to live, so Gregory embarked on a strategy of capitalising on Moss's fame in order to accumulate extra income. In doing this he was to set a pattern followed by all professional managers ever since. He was not a racing manager per se – that was to come later – but he knew the life to an extent, via the RAC and the British Racing and Sports Car Club and its precursor, the 500 Club, so he realised that the key to extra earnings for Stirling lay firmly in the motor industry. The first step was to attempt to address the 1956 season. Moss was clearly a contender for one of the top places in the Championship and there was no point leaving things until the last moment. Mercedes had already suggested that their Formula 1 effort would only last two seasons, so that Stirling would be free in Grand Prix terms for 1956. The Stuttgart strategy was stated to be that they would persist with sports car racing for longer, but Moss would still need a single-seater drive, so Gregory started to look around. He started at home.

Depressingly, little had changed. Connaught were pressing on with their Alta-derived four-cylinder car, experimenting with fuel injection to eke out more power from the essentially pre-war design. BRM were re-entering the fray, working on a 2½-litre 'four' of their own, and Vanwall were moving away from their Ferrari phase and developing a similar layout which owed much to Norton motorcycle engine experience, also with fuel injection, powering a Cooper-derived chassis. It was a little less of a 'special' now, as the move to engine manufacture had taken place, but was not there yet. Both BRM and Vanwall were to develop these themes to their logical conclusion, although Connaught would be the firm to hit the headlines before the year end.

At Coventry-Climax, work was still under way to develop the Godiva engine, which both Connaught and Cooper were still awaiting, but the cautious engineers were reluctant to go public with it. As a V8 it was the odd one out, but all agreed that it had the most promise, on paper at least. Coventry Climax were, though, nervous of the extravagant claims made by Maserati and Ferrari, few of which had any basis in fact. It caused them to re-think the project into inactivity.

By this time, Moss had given up racing in Formula 3 events, which gave Gregory less to do on that front. There had been talk that he was, as a Formula 1 and World Sports Car Championship driver, outstaying his welcome in this uniquely British cradle of talent, a view with which he heartily concurred when it was pointed out to him. He had mainly stayed on out of sentiment, as the few pounds of starting money was obviously barely worth the effort, which was still considerable, given the keenness of the opposition. Another reason for staying as an occasional Formula 3 driver, though, was to boost the popularity of the class, as well as qualifying for the coveted BRDC gold star awards, of which he would win an unprecedented 10 in his career.

Gregory was still deeply involved with Formula 3, by now no longer the Half-litre Club, but the British Racing and Sports Car Club. Moss's presence was always worth a few extra thousand in attendance, but it seemed that the dead hand of parochialism was setting in. The Formula 3 crowd were perfectly happy with their noisy, smelly and cheap little racers, and the BRSCC was hard put to stimulate much interest in other types of racing. It was interesting, though, that other drivers, who were contemporaries, frequently drove in Formula 3, sports cars, Formula 2 and saloons, without attracting resentment. They, though, were neither works Maserati nor Mercedes drivers.

The hard core of conservatives in the club had been, in fact, rather loath to widen its horizons, perhaps failing to realise that with racing at higher levels becoming more accessible to the public, the little 500cc cars, which hadn't really changed since inception, were unlikely to keep attracting spectators at any kind of commercial level. The races were noisy, slow and by now relatively dull. The arrival of the 2½-litre Formula 1, particularly in the form of the elegant Mercedes had played its part in this.

That stick-in-the-mud attitude was to be rather changed by August 1955 when the BRSCC organised its first international competition at Oulton Park, sponsorship for which Gregory had agreed with the *Daily Herald*. Moss turned out in the Peter Bell-owned Connaught in which Les Leston and Archie Scott Brown had just won their class in the Goodwood 9 hours. It looked like a late decision, as Leston offered Moss the car more or less at the last minute. In fact, Gregory bribed Leston with a drive in Stirling's Maserati. The race attracted around 50,000 spectators, most of whom paid to get in, so it finally proved the point to the die-hards that if the club was going to prosper, they would have to diversify its interests, and Gregory gave notice that he would brook no arguments about the issue; which won him many admirers and not a few detractors. He was becoming a man of some influence.

None of the club's profits went to improve the BRSCC home circuit at Brands Hatch, though – all that investment came from the circuit's own revenues. Brands was, by comparison with Silverstone, Oulton Park and Aintree, looking a little like a poor relation by now, despite the addition the previous year of the section now known as Druid's, which had extended the circuit by 25 per cent. A stand was installed – bought for a few quid from the Northolt pony trotting course (an organisation with delusions of grandeur), knocked down and reassembled on site. It was the start of a comprehensive updating of the sinuous little Kent circuit, which was not completed until the final modifications in 1960 up to Grand Prix length. Gregory's role in all this was to be recognised quite soon by the offer of a directorship in the holding company, an event which, by a circuitous route, would make him first an entrant and team-owner, and later a manufacturer. For the moment, though, he was the clubmen's clubman, and the members, whatever their feelings, sat back as Gregory ran their affairs with a brio to which they were entirely unaccustomed.

Moss, meanwhile, had time to enter his Maserati three times, twice at Goodwood and once at Bordeaux, before the serious preparations started for the blue riband event of the sports car calendar – the Mille Miglia.

This extraordinary event, which in terms of contemporary notions of political correctness would probably lie somewhere between fighting a bull while wearing an ocelot coat and betting someone else's pension fund on a dwarf-throwing competition, was one of the two major road races held in Italy at the time – the other being the Targa Florio in Sicily. The event was simple. The public roads were closed for a distance of 1000 miles, starting and ending at Brescia. There was no attempt to repair the roads or to enforce standards of safety, which would have been elementary even at a boxing match, for the spectators. Jolly good fun for the participants, of course, but perhaps a little sloppy on the organisation front.

The race was generally held to be the preserve of wealthy Italian sportsmen and the manufacturers who made their cars, not to mention the mass-production players, particularly Fiat, always there for a dimly-remembered class win. It was the chance for the well-heeled, who always ended up paying for Enzo Ferrari's racing operations one way or another, to pit their skills against the professionals. Factory-backed (if not entered) teams from Aston Martin, Healey, Maserati, Lancia, Alfa Romeo and Ferrari all turned out. Mercedes had made an entry in 1952, but the improbable, chain-smoking Giovanni Bracco, driving his own Ferrari

250, had beaten Karl Kling by over four minutes. Stuttgart paused for reflection and had not entered in 1953, and Giannino Marzotto had triumphed, again for Ferrari. There was a rumour – theory, even – that Marzotto, the scion of a huge Milanese textile combine, had been guided by coded Marzotto hoardings at key points, but the Mille Miglia had always generated such speculation, one of the most amusing being the theory which someone was later to put forward about Moss's navigator. Giannino's brother Vittorio was, though, beaten by Ascari in a Lancia in the 1954 event, at least punctuating Enzo Ferrari's post-war domination of the race and proving that the cars from Maranello were not totally unbeatable, which was encouraging for Mercedes in this most macho of events. It is estimated that perhaps eight million people lined the course in 1955, which made the Mille Miglia the most widely spectated live sporting event in the world, bar none. It must, I think, still hold that record.

Mercedes' preparation was typically thorough. It needed to be. As well as the SLRs, they brought 300SL and 190SL models which could be used for practice and familiarisation. All in all, the firm spent almost three months preparing for the race. It was usually some sort of Italian benefit, but Stuttgart were keen to prove that they could do to the Italians in road races what they had already done to them on the circuit. Success in the big endurance races also sold more cars than any other class of event; the Mille Miglia and Le Mans were core to a European sales strategy. The road cars which Mercedes were offering, particularly the slightly tame 190SL, were designed to resemble both the 300SL and the SLR, and the association worked well – the little tourer, although relatively sluggish, was beautifully put together and was to be a best seller.

Gregory and Moss had briefly discussed the faint possibility of Ken navigating, but it was decided that motor racing journalist Denis Jenkinson, the ex-partner of Eric Oliver, the motorcycle/sidecar World Champion was more qualified, or perhaps had less imagination. He had entered before, partnering George Abecassis the previous year in an HWM, and his previous experience, as well as his lack of nerves, in this formidable one-lapper, were to be vital.

The puckish Jenkinson, who resembled nothing so much as a rather badly-dressed garden gnome, complete with a great beard, had picked up an idea from the American driver John Fitch, who had tested it in the previous year's race, as an aid to navigation which might serve to even out the differences between the Italian and foreign drivers' experience of the circuit, which would always give the Italians a potential edge.

While repeatedly trundling around the course in a practice car, being driven by either Moss or a stand-in, Jenkinson compiled a vast amount of pace notes, which were strung together on an 18 ft length of paper. This was loaded into an alloy case, specially commissioned by Moss, with rollers. As each waypoint was reached, Jenkinson fed the course notes through the device and kept up with the pace. He used hand signals to communicate the up-coming course of the road to Moss so that the Mercedes was able to take blind bends and crests in the road at near enough maximum speed. It was an extraordinary achievement for both men, not to mention the car itself, and few sporting accomplishments come even close to it. It remains a classic example of teamwork.

Jenkinson had a very rough race. When the pair roared into Brescia that evening, he had lost one pair of glasses overboard, was covered in spilt fuel and his beloved beard was stiff with vomit, caused by motion sickness as Moss drove so fast that he outpaced the aeroplanes which were attempting to film their progress. The Mercedes was geared to do around 170 mph at 7500 rpm and Moss used its facilities to the full. Neither of the men wore a safety harness, of course, which made the small shunt they had at Pescara even more character-forming. The Mercedes hit a pile of straw bales and dented its nose. But for that, Moss might have managed to average the magic 100 mph.

The Moss/Jenkinson effort had comprehensively smashed all records for the Mille Miglia as well as firmly nailing the famous superstition that he who leads at Rome never goes on to win the race. Of course, the whole effort had cost a huge amount of time and money, but such was its importance in the racing and motoring calendar, with a commensurate effect on sales, that the cost was considered easily justifiable.

The late Jenks had an extraordinarily analytical mind. He later remarked, upon being asked whether or not he had been scared by the experience, that, as he had never actually driven the Mercedes, he had no yardstick by which to measure Moss's performance and assumed that he was driving the car within sensible limits. He himself drove a Porsche, and he added that if Moss had been driving a similar car, then he would have found the journey terrifying, or words to that effect. A total perfectionist in all things related to the motor car, its history, construction and performance, Jenkinson could be spiky with those whom he considered not quite up to snuff, or who considered themselves rather better than they really were. He would have a rather nasty run-in with Gregory before long, which both men would regret. He thought the world of Moss, though. He died aged 75 in November 1996.

145. *Olivier Gendebien, before the French Grand Prix, 1960. On the left is Dick Johnson, on the right Aidan Jones. (Ken Gregory).*

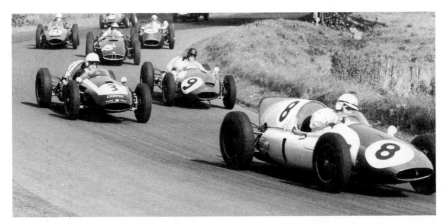

146A. Tony Brooks at Silverstone, 1960. (T.C.March).

146B. Henry Taylor leads round Brands Hatch, 1960. (T.C. March).

146C. Bruce Halford holding off Henry Taylor, Brands Hatch, 1960. (T.C. March).

147. Goodwood 1960. Stan Collier, John Gimmelli and Ken Gregory with a Yeoman Credit F1 car. (Ken Gregory).

148. A charging Chris Bristow leads Graham Hill and Stirling Moss, Brands Hatch, 1959. (Autocar).
149. Highgate. The UDT Laystall workshops. In the foreground is Bruce McIntosh, with Peter Downie walking away from the camera. The cars are Lotus 19s. (Motor).

150A. Tony Brooks pursuing Wolfgang von Trips, Monaco 1959. (Bernard Cahier).
150B. Brooks again, this time at Oporto, Portugal. Note the tramlines and cobbled surface. (Ken Gregory).

151A. *The wreckage of Henry Taylor's Yeoman Credit cooper at the Portuguese G.P. (Bernard Cahier).*
151B. *Olivier Gendebien leading Bruce McLaren's later works Cooper at Reims in the 1960 French G.P. Gendebien finished second. (Bernard Cahier).*

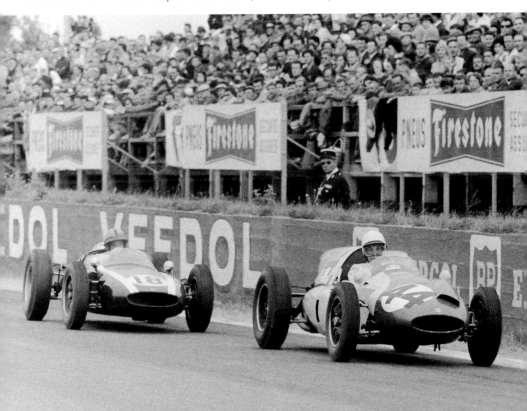

152. Harry Schell looking determined in the Yeoman Credit Cooper. Goodwood 1960. (John Brierley).

Moss's victory, 30 minutes ahead of Fangio, who was, it should be remembered, driving alone, preferring open-wheeled cars, was possibly the high point of his career. Only one other foreigner had ever won the race before, and that was Rudi Caracciola (who was often, but wrongly, assumed to be Italian) in 1931; so the celebrations in Britain, not to mention Stuttgart, were predictable.

One of the things which aided Moss apart from the presence of Jenkinson, without whom, he later said, he might well have finished, but would never have actually won, was the 'Dynavit' tablet which Fangio had given him. The Argentinian maestro had cut his teeth on huge road races in South America before the war and knew the dangers of falling asleep and never waking up. He clearly got the dose wrong, though, as Moss cleaned himself up, sat down to dinner and then drove all-out to Stuttgart, arriving at the Daimler-Benz works in time to have an early breakfast with the startled directors, before driving up to Calais to catch the cross-Channel ferry. Another pleasure at Stuttgart was to pick up his road car, a British Racing Green Mercedes 220. He was gratified to discover that a three-spoked wheel had been installed, never mind that the original had only had two. A literal interpretation of his wishes. Jenkinson later wrote that when he returned to Italy years later, when the locals were still talking about the race, that he overheard a bar-room sage commenting that Moss had had divine help; it was clear that he had had a bearded priest with him in the car, who was reading to him from the bible. It was a doubly amusing episode for Jenks – he was an atheist.

The stock in Daimler actually rose on the bourse as the news came through, in anticipation, correctly, of future sales. The rally, of both the equity price and the company morale, was corrected six short weeks later.

Stirling's stock rose even higher. The offices of Stirling Moss Ltd were besieged, not just by the media looking for a quote, a thing they still do, but by a deluge of serious commercial offers, all of which were sifted through by Gregory, and most of which were weighed in the balance and found wanting. One which was not was a patent device, fixed to a car dashboard, which would automatically roll and light cigarettes. Had the enthusiastic sponsor of this improbable piece of kit ever heard of Giovanni Bracco, he might have approached him, if only to sell him one; allegedly the Milanese millionaire had consumed seven packets of gaspers during his own winning drive in 1952.

Six weeks later, though, was Le Mans. The Mercedes team arrived in good spirits, more or less straight from the Nürburgring, where they had established a good 1-2, and set about preparation with their usual thoroughness.

Mercedes, not present at the 1954 event, had yet to come up against the works D-type Jaguar and Ferrari 375 teams at the Sarthe circuit. They were well-staffed, with Stirling and Fangio sharing one car, Karl Kling and André Simon the second and John Fitch partnering Pierre Levegh in another. Levegh was not his real name, but an anagram of Velghe, his uncle's name. It was a talisman; his uncle Alfred had been a pioneer racer, driving a Mors car in long-distance races at the turn of the century. Levegh, whose surname was actually Bouillon, had come to the notice of Mercedes in 1952 when he had driven the Le Mans race for 23 hours single-handedly before his Talbot expired with a broken crank. He was, in June 1955, 50 years old, and a racer through and through.

The meeting started badly with the announcement of the death of John Lyons, the son of Jaguar's chairman, who, in his road car, had collided with an army truck on the

Monday before the race. This had cast a pall of gloom over the Coventry team. That was bad enough, but what was to follow soon eclipsed it.

The regulations at Le Mans stated then that a car could not refuel less than two hours after the start of the race, and so at 6.28 p.m. Mike Hawthorn made his preparations to bring the Jaguar in, as instructed. It should be borne in mind that the pits straight at Le Mans had not been modified since the circuit was first used in 1923, when a Bentley had set fastest lap at 66.69 mph. The fastest lap time had almost doubled by 1955 to over 122 mph and, more important, the maximum speeds had increased to the order of 185 mph in the case of the Mercedes-Benz, nearly the same speed as a modern Formula 1 car – with drum brakes and a peculiar air brake mounted on the rear deck; they hadn't quite mastered discs in Stuttgart then.

Lance Macklin, in a Healey 100S, sluggish in Mercedes-Benz terms, was behind Hawthorn as he started to brake for the pits. The D-type, fitted with disc brakes, slowed fast, and Macklin's Healey moved swiftly to the left to avoid him as he was not following him in to refuel. The car moved quite sharply into the path of Levegh's Mercedes and was dawdling by comparison with the German car. Levegh was travelling at approximately 150 mph, and was far too close to use his patent airbrake device when his car hit the left rear of Macklin's Healey. The rear deck of the Healey was long and sloped, ramp-like, and the Mercedes was launched into the air at 30°. It flew, and came down on the low safety wall, exploding in an awful welter of fuel and blazing magnesium, killing poor Pierre Levegh instantly. The engine, front suspension, wheels and front body of the car were ripped out by the sudden deceleration and scythed through the tightly-packed crowd like so much hot shrapnel. The carcass of the beautiful machine was left blazing like a roman candle on the safety wall. In the pits opposite the stands, the mechanics, team members and gendarmes could only stare in mute horror as scores of people were mown down. The carnage was so great, the manner of death so violent, that no accurate body count was ever made; the accepted total of fatalities was 89, including Pierre Levegh, but it may well have been many more. Hundreds more were certainly hurt, some of them very badly. Some commentators have mentioned a death toll of as high as 120, but it was such a bloody jigsaw that no-one will ever be sure. Lance Macklin, though, astonishingly, was unhurt.

Hawthorn immediately assumed that he was responsible for the crash. He was not, as study of the film of the disaster shows, but that did not stop a lobby developing who tried to blame him. It was simply a tragic accident, and if there was any particular cause, it was surely the narrowness of the track and the inadequate safety measures at the circuit, which had simply not kept up with the speed and power of the cars which raced upon it. The revision of regulations concerning the pit lane and access to it rather suggest that the authorities had in fact worked out what had happened and quietly acknowledged their own responsibility. Certainly the lobby which had attacked the obviously Anglo-Saxon Hawthorn subsided quite soon. The examining magistrate appointed later, one Zadoc Khan, was to find no single driver responsible.

The witnesses to this uniquely awful episode were poleaxed, of course, and none more so than the Mercedes-Benz team. A distraught John Fitch, partnering Levegh and thus completely unmanned by what he had seen, insisted that the team withdraw. Few actually agreed with him, particularly Moss, for a variety of reasons, the main one being that a withdrawal would constitute some sort of admission of guilt or liability, which was not a position Neubauer was prepared to take. Reluctantly he telegraphed Stuttgart with the news (as if they didn't know already) and anxiously awaited the response, which came in the small hours of the Sunday morning after an emergency meeting. Neubauer was ordered to withdraw the remaining cars as a mark of respect, and they pulled off the circuit, with Moss and Fangio 20 minutes in the lead, at 2.15 a.m. They were on their way back to Germany by the time the race was over. If the delay of the response from HQ seems odd, then it should be remembered that the full horror of what had happened was revealed, as is the way with disasters, slowly, as natural optimism gives way to stunned disbelief.

Even those in the pits, right opposite the site of the crash, were unsure what exactly had happened. Moss was waiting about for Fangio to come in so that he could take over the car and, while he didn't witness his colleague's narrow escape and heard, rather than saw the accident, he had no particular reason, not being a prurient ghoul, to investigate. Visibility was reduced to almost zero anyway, with dust and a huge pall of smoke and glittering flame rolling over the track.

Gregory heard the news at home on the radio and like everyone else, could scarcely credit it. Hour by hour the news was worse, but the initial announcement, that a Mercedes-Benz had broken up and ploughed into the crowd opposite the pits, nearly gave him heart failure. All was confusion for some time, and it was not until eight o'clock that he could assure himself that Stirling was not involved.

The Le Mans accident, like the Hillsborough horror, revealed some basic inadequacies about the safety of mass audience sports which organisers and entrants alike had been happy to ignore previously. The Italians would discover this within two years. To bring the circuits up to the safety levels that they enjoy today was, of course, beyond the financial resources of the organisers, and the efforts went more or less entirely into managing the safety of the spectators, not the drivers. Stands were moved back and safety walls were put up, none of which made the actual task, or safety, of the driver any easier.

The manner of the response elsewhere to the Le Mans catastrophe, which a distressed Mike Hawthorn and Ivor Bueb won, courtesy only of the Mercedes-Benz team's withdrawal, was mixed, and with hindsight inconsistent, save the overwhelming sense of shock. In Switzerland, for example, the Grand Prix was cancelled and motor racing immediately banned, a prohibition which continues to this day; but the Dutch Grand Prix went ahead a week after Le Mans, after which Mercedes confirmed their decision to withdraw from Formula 1, which surprised no-one. A cynic might remark that the Bremgarten circuit outside Berne, which was poorly laid out and potentially lethal even on a good day, would cost so much to redesign that the enforcement of a total ban would be more cost effective; it is possible that the same thought occurred elsewhere. The horrified reaction of European governments had a negative effect on Stirling's finances; like most drivers, his deal was on a race-by-race basis.

The German, French and Spanish Grands Prix were cancelled. The dreadful episode at Le Mans caused Mercedes-Benz to rethink its previously stated commitment to sports car racing as well, which they had previously thought would continue after their two year re-entry into Grand Prix was over, but not publicly, and certainly not yet. Behind the scenes at Stuttgart, Rudi Uhlenhaut was fighting a rearguard action to remain in the sport, with a new car on the drawing board, but racing was expensive and the boom was lowering.

Another casualty of the sudden nervousness about the sport was Lancia. They were gobbled up by Fiat in July, partly through being in a parlous financial state because of the cost of building their beautiful machines. Fiat agreed that Ferrari could have the cars and an annual payment to develop and enter them in races. They were far better that anything in Ferrari's own stable, being, as with all Lancia cars of the period, astonishingly well-built. Indeed, Eugenio Castellotti had put one on pole position in the Belgian Grand Prix against the Mercedes team, only the second driver to do so that year.

So, gloomily, the truncated season went on. Oddly, the sports car calendar was unaffected. Those supremely dangerous grand road races, the Dundrod TT and the Targa Florio, went ahead as scheduled. With the Le Mans retirement, Mercedes were trailing both Ferrari and Jaguar in the World Sports Car Championship, so a change of tactic was called for. At Dundrod, Moss and Fangio drove a car each instead of sharing one and Stirling won by a lap from his team-mate, with Wolfgang 'Taffy' von Trips a pleased third. Mercedes 1-2-3.

It was, of course, a fine win, but the sensation of the race was the relatively unknown Ulsterman Desmond Titterington, who tigered in the sole works D-type Jaguar, in which he was co-driving with Hawthorn, until it uncharacteristically snapped its crankshaft on the last lap, which allowed a relieved von Trips to sneak home. Titterington was the son of a Belfast flax merchant and was thus, despite his Scottish education (he went to Glenalmond and St Andrews, where he shared digs with Archie Scott Brown), the local hero, which may have inspired him. It certainly gave Neubauer pause for thought.

No spectators died at Dundrod, but three drivers did – Jim Mayers, Bill Smith and Richard Mainwaring. The organisation of the race was, frankly, poor and the TT race was never held at Dundrod again. The Ulster AC had, in the opinion of some, blotted its copybook by refusing the entry of the Lister team, who had won the British Empire Trophy in the spring, on the grounds that Titterington's friend Archie, who drove the car was one-handed. The Hon. Charles O'Neill was to wince somewhat at some of the editorial lightning-bolts which were thrown at him and his club, which culminated in the TT being moved to Goodwood.

There was one race left on the sports car calendar and the Mercedes team had drawn dead level with Jaguar. Ferrari were three points in the lead, and Neubauer, taking the view that one should always leave things as one would wish to find them, performed a fairly brutal reshuffle in the Mercedes team. Gone were von Trips and André Simon, so Ken Gregory was asked to find and deliver two top line drivers, one to partner Moss, the other Fitch. This was heady stuff; Neubauer was in effect allowing Gregory to select two drivers for the race which would decide the World Championship – not a task to take lightly. Gregory and Moss put their thoughts together and came up with, unsurprisingly, two Brits, Peter Collins and Desmond Titterington.

Peter Collins, chum of both Ken and Stirling from the 500 days, was a works Aston Martin driver and something of a veteran. Like many British drivers, he was frustrated at the lack of a home-grown product. Like Moss, he had spent two years with HWM and had driven a Maserati (for Alfred

Owen). His Formula 1 mount for 1955 had been the Vanwall, but he had had little success with it. Moss would drive its successor.

But that is where the resemblance between the two men ended. Whereas Stirling Moss was (and is) a focused, introspective man, given to intense self-criticism, and fanatical about such social imperatives as punctuality, Peter Collins was, ahem, not. He got away with it, though. Even the vinegary John Wyer, team manager at Aston Martin and disciple of Neubauer, couldn't find it in him to stay angry very long with this charming, affable fellow, even when he was hours late for an appointment. Collins pursued his social life with the single-minded resolution which characterises the true Hedonist. The completely carefree sybarite is a rara avis in Britain, but commoner south of the Alps, so a trip to Italy was perfect for him. Gregory was, of course, concerned that he would miss the plane, or meet a girl, or forget, so virtually frogmarched him to the airport, rather as you would see off a nine-year-old to school.

Of all the races on the calendar, the Targa Florio, since its inception in 1906, was arguably the most challenging; a 45-mile circuit, much of it dirt track, with 800 corners linked by a single straight. The prize, money aside, was the Florio shield (Targa) which had been put up by Vincenzo Florio of the local shipping family. Times were fast – suspiciously so, in fact – but there was more than a slight possibility of being shot at, which kept drivers very alert indeed. As much a rally as a race, it was hard on cars and drivers. Aston Martin were not entering and never had, but Gregory had requested David Brown's permission anyway as a matter of courtesy. Happily, he gave it and Gregory was rewarded by the news that his two chums had won the race in record time, the other two Mercedes had come second and third and that

Mercedes had won the World Sports Car Championship. Put that together with the Formula 1 results and the World Rally Championship and, Le Mans aside, the Stuttgart team had an unparalleled year, the like of which has not been seen since. There were some naïve enough to think that they would rethink their two-year Formula 1 strategy, but that was not to be.

Nor, actually was anything else. The entire team was summoned to Stuttgart for a Press Conference, held in a theatre hired for the occasion. Expectations were high, given the racing results in both sports car and Grands Prix, but it became clear early on, as Artur Keser, the Mercedes-Benz head of public affairs, made his presentation, that the strategy had been rethought. Moss sat there in blissful ignorance, until a journalist nudged him and started to translate, that Mercedes-Benz were henceforth withdrawing from all motor sport. Not only was he out of a Formula 1 seat for 1956, there was to be no sports car either. As he was the de facto sports car champion of the world at the end of that traumatic season, the unilateral lowering of the boom on the glorious if tragic effort was depressing. He would miss the money, too.

Chapter 11

TWO FAT YEARS

*'I don't want to achieve immortality
through my work ... I want to achieve
it through not dying.'*
WOODY ALLEN, 1975

The Mercedes withdrawal left both Fangio and Moss without a Formula 1 drive. Peter Collins had driven the Alfred Owen-owned Maserati 250F in 1955, and Ken Gregory tried to get him a drive in the works Maserati team, but a confusion over a telegram allowed Ferrari to snap him up. Colin Davis, son of the famous S. C. H. Davis, had been lurking about the Maserati works hoping for a trial drive and the telegram which Gregory sent about Peter Collins was misinterpreted. The Maserati factory had for some reason assumed that Gregory was referring to Colin Davis, and they refused. By the time Gregory had corrected the misunderstanding, Collins had been approached by Ferrari and had accepted his meagre offer. Fangio went there, too, which he would come to regret. The Ferrari team – now Lancia-equipped and saved from ignominy with both cars and money (the latter from FIAT) – was expanding. Gregory winced when he heard how much – or, rather, how little – Collins was to be paid, but the contract was a fait accompli and he was too late to even attempt to amend the awful deal. Enzo Ferrari did not pay like Mercedes-Benz.

The Ferrari team looked, and was, strong. Allied with Collins and Fangio were Eugenio Castellotti, Luigi Musso, Olivier Gendebien, Paul Frère and the Spanish grandee, the 17th Marquis de Portago. 'Fon', as he was called, belonged to that set of people which included Aly Khan, Gianni Agnelli and Porfirio Rubirosa, swordsmen all, whose pursuit of simple pleasure would mark them out as antediluvian now, but made them a benchmark then. Their spiritual home was Monte Carlo. Rubirosa is immortalised in the catering business, of all things. The giant pepper mills familiar to all diners in Mediterranean bistros are, up and down the Ischian coast, known as 'Porfirios', for reasons which need little explanation. Rubirosa actually shared a car with Roberto Baggio in the 1954 Le Mans race, but he had parked it in the sand at Tertre Rouge and the car wisely refused to budge.

Stirling, back in a Maserati 250F with no hard feelings, had a very good 1956 and so did Peter Collins. Interestingly, the absence of Mercedes-Benz made little difference to the competition level, with several races being completed at rather higher speeds than the German cars had done – notably the Italian Grand Prix, which Stirling won. He was to come second again to Fangio in the Championship, with Collins, driving his first full season, only three points behind. In fact, Collins might easily have won the World Championship himself if Stirling had not finished, but he threw any chance of the opportunity away by handing his own car over to Fangio at Monza so that 'the old man' could keep in the points after his car let him down. It was a generous gesture, honestly made, and it caught a mood in both Italy and Britain which made Peter Collins an extremely popular young man indeed, not the least with team managers. No pit signals had been made to call him in; he had merely observed the situation and used his imagination to work out what was probably happening. Such an astonishing lack of side in a sport which was becoming ever more personality-driven was a thing to be treasured indeed. Here, clearly, was a young man who understood the nature of teamwork. It was typical of him, and Fangio was never to forget it.

Enzo Ferrari had lost his only (legitimate) son, Alfredo†, to illness on 30 June and, according to some observers, was so distracted by grief that he was tempted to give up racing altogether. Collins had actually won the French Grand Prix (by three tenths of a second from Eugenio Castelotti) the day after 'Dino' had died, and had driven his heart out later at Silverstone and the Nürburgring. The decision to give his car to Fangio at Monza and split the six points for second place with him rather than take them all himself allowed Fangio to win the World Championship by three points. Stirling thought it the most professional thing he had ever seen.

So did Enzo Ferrari. While there is no thought that Collins' action actually pulled Ferrari back from any brink, from that moment on the young man from Kidderminster could do no wrong in Modena. He was given a comfortable apartment in which to live and Laura Ferrari, Enzo's wife, even did his laundry. He became, after Monza 1956, a star in the Ferrari firmament like no other had ever been. It would not last, though.

Stirling's own Maserati 250F had been sold by now, for more or less its purchase price. Alf Francis had attempted to dispose of it over the winter of 1955-56 while he and Moss were racing in New Zealand, but to no avail. Ironically, it would go there anyway, but later in the year from Modena,

†The diminutive of Alfredo is Alfredino, hence Dino. Enzo Ferrari chose to name the family of V6 motors which were developed for racing and, later road cars, after his son, who was an enthusiastic engineer, and there was some claim that he had helped to design the brilliant engines, but no one is certain. As likely is that Enzo named them, and the cars which were later powered by them, after him as a tribute.

when Gregory sold it to Ross Jensen. There was some unpleasantness about this involving Ken Gregory and Denis Jenkinson.

Maserati, still receiving export credits from the Italian government for every car sold overseas, had artfully changed the chassis number so that they could put in a second claim. When Jenks was researching the Maserati 250F for a book on the subject, he discovered the difference between the chassis number on Jensen's car and the one that had been on Moss's car. He immediately assumed that Gregory had pulled a fast one, and in the Vintage Sports Car Club Newsletter he rashly compared Ken to a 'creature crawling from under a stone'. (He was never much of a Gregory fan, anyway. Managers, he felt in his purist way, were surplus to requirements for any racing driver.) It was a serious mistake. Gregory threatened to sue for libel, and recourse to law was only avoided by the printing of a full apology and retraction in the pages of the VSCC bulletin. The VSCC paid damages, including Jenk's share, which he could ill afford anyway, and the whole episode left a very sour taste in everyone's mouths. Jenks, as a Maserati fan since he was old enough to pronounce the word, was mortified to discover the truth about the bureaucratic antics. Stirling's old car went on to achieve one more distinction in Jensen's hands, albeit a poignant one. It would be the last Maserati 250F to win a fully accredited international race, at Teretonga Park, New Zealand, in February 1958.

For Moss, sports car racing was rather less fulfilling in 1956. He had signed for Aston Martin, and although it may have been a great catch for them, it was not as wonderful for him. It was not a disaster financially, as he earned something just over £3,000 for the year. However, he had been de facto sports car champion in 1955, winning virtually everything, but the cars which the Feltham team were using, the DB3Ss, were in the fourth year of their evolution. While sports cars were not evolving as fast as other types, the DB3Ss had already peaked in terms of development, and there were also regulatory changes at Le Mans which handicapped them. On top of this, Aston Martin did not always enter races such as the Targa Florio or the Mille Miglia, so his dance card was split between Aston Martin and Maserati. Of the two, Maserati were rather more entertaining. He had been invited to lunch by David Brown to discuss this deal and had turned up, 30 seconds before the appointed time, as is his habit, to be told that it was to be orange juice and a boiled egg in Brown's office. However minimalist Moss's eating habits may be now ('I don't eat lunch', he says), he was severely unimpressed.

To many informed observers, particularly those at Feltham, Peter Collins – who had been a works Aston Martin driver since 1952 – seemed to have lost his enthusiasm for the British team. Also, 1956 was not to be his best sports car season, which was ironic given his astounding performance in Grands Prix. He would happily switch to Ferrari for sports cars as well as Formula 1 in 1957. His action at Monza had endeared him not only to Fangio and Ferrari, but to most of Italy; and he would stay with Ferrari for the rest of his tragically short career. Ken Gregory would manfully attempt to renegotiate Collins' contract for 1957.

But 1956 was not merely about motor racing for Moss, Collins and Gregory. They had all met the women who would become their wives. Moss had met Katherine Molson, a Canadian brewing heiress, Peter Collins had met Louise Cordier King, daughter of a senior American United Nations official, and Ken Gregory met Ann Tyrrell, a showgirl. All would marry in 1957.

There was one separation, though. Alf Francis resigned from Moss's employ after the French Grand Prix. Within weeks he had been snapped up by Rob Walker's garage at Pippbrook, near Dorking, to head up Walker's competition effort. He would meet up with Moss again soon.

*   *   *

The search for a quality British racing car with which to beat the Italians had been carrying on. The contenders, Connaught, Cooper, BRM and Vanwall had been quietly plugging away. Of all of them, the Vanwall seemed to have the most promise. Mike Hawthorn and the rising star Tony Brooks had been less than happy in the BRM in 1956, Connaught were functionally broke and Cooper were yet to become relaxed about committing wholeheartedly to Grands Prix. Interestingly, Coopers was the only firm seriously developing a rear-engined car.

David Yorke, the Vanwall team manager, and Ken Gregory had discussed the possibility of Stirling at long last taking a seat in a British car, and in December 1956 one was prepared for him. He had already driven the marque to victory in the International Trophy Race at Silverstone in May 1956, but that was a non-Championship event, but here was the possibility of a reliable Formula 1 drive for an all-British entry. The prospect, so long in the making, was irresistible.

His place at Maserati was taken by Fangio, who could not wait to escape across town from Ferrari. The World Champion's phlegmatic patience had been stretched to twanging point by the hysterically self-serving attitude of the Ferrari management team. At Mercedes he had encountered cool, even chilly, professionalism, and at Maserati something agreeably quite the opposite – but enjoyable, none the less. At Ferrari the Byzantine intriguing disturbed him. He was not an arrogant man, but he had delivered Ferrari's first Championship in three years and his own win was his third in a row. He really felt that the Machiavellian way in which drivers were set against each other was somewhat beneath him. Hardly had the cooling engine block of his, or rather Collins', car stopped ticking after the Monza race, than he was off as fast as his bandy legs could carry him. He was replaced by Mike Hawthorn.

A huge amount of work had taken place at the Park Royal Vanwall works since the days of the early 'Thinwall Special'. G. A. Vandervell, who had been involved in the trust company which ran BRM had decided to abandon them to their fate, and he turned to making his own car. He was, as chairman of the Vandervell bearing company, offered unique access to the great and the good in British industrial circles. His initial efforts, clearly derivative of Ferrari, but better-engineered, were disappointing, but he called in Colin Chapman and Frank Costin – the former for the chassis, the latter for the bodywork – while his own engineers, in co-operation with both Rolls-Royce and Norton motorcycles, developed the engine.

The result was a chubby, four-cylinder, fuel-injected machine, with a high head-fairing and a very narrow air intake. It was, of course, green. It had performed quite well in the hands of Harry Schell in 1956, but Harry was off to join the great Juan Manuel at Maserati to participate in an effort which looked suspiciously like an expansion. Moss was joined at Vanwall by Tony Brooks, Stuart Lewis-Evans and Roy Salvadori, the latter on an occasional basis. All-British car, all-British drivers; it was a mouth-watering prospect and one which had come into being by a combination of almost limitless money, total commitment and sheer hard work – not to mention a great deal of lobbying, bordering on emotional blackmail, by Vandervell within the British motor industry.

So, there were but six manufacturers contesting Formula 1 in 1957, which would drop to five as Connaught finally bowed to the inevitable and withdrew under the huge financial strain of carrying on unsupported. Kenneth McAlpine had personally invested over £40,000 in the firm in 1956 and, despite his keenness – supported by the skills of Mike Oliver and Rodney Clarke – it was simply uneconomical. Bernie Ecclestone would buy most of the works at auction and campaign the cars privately. It was, in retrospect, a national tragedy, but no backers could be found. G. A. Vandervell, though, would fill the gap and take over from where Connaught had left off. It was a sign of both financial exhaustion and the inevitable rationalisations and shakeouts which take place in a competitive industry. Significantly, of the surviving five marques, three were British, two Italian. Both the Italian makers, though, sold road cars; but none of the British ones did, so winning for them was a commercial necessity.

The Suez crisis in October 1956 and the subsequent fuel rationing which was spawned by it, threatened not only motor racing, but the very future of the internal combustion engine as a means of transport, but it was an event which, by total coincidence, did Ken Gregory no immediate harm at all.

He had been approached, along with Stirling, to become involved with a company called Noble Motors, whose principal activity was the importation, preparation and distribution of Heinkel bubble-cars from Germany. Stirling did not think it fitting to be involved, so accordingly, in early 1956,

Ken Gregory had been offered the post of technical director of the firm, along with a shareholding.

There was much to direct. The firm was in something of a shambles. Yorke Noble, the owner, was a clever, multilingual man, who had spotted a gap in the market for these quirky little machines, but had little idea of how to exploit it. The firm had decent premises, in Chelsea's Lots Road, but little infrastructure. Pilfering was rife, and Gregory was tasked with organising it properly. He needed help, and he engaged the services of one Robert Thornton, who had worked for a freight forwarding company, the owner of which was known to Ken, and known to be difficult. There was little reason to suppose that he should need to take up references on Thornton, as his acquaintance's standards were famously uncompromising. This was later to prove to be a mistake.

Gregory and Thornton worked well together. Within months, and certainly in time to meet the fuel rationing which started to choke off the transport system, Noble Motors was flourishing, with a full spare parts operation, a repair facility and smoother distribution. It benefited particularly from the strategy employed by many owners of larger cars. They would claim the petrol coupons for their regular cars and actually use the fuel in their bubble cars; thus they would have infinite mileage available to them. The bubble car would, for a while, become deeply trendy. It was an irony lost on very few that the main manufacturers of these weird little machines, Heinkel, Dornier, Messerschmitt and BMW had, a scant dozen years before, been a signal part of the Luftwaffe's war effort. Whatever – the firm did well – too well, as it turned out.

Although 1957 would not be as tragic a year in motor racing as 1955, it was depressingly similar; this time to no-one's surprise. The disaster took place at the Mille Miglia. It had been a long time coming.

Moss and Jenkinson were back, this time in an unwieldy and, it transpired, rather hastily-prepared Maserati 450. The entry list was vast, nearly 300 cars, and the British pair, driving the most over-engined conveyance, started towards the back of the field. They managed nearly seven miles before the brakes disappeared, not through fade, but because the brake pedal had snapped clean off, with nearly terminal results. Hopped-up with adrenalin and stress, Moss and Jenkinson turned round and, with the last starters having gone by, headed back to Brescia, and arrived at the astonished Maserati pit, Moss waving the broken pedal like an assegai, speechless with rage. One look at the expressions on the faces of the Maserati crew calmed him down. So mortified were they that many were in tears and unable to say anything at all.

Thus Moss did not witness the disaster between Goito and Guidizzolo as de Portago's Ferrari flew off the road, its left front tyre burst, killing de Portago, his co-driver Ed Nelson and nine hapless spectators, five of whom were children. It was the last Mille Miglia. In the manner of Italian jurisprudence, charges for manslaughter were brought against Enzo Ferrari and were not dropped for three more years.

The 1957 season would see Stirling come second again in the Championship to Fangio, whose last full season it was. The high point was the German Grand Prix, during which the Argentinian master gave Collins and Hawthorn a driving lesson which they would never forget.

After a botched pit stop while in the lead on lap 16, Fangio lost the 30-second advantage which he had carefully built up by running on a half-full tank. The 'mon ami mates', assuming that he was out (he certainly looked out, sitting serene and calm on the pit counter while the mechanics panicked), set out to entertain themselves, and they paraded around, swapping the lead. As they came around one lap later, however, Fangio's Maserati was no longer in the pits. He had dropped a 30-second lead into a deficit of over a minute. The pair speeded up, but Fangio reeled them in like a pair of Tuna. He caught them on the 21st lap and went through to win. It was his last Grand Prix victory and his finest race. He had done something which simply could not be done. Hawthorn and Collins thought it was marvellous.

What was it about Fangio? Hear Masten Gregory on the subject, telling Ken Purdy in 1969, and perhaps some of the man's sorcery comes through:

'Fangio psyched you, too, but differently; he came on like a tired kind of fat man, a very nice man who was sorry he was going to have to run away from you, but that was the way it was … it was inevitable, too bad.'

By the end of 1957, Collins, Moss and Gregory were all married. In time Louise Collins would become a widow, Moss and Gregory would revert to bachelorhood; and for Gregory a whole new chapter would begin, which would bring with it more pleasure and more pain than most people could imagine. The Ken and Stirling show still had plenty of material left in it and a long time still to run.

Chapter 12

THE BRITISH RACING PARTNERSHIP

'Something will come of this.
I hope it mayn't be human gore.'
CHARLES DICKENS,
BARNABY RUDGE, 1841

When looking at history, it is academically unacceptable to refer to any event as inevitable but it was, shall we say, always a possibility that Ken Gregory would attempt a foray, and a serious one, into team ownership and management. After all, he had been a driver – qualifying as a British Racing Drivers' Club member in 1952 – as well as an administrator of the sport with the RAC and the British Racing and Sports Car Club, and he had invented a category new to motor racing; that of personal manager. On top of this, he was a director of Brands Hatch. His knowledge of the sport and its procedures and imperatives was thorough, probably second to none then, and he possessed rather more than a cursory grounding in engineering. He had also seen the best, Neubauer, at work, and the acknowledged British contenders for management honours – England at Jaguar, Wyer at Aston Martin and Yorke at Vanwall. Above all, though, he was an exceptional organiser.

His chance to show it came during a conversation with Alfred Moss on the way back from Brands Hatch one day in November 1957. Their conversation moved onto the subject of the two of them forming their own racing team. Both men had been impressed by the way Mercedes-Benz had produced and managed their racing effort. Of course, as a manufacturer as well, the Stuttgart company were better able to control the entire process than certain others; Maserati had not the budget, the episode over the sale of Moss's Maserati providing eloquent testimony to that. A better parallel would be the efforts put in by Whitney Straight before the war – immaculate presentation and a sensible organisation with which success could be delivered. Straight had used Maserati cars for his effort, but both Alfred and Gregory knew that the sport was changing rapidly and that the clever route would be through Formula 2, using a Cooper chassis, almost certainly powered by a Coventry Climax engine. The car was affordable and eligible for a multiplicity of events, both foreign and domestic. Both men also knew the Cooper family and their works very well, which was a big advantage. There were other manufacturers who, despite their obvious technical strengths, were more or less untested. There were, in fact, plenty of Formula 2 constructors, of varying abilities, but Coopers were clearly the best.

There was a small technical problem for Gregory, though, which was that he could not actually afford to participate, being, as it were, rather finely drawn at the time. Alfred Moss suggested that he himself should actually put up the £2,000 required by the agreement, and that if profits were to be split 50:50, then Gregory would repay him via his own share. It was an arrangement which would and had worked very well in other ventures which the pair had launched, and would do so again surprisingly soon. The initial investment was boosted by a fuel and oil support offer from BP, which produced £2,000 a year as well, so that the tiny operation was well-funded from the start. In fact, that £2,000 was the only equity investment made until the end. Gregory got on very well with Bryan Turle, and the Shell Mex & BP competition manager did not even hesitate to offer the sponsorship. It was pleasing for Shell Mex & BP to support a British team with British staff and drivers, particularly because Coopers themselves, the manufacturers, were already supported by Esso. If the new arrival proved to be a success, it would neatly serve to dilute Esso's efforts.

The question as to where the new entrants would be based was easily solved. The Moss family farm at Tring was ideal; workshop space would be provided in one of the luxurious barns, free of both pigs and chinchillas, which were another of Alfred's many and varied passions. The pair decided that Tony Robinson, by that stage working for the privateer Bruce Halford, should be offered the job of chief mechanic, with an assistant in the form of Derek Spencer, who lived close to Tony in North London. All they needed was a driver.

Stuart Lewis-Evans had made a good name for himself in Formula 3 and had been driving for Vanwall since the summer, and also for Bernie Ecclestone once the Connaught works effort had finally succumbed to economic fundamentals. He was extremely quick and committed, as Ken Gregory knew from when they had raced against each other. He was also very light, which was a bonus.

Lewis-Evans is a name too-often forgotten today, but it is fair to say that he was one of the greats of British motor sport, particularly when one remembers that he was never a particularly fit man. As a child he had suffered from a disease known as spondylitis, an unpleasant, painful and debilitating inflammation of the spinal column, which had confined him to a wheelchair for lengthy periods. As an adult he suffered from severe stomach ulcers, both of which conditions conspired to prevent him from ever being as perfectly fit as Moss, for example, despite the clear fact that his arms were very strong. Overall, Lewis-Evans had a major difficulty with stamina, but he was a tiger. He had a problem coping with long-distance sports car races, which is why he never really shone as a driver at Aston Martin, but limited-duration single-seater events were more acceptable to him, as he had proved in Formula 3.

Lewis-Evans was not, therefore, handicapped in the way that Alan Stacey or Archie Scott Brown were, for he was physically intact, but his courage in simply driving a car was undeniable. His career, from the 500cc movement, followed by success with Connaught, Vanwall and the new Gregory/Moss team is not perhaps the matter of public record that it should be, but there is little doubt that he deserves mention in the same breath as others much more well-known.

After some discussion, the new entity was christened the British Racing Partnership Ltd. Perhaps a little grand, given that there was but one car, looked after in a barn (albeit a luxurious one); but one must start somewhere. Certainly, the registrars at Companies House thought it a little over the top, but eventually they would be persuaded by dint of much lobbying and hard work. Even in the 1950s, when motor racing cost a pittance compared to now – but was still expensive – there were risks of overindulging. The real dangers were in manufacture, at least financially, as Connaught had found and BRM were discovering, but the 1958 season, like others before it, was to be a particularly hard one on the drivers, with a 'butcher's bill' which many observers, including Ken Gregory, were to find completely unacceptable.

The choice of a Cooper was a good one, as Moss was to prove in the first Championship Formula 1 race of 1958, and Roy Salvadori had already proved in the British Grand Prix of 1957 by coming fifth in a Formula 2 T43, providing the first World Championship points for the new school of design. But, first things first, the équipe's home had to be organised properly, after they had actually acquired a car. The one they did buy, a Cooper T45, chassis number F2-10-58, was fitted with a Coventry-Climax FPF 'Firepump Featherweight' 1500cc engine at the Cooper works, and Robinson and Spencer set about it. It was painted a very light colour, meadow green. Actually it was Alfred's choice and, however questionable its visual impact, it at least served to make the car easily distinguished. Several innovations were considered, but the most prescient, years ahead of its time, was the attempt to build a two-way transmitter/receiver, using Pye components, into the car so that Lewis-Evans could communicate with the pit and vice versa – a sound idea, developed by John Gregory, Ken's brother, but one which suffered from the environmental noise levels in the cockpit of a single-seater.

Bolstered with the impact of the Vanwall success in 1957, much of which had been down to Stirling, Britain was now rapidly donning the mantle of leader in international motor sport, which it has not since lost. Gregory and Alfred Moss were, with hindsight, in on the ground floor. What they would make of this new enterprise was entirely up to them, but they were to be ably assisted by Lewis-Evans, Robinson, Spencer, and Tommy Bridger, who they brought in as support driver to Lewis-Evans, who still had Formula 1 obligations to Vanwall in Championship events and Bernie Ecclestone in other Formula 1 drives. In fact, as the Cooper was being fettled, Lewis-Evans was in New Zealand with Roy Salvadori. Their purpose was simple; Ecclestone had bought two type B2 Connaught Formula 1 cars at the liquidators' auction of the company assets and Salvadori and Lewis-Evans were to race them in the non-Championship New Zealand Grand Prix and sell them locally. There was little thought of the B2s being truly competitive in Britain or Europe, despite their beautiful engineering, as they had been designed some four years before, but several drivers had had some success with them. As things turned out, there were no takers, although Lewis-Evans nearly swapped one for a stamp collection, which was not quite what Ecclestone, who was merely a motor trader back then, had in mind. As it transpired, the result of the New Zealand event, a win by Jack Brabham in a 2-litre Cooper-Climax, was to be totally overshadowed by something which happened the very next day, thousands of miles away in Argentina, ironically involving the same type of car as Brabham's.

At the White Cloud farm, Robinson and Spencer were equipped with typical thoroughness – lathes, welding plant, workbenches and a formidable array of tools were assembled and moved into an outbuilding, while the pair of mechanics spent a large part of the 1957-58 winter at Surbiton, watching the car being built. This was quite normal, and suggested no supervision, but merely familiarisation with the manufacturing process, particularly welding, so that they would be able to repair the car properly should anything untoward happen, which it was, quite soon. To complete the equipment, an Austin Omnivan with a purpose-built trailer was bought as a transporter. The BRP was not scheduled to compete until Easter, so Gregory was able to devote more time to his two clients, Moss and Collins.

Tony Vandervell, boss of the Vanwall concern, was vexed by the change of regulations governing fuel, and he declined to enter the season's opener in Buenos Aires. Nothing new here, in fact, as the Vanwall team had never made it to Argentina anyway, but the switch over to AvGas from the potent methanol/petrol cocktail of the previous year was to have the effect of limiting the advantages offered by fuel injection which the team had continued to use. Broadly, the methanol mix was less sensitive to mixture than the AvGas which was simple if you used carburettors – a mechanical fuel injection system, the only kind available, would have to be more finely tuned, possibly even re-engineered.

Moss was therefore short of a drive in Argentina. An extremely expensive telephone conversation between Moss, who was in Nassau building a holiday house, and Gregory, who was in London, came to the conclusion that Gregory approach Rob Walker with a view to Stirling piloting Walker's T43 Formula 2 car for the Argentina race. With its small engine and light weight, as well as its wonderful Climax engine, designed originally to run on petrol rather than alcohol, but theoretically suited to both. The Cooper suffered fewer penalties than the larger cars with this new arrangement, but that is a matter of hindsight; the Walker Cooper was never actually track-tested on AvGas before its attempt in Buenos Aires.

The 1958 Argentinian Grand Prix was, as it transpired, a watershed. The Walker car was the only non-Italian entry, which was not a situation which would persist after that race. It was to be Fangio's last race on Argentinian soil and his last but one Grand Prix. The deal offered to the Walker team, negotiated by Gregory, included good starting money as well as air freight for the car, its spares and the driver and mechanics. Just as well, actually, as the entry was not confirmed until all available steamship space had already been booked. It was to be the start of a long and fruitful association between Moss, Gregory and the R. R. C. Walker Racing team. From then on he played a significant role in organising their team entries, their starting money and the supply of both cars and engines. The last event in which Walker and Gregory were to participate, with a commercial and sporting intimacy honed by four more seasons, was to be Goodwood in 1962.

At Buenos Aires the reception accorded the little car was predictably patronising. The similarities between Cooper Formula 1 and Formula 2 were striking – in most cases teams used one car with a choice of engines, so that an engine upgrade was the way in which Formulae were swapped. It certainly saved the teams money and served to focus attention, particularly abroad, upon the flexibility of these peculiar little cars. Fangio, who never drove one, referred to them as 'spiders', not in the sense of open cars, but in the sense that he thought them scuttling arachnids. It was a view shared by many present; even Alf Francis, who disliked the tiny cars when compared to 'proper' Grand Prix machines. But the performance which Moss put in, in what was actually a Formula 2 car with a 1500cc engine bored out to just under 2 litres, was to startle the sporting world, and still should.

Gregory, Cooper and Walker all stayed at home, resigned to the view that the trip would be marginally profitable and merely good experience for car, driver and crew. The Cooper could not really be expected to be competitive, as it was really only set up for shorter races and had never competed head to head with the major factory-backed teams at an important race.

The essence of the Moss/Francis strategy, though, was to run the 200 mile race non-stop. The fact that the little car was giving away more than half a litre to the opposition was offset by its relative lightness and by its far greater range – by comparison merely sipping fuel like a Ronson lighter. On the debit side, the car used four-stud wheel fixings, so

Francis could not change wheels without a huge time penalty, as against the quick-change hubs used by Ferrari and Maserati. It was a finely balanced judgement and involved some gamesmanship by Francis. Also Moss was injured, the result of a trivial domestic accident involving the insertion of his wife's thumbnail into his eye. This had scraped his cornea, so he had to practise with a rather sinister eye patch.

He qualified, one-eyed, seventh on the grid and, after gearbox trouble, he was in the lead by a good margin at halfway. Now came the gamesmanship. The Ferrari team assumed that he would have to stop for tyres, and Alf Francis did not disabuse them of the notion, even going through the pantomime of having them ready in the pits. This reassured the perplexed Italians, who were increasingly nervous about the performance of this ridiculous little car. By the time it was clear that Moss was not going to stop and would run the race on one set of tyres, it was too late to catch him – not that Luigi Musso didn't try. Moss finished less than three seconds ahead of the Ferrari, his tyres shredded down to the canvas and the engine running off a merely damp fuel tank.

It was scarcely credible. Gregory heard the news from Reuters news agency and called Walker, whose home was in Somerset. John Cooper heard from the *News of the World* news desk. He was having a drink with Keith Challen, that paper's motoring correspondent, which quickly turned into several when Roy Salvadori turned up. Soon, the whole sport knew, and by Monday morning the whole country. The significance of the race was naturally lost on some (and still is) – merely another Moss win, to which the public were becoming quite accustomed – but others understood exactly the magnitude of what he, Walker, Cooper and Francis had done. It was in many ways an even more important win than the Mille Miglia had been. Not only was Walker a private entrant, but the car was a 1957 model built originally for Formula 2. A child might as well have won a marathon.

Maserati were philosophical and gave a primordial shrug; they had more or less given up racing anyway and were only at the event to support Fangio and to attempt to collect some bad debts, of which they had many. Ferrari, on the other hand, was horror-struck and, unsurprisingly, the recriminations started more or less immediately; but to little effect, as Ferrari was to have a miserable 1958 season in Formula 1. By the end of it he would have lost all three of his drivers, two of them on the circuit and the third retiring, later to die in a stupid road accident, ironically witnessed by Rob Walker himself, who was travelling on the same road at the time.

Walker won again at the Monaco Grand Prix on 18 May, this time the driver being Maurice Trintignant, who set a new circuit record in the process. Stirling retired, as did many others. Only six cars finished, none of them a Vanwall. The jubilation was rather muted by Monday as news filtered back that the brave and popular Archie Scott Brown had died of his burns after crashing his Lister-Jaguar at the Spa Sports Car Grand Prix, held on the same day as Monaco. Salvadori was particularly upset by this, as the two had been both friends and rivals, and Ken Gregory himself was also to rue the day he ever set eyes on Spa-Francorchamps. But that was later.

Thus, the twin leitmotifs ran intertwined through the season; mortality and progress. It is ever thus in motor racing, but by the end of the year it was to become clear that the little cars from Surrey had set a new benchmark and changed the rules completely. But it was a trend against which some were to struggle, in an expensive but hopeless endeavour to maintain the status quo. For drivers – many of whom would not try the Cooper school of design for some time, if ever – the debate as to where the engine goes was fairly academic. Their input revolved around power and acceleration for the most part, and in this they were supported by Enzo Ferrari, whose view was that the engine was not only 90 per cent of the car, it would have to be in front. 'Whoever heard of a horse pushing a cart?' he is said to have remarked. He would eventually change his mind, but only when events forced his hand, after the lions who drove for him in 1958 were all dead.

A rear-engined car is inherently lighter; the drive train which connects a front engined car to its rear-wheel drive is heavy and power is lost along its length. A rear engine also acts as a chassis component of itself and allows less structural mass for a given rigidity – this last element was to be refined by monocoque design and brought to a fine art by Colin Chapman at Lotus and Tony Robinson at BRP (and elsewhere). Further, as the car is lighter in terms of its basic structure, so can its engine and unsprung parts be lighter, for a given power/weight ratio, so that the Cooper-Climax with which Moss won at Argentina and Trintignant won at Monaco weighed something in the order of 400 lb (the weight of 2½ drivers) less than the Maserati 250F or Vanwall. Thus, they could afford a smaller engine which used less fuel and oil, and so on.

Purists, particularly in Italy, disliked on sight what they perceived to be the crude little Coopers, and were quick to point out the humble origins of the Coventry-Climax engine, conceived as a fire pump – which was to rather miss the point. The Italians took great pride in the 'tool room built' aspects of their cars, which goes to show that some may not have looked too closely at them – the engineering integrity of a Ferrari or Maserati was poles apart from that of a Connaught, Vanwall or BRM, after all, but it was clear that the British builders, who engineered their cars to last, Royce-style, forever, were also rather caught out by the Cooper, not that it was exactly disposable.

These were not the days of tearing an engine down after each race; rather, a power unit would be expected to last several Grands Prix and, unless the car had been bent, much less would be done to it than is the case now. Racing cars, of the 'Grand Constructor' type were actually built to last in Britain, too, until Cooper came along. An engineer's pride would not let him build a car which fell apart as it crossed the line. Tony Rudd, the man who finally got it right for BRM, noted with interest when surveying a Cooper-Climax, that 'life has been sacrificed for lightness'. He meant component life, of course, but the statement could easily be philosophically reassessed in the light of subsequent events. Modern motor racing had arrived, but without the hyperinflation. Although not entirely modern, since the newly-inaugurated Constructor's Championship was to be won in 1958 by Vanwall, with Ferrari second – both front-engined types – but 1958 was to be the last year that it happened.

Ken Gregory was now firmly involved in the sport as a principal entrant, and as the 1958 season progressed he found that, after only three events, he could pay Alfred Moss back his original share of the investment, and from then on they were genuine 50:50 partners. It was an agreeable arrangement, as it afforded Gregory a more direct involvement in the sport, which he surely adored, and it allowed him to exercise his formidable organisational skills on more than one level, which was both pleasing and a better use of his time. The commercial management of Moss was a job which needed less and less work, now that Stirling was under the wings of both Aston Martin and Vanwall, and the issues of endorsements and appearances were not ones he ever flogged over-hard – too easy for Moss to become devalued into what today would be called, rather impolitely but nonetheless with powerful imagery, a 'media tart'.

There were already some eyebrows being raised at the frequency with which Stirling's endorsements were appearing (It's That Man Again), which was rather unfair, given that the majority of the drivers at his level in Britain were automatically endorsing their own business activities via the motor trade, but car-dealing was one area which Moss and Gregory resolutely stayed away from, or at least tried to.

Broadly, Gregory took the view that saturation was a bad thing and that such endorsements that were undertaken were not to be for products or services which competed. So, one make of spark plug, one type of driving glove, one type of brake lining, one make of plastic construction kit, and so on. The obvious area of endorsement directly via motor racing which strayed into sponsorship, though, was fuel and oil. The long-term contract later drawn up by Gregory with BP was a masterly piece of work and, eventually, its very existence was to have a radical effect on Stirling's life when he reached his own personal and agonizing Rubicon four short years later.

For Gregory, though, the 1958 season was to be a shake-down in terms of his new racing venture, but an endorsement of his faith in the Cooper company, a decision reached well before the Walker car triumphed in Argentina – the new firm clearly had the right vehicle. On the other hand, his exposure to motor racing as an entrant was to be a traumatic one; the first step on a long road paved with misery and loss, a road from which he would start to seek turn-offs relatively soon.

Not being a constructor in his own right – yet – he had come to know the participants in this supremely dangerous game rather more personally than was perhaps good for him. He lacked that essential hardness that seems so necessary to get the most out of people. Enzo Ferrari and Colin Chapman had it in abundance, but the people to whom Gregory would turn to drive his cars were essentially friends from a very small world. This was to govern his view of both the sport and the business which it would shortly become, and it would eventually cause him to leave it with few regrets – its undeniable attractions in terms of perks and lifestyle notwithstanding. Despite the appearance of the British Racing Partnership to the public, it was to be a nightmare for Ken Gregory, who never really got used to the price which even trying to succeed in racing was to exact from the enterprise. If we think that that price is high now, then it is as nothing compared to the loss of life which resulted from trying to define excellence without enough imagination.

It is fair to say that Tommy Bridger did not shine as a BRP driver. After Lewis-Evans came fourth on the occasion of the car's debut in the Lavant Cup race at Goodwood, Bridger was entered in the Glover Trophy, and he almost totalled the car at Madgwick corner, which was depressing. Tony Robinson and Derek Spencer managed to rebuild it in time for the Aintree 200 miler a fortnight later, when Lewis-Evans shone again, coming second to Tony Brooks in the Formula 2 class. Moss won the Formula 1 section in Walker's Cooper, thoroughly in the groove by now as, of course, a 10-year veteran should be.

Collins, Gregory's other client, was having trouble, though. His relationship with Enzo Ferrari, via the team manager Romolo Tavoni, was deteriorating somewhat.

There is a view that this was because of his marriage to Louise King, an event which Ferrari famously disapproved of – but that had been in February 1957. Another explanation was that Collins had lost some of his aggression. Either way, there was something of a crisis in Collins' career in the summer of 1958 after Le Mans. The 'mon ami mates' were sharing a Ferrari Testa Rossa, and Hawthorn may have singed the clutch at the start. Whatever the truth of it, the clutch seemed so badly damaged when Collins took over the car that he pulled up and, unable to get the car moving again, retired. Hawthorn had certainly been pressing on, as evidenced by his fastest lap at 121 mph, which, given the torrential conditions of the race, was a remarkable effort. With no car, the pair simply left the circuit. Tavoni was scandalised, particularly when the mechanics loyally reported that the car seemed perfectly fine (once it had cooled down). Collins bore the brunt of the blame for this gross dereliction of duty and he was to pay the price at Reims the next month.

It was a typically Byzantine Ferrari ploy, enthusiastically executed by the toadies with whom Ferrari surrounded himself. Collins, fortunately accompanied by Ken Gregory, who was there to watch Tommy Bridger in the Formula 2 race, arrived at the circuit for practice to discover that Collins did not have a Formula 1 drive at all. Instead, a Formula 2 car was prepared for him to enter in the supporting race. Collins was predictably upset; it was a cruel and petty thing to do to a man who was, for all his cheery unreliability, a paragon of loyalty. Happily, after a heated session in the Collins's hotel suite, with Hawthorn, Romolo Tavoni and Ken Gregory present, Tavoni was persuaded to call Modena and explain that Collins had not been responsible for the retirement at Le Mans and that Hawthorn had actually

wrecked the clutch. Ferrari assented and Collins was rein-
stated for both races. All seemed well, but the episode had
put a large wriggling worm of doubt in Collins' mind. He
managed fifth place, but the whole Ferrari effort was cast
down by the accident which killed Luigi Musso on the
ninth lap.

If he felt under pressure, it didn't show at Silverstone,
though. Or perhaps it did – Collins romped home in the
British Grand Prix by 24 seconds from Hawthorn to give
Ferrari their only 1-2 of the season. He led the race from the
grid to the flag and all were certain that he was firmly back
in the groove and reconciled with Ferrari.

Gregory was not at Silverstone to witness this, as he had
preparations to make at Caen for a BRP entry in the Formula
2 part of a meeting which almost overlapped. He did hear
the news on the radio in his Austin-Healey, though.
Raymond Baxter, the BBC commentator, assumed, like
many others, that Collins was running on very light tanks,
so fast was his progress, which made for some tension if you
weren't there. When he just pressed on and won, few could
believe it.

Many drivers were engaged for both events, Silverstone
and Caen, which meant that there was some nifty work to
be done with a de Havilland Rapide to ferry the growing cir-
cus across the Channel. The ease with which this was actually done started the germ of an idea in Gregory's mind.

On 3 August, any sense of optimism which Gregory was
getting out of either the success of his clients or of his new
racing enterprise was cruelly dispelled – Peter Collins was
critically ill in a Bonn hospital with appalling head injuries
after a crash at the Pflanzgarten curve at the Nürburgring,
on lap 11 of the German Grand Prix. He had been struggling
to keep up with Tony Brooks' Vanwall and made an unchar-

acteristic error. Brooks had been very much the junior to Collins in his early days at Aston Martin and there is some thought that Collins took their role reversal rather too seriously.

Immediately, Ken Gregory attempted to find out more by phoning Moss in Germany, but Stirling couldn't tell him very much. He then called the Police in Dartmouth, where Collins' parents were staying on their ketch, the *Jeannie Marie*, and two officers actually rowed out to the vessel, which was at anchor on the River Dart, but poor Collins was actually dead before they could even put in a call to Germany. The news that Collins could not have suffered much and never regained consciousness was no consolation; not to Gregory, and certainly not to Mike Hawthorn, who had witnessed the crash. The two of them, the 'mon ami mates', had clearly come to dominate the Ferrari team since even before the sad demise of Luigi Musso at the French Grand Prix three weeks earlier. Hawthorn had seen that crash, too, and was rapidly becoming traumatised by the whole process, despite the teasing which he and Collins routinely handed out to poor Musso. Hawthorn, after the death of Collins, made up his mind to retire at the end of the season, indeed he nearly quit right then and there.

For Gregory as well as Hawthorn, Collins' death was a hammer blow. Worse was to come, though, at the last Grand Prix of the Formula 1 season, at Casablanca, against a background as exotic as it was dramatic – the deciding race of the 1958 World Drivers' Championship.

The story is well-known. Moss had the chance of being the first British driver in a British car to become World Champion and make a clean sweep, combining the inaugural Constructor's Championship for Vanwall with the driver's crown for him. That it was not to be was a particularly cruel irony, not only because he had won more races than his nearest rival, Hawthorn, but also because the race was to cost the life of a team-mate.

The Moroccan Grand Prix may not have been the most well-organised event in the history of the sport, and the reason for that may not have been entirely cultural. The Ain-Diab circuit at Casablanca had been completed, using public roads, the year before, and the 1958 race was its first (and only) Grand Prix. It was both very fast and somewhat ill-prepared. Dust, of course, was a predictable problem, as was sea spray and fog on the coastal section (almost half the circuit). The length of the track, 4.7 miles, militated against efficient marshalling, and medical facilities were elementary.

The Vanwall team had justifiably high hopes. The Moss/Brooks/Lewis-Evans combination of drivers provided for most contingencies and, while Vanwall would probably win the new Constructor's Championship, there was the added thrill of which British driver would take the Championship. The top four contenders were all British – Moss, Hawthorn, Brooks and Salvadori – but only Moss or Hawthorn could actually win it. Brooks was one point adrift from possibly winning, with 24 points against Hawthorn's 36 and Moss's 32. Lewis-Evans, who had grown a goatee beard in honour of the venue, was rather adrift with 11 points. Crucially, Moss had to both win the race and set fastest lap, which was worth a point in those days, with Hawthorn no better than third, in order to take the Championship. Well, in the event, he got two out of three. Not bad, but not enough.

The Ferrari team were over a minute behind Stirling as the race entered its finale, with Phil Hill second and Hawthorn third. Hill, of course, moved over to let

Hawthorn through to cross the line a second in front of him, and Mike Hawthorn won the Championship. Ironically, the man running the Hawthorn pit at Casablanca was the famous F. R. W. ('Lofty') England. Hawthorn, so distressed was he at the recent death of Collins that he insisted that his old mentor from Jaguar should be on hand to manage the event for him; after Collins' experience with Ferrari politics, he would trust no-one else and needed the moral support. He had already decided to retire, in fact, come what may.

On lap 41, though, tragedy once again struck. Stuart Lewis-Evans' engine gave out and, at high speed, his locked transmission spun the car off the circuit. The fuel tank fractured and the car burst into flames. Poor Lewis-Evans, by now a human torch, struggled blazing out of the car and, unable to see where he was going, staggered around blindly. The marshals, inexperienced and reluctant to deal with such a horrendous situation, dithered. Eventually, a macabre chase ensued until he was caught up with and his clothing doused. He was, of course, dreadfully burned by then, the whole ghastly process having taken some minutes. And, as the facilities at the track were practically zero, he was taken into Casablanca. One look at the hospital there was sufficient for Tony Vandervell to decide that Lewis-Evans should be flown back to England immediately. The fate of Scott Brown at Spa earlier in the year had served well to point out that there was little hope for a burns victim outside England. Accordingly, Lewis-Evans, still conscious – chatting, even – was loaded on to a BEA Viscount, with some seats removed to accommodate his stretcher and a rather subdued British party went home. Lewis-Evans was whisked to The Royal Victoria Hospital, East Grinstead, where Sir Archibald McIndoe was still in charge of the burns unit which had been set up during the war. The work which he had done there (he virtually invented plastic surgery) with his famous 'guinea pigs' from the RAF was still the world's benchmark and he was Lewis-Evans' only hope.

There was little Sir Archibald could do to help, though, two days after the accident. Shock, dehydration and the punishment of both an arduous journey and some ineffective treatment immediately after the crash all combined to give McIndoe no choice but to make his patient's final days as comfortable as they could be. Stuart Lewis-Evans died peacefully on 25 October 1958, a week after his crash. He would, in all likelihood, never have driven again, possibly never even have walked. It is sadly true that victims of injury are, in extremis, seldom told the true extent of what is wrong with them, and the injuries which befell Lewis-Evans were so grievous, with major, deep burns over 85 per cent of his body, that they would have threatened him the rest of his life even if he had survived.

Vandervell, horrified by the price which racing had exacted, decided to stop there and then. The enterprise which he had founded, to build a car which would hold its end up internationally, had certainly worked well, but he was sickened by the cost – 1958 was Vanwall's last season.

Hawthorn, a totally lowered World Champion, still grieving for his friend Collins, announced publicly what he had already told Lofty England in private; his immediate retirement from racing. The 1958 season had been one of triumph, but it had also been depressing for all involved. Enzo Ferrari, subdued by the deaths of Musso and, more particularly, his golden boy Collins, became even more reclusive, if that were possible. Stirling Moss, as ever aware of the cruel ironies of life, learned much from 1958. After Casablanca, he retreated a little, accepting that the realities of racing are often subsumed by the realities of winning. To this day, he maintains that Phil Hill's driving was a masterpiece of gamesmanship. The man who had, by virtue of his victory in Argentina, literally changed the focus of motor racing, by repeating in his Cooper what had been done by Bugatti against the Bentleys and Mercedes before the war, had confirmed what before had only been a hint; that this was not the end of the line so far as cars were concerned; it was the start of the line.

As for poor Lewis-Evans, his success – not in a Vanwall, nor even a Connaught – had changed everything and would outlive him. His drives for Ken Gregory and Alfred Moss in a relatively humble Cooper-Climax Formula 2 car, were the catalyst for a sea-change in the sport which is still with us – that the racing team, by virtue of its success, becomes a magnet for other people's money, allowing an acceleration of technical development, which only proper funding can bring to fruition. In the inflation-free 1950s, the bulk of participants in motor racing, indeed all sports, were chronically unbusinesslike – even the manufacturers. The year 1958 was, sadly, to be Maserati's last season. Sponsorship, the mainspring of the sport today, was still a thing of the future.

But the near future. The success of the BRP effort was to bring to the sport a new imperative and a new agenda. That Ken Gregory and Alfred Moss started motor sport off as a business is a central theme of this book and, before long, the intrusion of a new medium – television – would give this new emphasis a life of its own but, unhappily, Ken and Alfred would not profit by it. The catalyst was another business which the two were planning, which involved the relocation of the British Racing Partnership from the Moss farm to that well-known London borough with a tradition of motor-racing; Chelsea.

Chapter 13

SOMEONE ELSE'S MONEY

*'Money ... is none of the wheels of trade: it is
the oil which renders the motion of wheels
more smooth and easy.'*
DAVID HUME, 1742

Gregory had decided to branch out into a little property speculation soon after BRP was founded. He had bought a house in Clabon Mews, Chelsea, which had a garage huge enough to quite easily accommodate the little racing team. While they laboured in the garage, Gregory had the house restored.

The BRP was not the only commercial enterprise on which Gregory and Alfred Moss were working, though. Noble Motors was, sadly, no more; it had been bought by a publicly-listed conglomerate, Peña Industries, who clearly needed the cash cow which Noble represented. They were nearly bust at the time, a fact that Gregory only appreciated when he was forced to sue them for his director's fees. It was a shame, but it had led to a new situation, about which there was every reason to be optimistic.

The collapse of Peña Industries had left Robert Thornton out of work and it was he who suggested to Gregory that the experience they had gained in repairing and servicing cars could be usefully exploited in rebuilding them for profit. A first-rate idea, in fact. The object was straightforward; to repair damaged cars to be sold to the trade on a wholesale basis. Gregory and Alfred Moss were well-connected at both ends of the process, particularly at the buyer's – the trade. The motor trade provided many good journeymen drivers as well as many excellent ones, and Alfred and Gregory knew most of them. By operating an insurance-approved repair facility for the use of the wholesale market, the pair, alongside Messrs Nabarro and Nathanson, as well as Peter Jopp, were set fair to exploit that lucrative middle ground, knowledge of which was and still is virtually unknown to the car buyer.

Well, it all went horribly wrong – but that was later. It was clear, though, from the outset that the premises were too large, even if you chucked in a racing team as well, to soak up the business. In the slack times the building, which was literally down the road from the Noble Motors premises in Lots Road, still had to be heated, lit and insured, for example. The turnover in used, undamaged cars was also rising fast because of the ever-expanding presence in the market of a huge assortment of hire-purchase companies, who would finance, at fat margins, the acquisition of love's young dream on four wheels for the man whose mobility heretofore had been confined more to the Clapham omnibus. The two market leaders in the minor post-Suez boom were United Dominions Trust and Bowmaker. A relative newcomer was the much smaller, but rapidly expanding, Yeoman Credit.

The other shareholders in Gregory's new enterprise (which didn't include Stirling) were somewhat iffy about the venture – they were faced with heavy start-up costs and small, but mounting losses – and they were reluctant to put in any more capital. However, it is not in Gregory's character to give up on a project until every possibility has been exhausted, and he persuaded them to persist. He had confidence in his staff, and the business, once it was over its initial hurdles (it was a little undercapitalised), started to pick up and appeared, on the surface, to be going rather well.

The presence there of the BRP workshop, which was moved from Clabon Mews, actually served as a first-class advertisement. Robert Thornton, who was the general manager, had worked for Gregory before, of course, and he seemed able and well-liked within the car business; so Gregory was happy to delegate to him. But, quite soon, his activities were to threaten Gregory's very commercial existence.

In racing terms, the 1959 season, after the horrors of the previous year, held much promise. Moss, Salvadori and Trintignant had given a clear signal, with Cooper's third place in the Constructor's Championship, that the new architecture developed by the Cooper Car Company was where the future lay. However, Lotus were to persist with a front-engined layout for the 1959 season, as were Ferrari and Maserati. Vanwall had withdrawn completely, retiring their cars rather than selling them. That they had won so convincingly perhaps persuaded Colin Chapman to continue with a traditional layout, given that he had had so much influence upon their design.

Before the season even started, though (there was no Argentinian Grand Prix) a further disaster struck. On 22 January Mike Hawthorn died at the wheel of his Jaguar road car while barrelling along the Guildford by-pass. The crash was witnessed by Rob Walker, who was close behind him. The champion from the casualty-strewn 1958 season had had a bare few months of retirement. It later emerged that he was seriously ill with kidney disease and might not have lived much longer, but now, sadly, both the 'mon ami mates' were gone – dead within months of each other.

For 1959, the main imperative for BRP, now running a team of two cars, was to find a replacement for poor Stuart Lewis-Evans. Gregory and Alfred Moss already had their eyes on Ivor 'The Driver' Bueb, with George Wicken, the

500cc veteran as a potential No. 2. Nobody felt that Tommy Bridger could be asked to go through another trauma, so dire had his 1958 season been, so Wicken was shortlisted purely on a pro tem basis. It was not an agreement made for more than one race at a time, which was convenient, for Tony Robinson had discovered a new prodigy – Chris Bristow.

Christopher Bristow had risen very fast in the sport since coming third in an unpromising Hume-Cooper special at Crystal Palace on Whit Monday 1959. When unleashed in a proper car in a test at Brands Hatch, all present had to check their watches. He was almost frighteningly fast. He hailed from Streatham in South London where his family were involved in a car hire business. Although Bristow was to take part in only four Championship Grands Prix and score no points in any of them, his career was meteoric in other ways.

The cars which BRP were to use in 1959 were still Coopers, but they were to be engined not by Coventry-Climax but by Borgward. If this sounds improbable now, then it should be borne in mind that the Borgward concern, of Bremen, Germany, was the producer of several fine motor cars, notably the Isabella, all of them somewhat underrated now. It is a niche which the firm lost with the resurrection of BMW, but at the time they were possessed of a fine four-cylinder, twin-cam, four-valve engine, designed by Karl Ludwig Brandt, which had proved to be outstanding in sports cars the previous year. It was a complicated little thing, to be sure, and even had twin ignition and fuel injection, to produce 150 bhp at 7500 rpm. One hundred bhp per litre. Its four-valve layout allowed 8000 rpm; the lighter individual weight of each valve, literally tons when under load, allowed some relief on the hard-worked springs. This is 1959, remember. Four-valve layouts are common now, with even the most mundane engines employing them, but the layout was relatively exotic then.

Accordingly, early in 1959, Gregory approached Teddy de Gebert, who ran the firm's UK agents, Metcalfe and Mundy, and a visit to Bremen was arranged. Borgward were very interested, particularly when it was pointed out that Stirling Moss was to drive a car with their engine in it. Moss, of course, was driving for Rob Walker not for Gregory, but organisationally there was very little difference. A deal was done, with Karl Borgward himself signing the agreement, for a package of three engines and spares – one for Rob Walker and two for the BRP, with the services of a factory engine specialist assigned to the two teams for the duration of the season.

The first Cooper-Borgward was Walker's, but only just. The engine was fitted into the Formula 1 Cooper in which Maurice Trintignant had won the Monaco Grand Prix the previous year, and shakedown tests were carried out to bring the car up to competitive levels ready for the meat of the season which started at Easter. Shortly after the completion of Walker's car the BRP versions were ready for Bristow and Bueb to race.

However, Gregory had ambitions beyond Formula 2, however exotically-powered. The departure of Vanwall and Ferrari left Stirling with little to drive in Formula 1. He was happy with Rob Walker, of course, but rather as Gregory was sceptical about the virtues of the Climax engine over the Borgward, so Moss was a little iffy about the 2½-litre Coventry-Climax as against the BRM engine. He held no particular brief for the BRM car itself at that time, although the efforts of Harry Schell and Jean Behra had proved that it had come a long way since inception. In earlier days many drivers had walked away from BRM in high dudgeon – Salvadori, Brooks, Hawthorn and, indeed, Moss – but there was little doubt that the engine, although rough, had merit.

Neatly by-passing the BRM company, Gregory went straight to Alfred Owen, who financed it through the Rubery Owen corporation. He agreed with the proposal, and an engine was made available on loan. Obviously, it was a good idea, but the installation of an engine from a front-engined car into a rear-engined chassis obviously poses some logistical problems, which Alf Francis had but a matter of weeks to solve; chief of which was a gearbox. Moss wanted a five-speeder, and the only man in the world who could scratch build one in the time was Valerio Colotti in Milan. Francis undertook the liaison and took the chassis and engine with him to see what could be done. He also took with him a specification sheet of metals to be used in the construction, and thereby hangs the tale of why the Rob Walker Cooper-BRM was more or less stillborn.

Inexorably, if not quietly, engine power had been creeping up, and as it did, transmission failures also increased. Moss admits now that the Colotti gearbox was a magnificent piece of engineering with a wonderful 'change, made from the wrong sort of metal – simply not hard enough to take the strain. He also admits to a tendency to change up at lower revs in order to save transmissions. Of course, peak torque occurs lower down than peak power, and feeding maximum torque through a fragile transmission will wreck it more certainly than anything else. Whatever, the mating of the Colotti 'box to the BRM engine in the Cooper chassis was an expensive but ultimately fruitless exercise, but it did later result in Francis and Colotti working together.

Or so it seemed. Owen was philosophical about the hybrid's apparent lack of success and was pleased at the effort. However, in terms of Formula 1, he had other things on his mind, the chief of which was the apparent failure of the BRM company to produce a car which was competitive in any way whatsoever. Of course, Owen would have been delighted to have Moss as a works driver, leading the team, à la Vanwall, but Moss, in consultation with virtually everybody who had had anything to do with the cars, was not persuaded to offer his services. It was not entirely a matter of the car, either, although he had frightful memories of the old V16 – he did not really trust Raymond Mays and Peter Berthon not to mess him about.

However, things had been changing at BRM. The original design of the P25, the current Formula 1 offering, was largely the work of Peter Berthon and Stuart Tresilian and far removed from the 16-cylinder effort of before. It owed something in appearance to both the Maserati 250 and the Connaught B-type, was a good deal less complex than its infamous predecessor and was even possessed of a stressed skin body on a tubular chassis, which was highly advanced at the time, even if many observers felt that it was mere gimmickry.

Trouble was, it didn't work very well. The designers had decided that, given that the rear brakes did less than one third of the braking work, then the BRM would only employ one rear brake, which they placed at the input shaft of the rear-mounted transaxle. It would, of course, have to stop itself from a far higher rotation speed than a wheel-mounted brake, which fact was to cause the car problems.

The other key design element was the engine, designed by Tresilian and interfered with by BRM. Tresilian designed the unit as massively over-square to assist high revving. With the same thought in mind he penned it to have four valves per cylinder. Problems with engine gaskets persuaded

Peter Berthon to opt for a two-valve layout after all, which left the motor a little short on breathing power for its bore. This was theoretically addressed by using huge enlarged ports, which lowered gas velocity; so the potential rpm was raised to offer peak power at 9000 rpm. Here, there were problems. The five-bearing crankshaft was not, it seems, properly balanced. Any advantages gained in lower frictional stresses by using a short crank were cancelled out by a distinct resonance at high revs. The relatively vast reciprocating mass created a huge vibration which was fed straight down the input shaft to the transaxle – and thence to the famous single brake. The brake disc, rotating at engine rather than axle speed, might just have survived without knocking out its pads, but the rigid pipes which carried the fluid could not. The result, not unnaturally, was consistent brake failure. That it was a design fault in the car rather than in the Lockheed brakes was something which BRM were totally unable to admit.

Tony Rudd had arrived at BRM at the end of 1957 with a brief to sort the P25 out properly before it became a complete laughing-stock. In effect he designed a totally new generation of car, redesigning the entire chassis, suspension, engine and even the bodywork. By working with Colin Chapman – who had already done similar work for Tony Vandervell on the Vanwall special – it was established, for example, that the roll centres front and rear were actually different, which could not have helped the handling of the original. By the time he had finished with it, at the end of 1958, BRM had quite a decent car. It had a tubular chassis, mind you, as well as a longer wheelbase, both of which might be seen as great leaps backwards, but it handled well and offered less vibration after the crankshaft was modified with four main bearings rather than five, and the air-filled

MANAGING A LEGEND

struts of the suspension were replaced with conventional coils and dampers. It was not unlike a cruder Vanwall in many ways, and the brakes would always let it down, but the 1959 season started well for the firm at the Dutch Grand Prix, which Joakim Bonnier won. Unsurprisingly, in the light of the apparent promise of Rudd's car, Alfred Owen was keen to have Moss on the works team.

Moss first tested the BRM at Goodwood, after the Easter Monday meeting in 1959. He drove two cars and decided that he preferred Harry Schell's car (Chassis No. 257). Moss has a superstition about seven. It was the number worn by Tommy Wisdom's XK120 at the 1950 Dundrod race and he has always favoured it, down to wearing '7' cufflinks even today. He agreed to drive it at the Silverstone international race, which was next on the UK calendar.

Obviously Harry Schell liked it, too, because 257 certainly wasn't the car BRM offered Moss at Silverstone. He could tell, too, which rather startled Peter Berthon, although this was a piece of gamesmanship on Stirling's part – he had made a mark on one of the chassis tubes, so knew which one he was in. This small deception annoyed him. Notwithstanding his irritation, Moss made fastest time in practice. Having made his point, he then asked for the engine, which he liked, to be put in the correct chassis for the race. All went well, and then the dreaded brakes failed on the fifth lap of the race, which rather put egg on everyone's face. It certainly did little for relations between Moss and Berthon when negotiations were started to run a BRM in BRP colours. Again, Alfred and Gregory by-passed Berthon and Raymond Mays and dealt direct with Alfred Owen to obtain the car and work out a management deal for it for BRP, in whose pale green colours it would be painted. Significantly, the car was not only for Moss, but he

SEE TONY RUDD BOOK ON THIS !

would have first choice in driving it. In fact, it would be entered for Moss in only two Grands Prix that year, because of – er – unforeseen circumstances.

Moss raced predominantly for Rob Walker in Championship races in 1959. The BRM engine had been returned to the works and the Colotti gearbox was recycled by being mated with the Climax engine which replaced it in the Walker Cooper. It was not, broadly, a success, and the gearbox let Stirling down a crucial four times that season.

It was clear, though, that whatever misfortunes befell the Cooper, the BRM seemed happy in BRP hands. Peter Berthon was less that pleased by this and, in correspondence between himself and Owen, took every opportunity to carp about the part played by the BRP personnel in looking after his precious car, not least the bills for expenses submitted by BRP for carrying out their function. He was not to know that the only basis upon which Stirling would drive the car was if BRP prepared it. If this seems an over-reaction to what appeared to be a small economy with the truth, then bear in mind not only Stirling's superstition, but the track record of the marque itself amongst his fellow drivers.

For Moss, though, no deception was too small to ignore, and while he had his doubts about the integrity of the BRM company on more than one level, he had no such doubts about BRP, which is why the car was torn down and rebuilt by Tony Robinson and his crew. It was less a statement by Gregory about BRM, rather more a means of allowing Moss to sleep at night.

It is clear that there was a measure of 'needle' in the relationship between BRM and BRP as the season went on. Berthon's litany of complaints makes depressing reading after the event, particularly when compared to the jocular relationship which the Cooper company seemed to have with its customers, but this can be partly explained by the zeal with which Berthon and Raymond Mays undertook their crusade to bring motor racing success to Britain. To Mays and Berthon, British Racing Motors was merely the reinvention of English Racing Automobiles, the company which Leslie Johnson had bought after the war. In truth, the enterprise was more about engineering than winning. The fact that Tony Vandervell had entered and exited the sport as a manufacturer, winning the Constructor's Championship in the process, within the time that BRM had taken to develop the P25 to the level at which BRP took theirs over, cannot have helped, but Berthon nit-picked persistently.

The BRM set-up at Bourne was strange in the extreme and it was neither Moss nor Gregory's cup of tea at all. It had little to do with the fact that Mays was a homosexual or that Berthon was something of an enigma; it was more to do with the sheer arrogance of the organisation itself. A whole series of drivers prior to Moss had tried the BRM and none had liked it much. The Rudd BRM was a better car all round – indeed, the best handling front-engined car that Stirling Moss ever drove – but it was, none the less, front-engined. The 1958 Argentina race had raised more than a question mark about Maserati 250 clones against Coopers, and to Stirling Moss winning was all.

None of Berthon's antipathy rubbed off on either Gregory or Alfred Moss; they were too busy ensuring the development of the Cooper Borgward. Also, Gregory was by now involved in a most significant undertaking, the roots of which lay in the rather improbable business which shared the BRP premises in Lots Road, Chelsea.

The main providers of credit to the car trade, UDT and Bowmaker, were both observing the growth in motor sport with some interest. UDT, which also owned Laystall, the engineering company which made virtually all the crank-shafts in the land, had flirted with sponsoring racing in an alliance with Col. Ronnie Hoare, who raced under the United Racing Stable banner. It was during the discussions over the BRM venture that Ken Gregory was asked to lunch by UDT's smaller competitor, Yeoman Credit, which had recently been merged with Bowmaker. Present were two of the principals of the firm, the brothers Fabian and Paul Samengo-Turner, who controlled this burgeoning money-lending operation within the Bowmaker group. Of course, Gregory knew them already; the business conducted by Express Coachcraft with the motor trade had ensured that the two firms' paths would cross. Possibly because UDT were experimenting with Formula 2, the Yeoman Credit proposal was for Formula 1, a full three-car team, no rehearsals.

The ticklish question of how much all this would cost did not faze Gregory at all. He was, in fact, unprepared for the question, as he had assumed that the lunch was basical-ly social. He knew, from having been a negotiator on both sides of a table, that the key was a firm, high price if you are selling and a firm, low price if you are buying. He told them that such a team would cost £40,000 to set up and half that again, per annum, to run – a total of sixty thousand pounds for the first year. He knew, because nobody blinked, that his suggestion was not totally out of court. In fact, it was accepted. There was one proviso – Yeoman Credit would keep the trophies. Gregory did a quick calculation on the back of his mental envelope as he left the meeting; he was now potentially a wealthy man.

It was a startling vote of confidence. The Yeoman Credit effort could have gone to BRM, Cooper or Lotus, all of whom ran works teams, all of whom were well run and all

MANAGING A LEGEND

of whom were perpetually short of money. That they offered such a tempting deal to an organisation which had but a season's experience was less a leap of faith on the Samengo-Turners' part, and more a statement of broad policy. The involvement of these two companies, UDT and Yeoman, was to have far-reaching effects, which the sport still benefits from. The success of the BRP team with Lewis-Evans as No. 1 driver the previous year had had more of an impact upon observers that anyone had thought, not least Ken Gregory and Alfred Moss. The BRM deal, conducted as it was at a high level and as a business as much as a sporting endeavour, had caught the imagination of the Samengo-Turners. They were interested in a high profile; they had done well out of their business and were seeking to capitalise upon it. What better way than Formula 1? The enterprise would enjoy its debut on 26 September 1959 at the Oulton Park Gold Cup. Before that was to happen, there was a chain of seminal events.

In the last week of July another tragedy struck. Ivor Bueb had a bad crash at Clermont-Ferrand – a touch of adverse camber had caught him out on a bend in a Formula 2 race – and he was thrown from the car to suffer massive internal injuries. Ken Gregory was in an agony of indecision. Bueb was clearly very badly hurt, with a ruptured spleen the least of the worries. He seemed too ill to move, and yet was clearly not receiving the kind of medical attention which his condition merited. Gregory stayed by his bedside until 30 July, when he had to leave for Berlin, and on 1 August Ivor Leon Bueb, 500 veteran, Le Mans winner, Connaught and Lister driver, bon vivant and racing stalwart, finally lost his grip on life. Chris Bristow, who stayed behind in France to be with him, was dreadfully upset. Ivor had been an easygoing colleague and, more important to a lad whose home life was never particularly happy, both mentor and father figure. Bristow nearly gave up altogether.

Meanwhile, the organisation of the Cooper Borgward and BRM efforts went on, with no particular good grace from Bourne, the BRM headquarters. A respite from all this was at hand, though. Whatever criticism Peter Berthon levelled at BRP was firmly nailed at the German Grand Prix held in August 1959 at the preposterous Avus circuit in Berlin. It was the day of Bueb's death and the mood among the British contingent was sombre as a depressed Ken Gregory put the news about.

Stirling was not to drive the BRM. While it had always been intended that Bueb would be the standby, as communicated to BRM, Gregory had offered Ron Flockhart as a hurried substitute. Flockhart had bags of BRM experience, in so far as anybody had, as he had campaigned as a works driver for two fairly fruitless seasons, but The Automobil Club von Deutschland, seizing the moment, countered with Hans Herrmann. If this seems highhanded, then it should be mentioned that there were only two German cars at the meeting, Porsches entered privately by Jean Behra and by the works for Wolfgang von Trips. They were, though, only in the supporting race. The AvD saw here the opportunity of strong-arming a German driver into a seat in the Formula 1 event. Herrmann was at least an ex-Mercedes driver, although he had only scored one point in the all-conquering 1955 season. The AvD would regret their enthusiasm, indeed they would regret the whole meeting, as it was commercially a failure. Herrmann would regret it more.

The reason was the circuit. It was five miles long with only two bends; the straights were actually part of a dual carriageway and, with lap speeds approaching 150 mph, (Tony Brooks still holds the lap record at 149.13 mph, set at this meeting) the consequent 300 mph closing speeds along the parallel straights, with no barriers, made it all insanely dangerous.

However, the accident which killed Jean Behra in the supporting sports car race was not as a result of a collision; rather he failed to get round the slippery, banked North curve, his car hit the retaining wall and he was catapulted high in the air and smashed into a post, dying instantly. It was an appalling crash, captured in a particularly grisly photograph which served as the main propaganda for the sport's critics for years to come.

More photogenic, but less persuasive evidence was given in the main race by the luckless Herrmann, though. If Stirling thought he had backed the wrong horse by driving Walker's Cooper Climax, retiring as he did on the second lap of the first heat, he was corrected by what happened to the BRM on the fifth lap of the second. It was the dreaded BRM brake syndrome – they failed, totally. Herrmann was barrelling into the South turn at something near 150 mph and started to brake. The entrance to the turn, normally taken at around 60 mph, was outlined by straw bales, themselves dangerous, and the car somersaulted as its wheel spinner bit into them. It went end over end half a dozen times and, as the car inverted at its apogee, an astonished Herrmann simply fell out of the cockpit on to the concrete road. The car, totally berserk, scrapped itself. A crowd-pleaser was that Hans simply got up, dusted himself off and limped away with a sore head.

Gregory was appalled. So was Berthon. The BRM had done this before. The earlier version of it had nearly killed Tony Brooks in 1956, terrified Hawthorn the same year and had given Roy Salvadori several undesirable moments in 1957. The three of them had more or less converged on

Archie Scott Brown and virtually dragged him away from it when he was tempted.

The incessant fiddling about which the BRM engineers had done with the Lockheed brakes was mooted to be the cause of the difficulties. They locked, bound, chafed and, as in Herrmann's case, went away altogether. Herrmann didn't, though, eventually retiring from Formula 1 in 1966 and pleasingly winning the 38th Le Mans in 1970, partnering Dickie Attwood in a Porsche.

Two days after the deaths of Bueb and Behra, Chris Bristow, energised as only the grief-stricken can be, did exactly what Froilan Gonzalez had done at the Nürburgring five years before, after the death of his friend Marimon, and stormed around Brands Hatch to win the Formula 2 John Davey Trophy from Roy Salvadori. It was another defining episode in the evolution of Bristow's accelerating career and he found himself unanimously confirmed as the successor to the great Stuart Lewis-Evans. He had 10 months to live.

The autopsy on the BRM, or rather what was left of it, was carried out in Lots Road. The conclusion reached by a glum Tony Robinson, that the vibration from the lusty four-cylinder engine was causing the pipework to fray on the chassis, letting out the fluid, was persuasive in calling a halt to the BRM adventure, particularly as the car was junk. The taste for Formula 1 was there in Gregory's mind, though. Slightly tongue-in-cheek, the 'car' was returned – er, here you are – to Bourne, to an enraged and embarrassed Berthon and Mays. Rudd was rather more fatalistic. It had not been a marriage made in Heaven, this. Perhaps the initials of the two concerns – or at least their ambitions – were too similar. The BRP-BRM exists today, restored, or rather totally reconstructed, in its distinctive colours at the Donington collection.

Gregory's association with the Samengo-Turner brothers was about to bear fruit, though. The debut of the new Yeoman Credit Racing Team was auspicious. Bristow came third in his Formula 1 debut at the Oulton Park Gold Cup in the last week of September, again beating a slightly rueful Salvadori, but behind Jack Brabham and Stirling Moss, the latter buoyed by his victory in the Italian Grand Prix a fortnight previously. It would have been some consolation to the *tifosi* that the winning car at Monza used an Italian gearbox, but this was a fact probably unknown to them, however much it pleased Valerio Colotti. Much re-engineering had taken place on the innards of this complex device, once it had been admitted that the actual gearsets had originally been machined by a sloppy subcontractor in order to save time, and it had finally found its form. No consolation to Enzo Ferrari, though, as Cooper won the second World Constructor's Championship, a trick they would repeat in 1960. The efforts of Moss, Brabham, McLaren, Trintignant and the other Cooper drivers had ensured that the pivotal moment in the evolution of the sport in Britain had, at last arrived. After the Vanwall, there was no certainty that another British manufacturer could repeat the trick, but Cooper's success hammered the point home firmly.

Gregory and Alfred Moss were doing their bit, too. The Yeoman Credit campaign was planned for 1960, in the light of the Cooper successes, to be a comprehensive one. That 1960 would be as tragic a season as 1958 or 1959, particularly for the BRP, was not a thought that inhibited anyone. Gregory's own griefs, the loss of Peter Collins, Stuart Lewis-Evans and Ivor Bueb, not to mention Archie Scott Brown, Mike Hawthorn and Luigi Musso and the whole host of others, did not at that stage threaten to annul his relationship with racing, but the events of 1960 were to test his resolve almost to destruction, on more than one front, in maintaining his role in this supremely dangerous sport.

Given the level of commitment offered by Yeoman Credit, there was a great deal of flexibility available. The essence of the deal was a development of the BRM venture, in that Yeoman Credit would own the cars, BRP would manage them, prepare and enter them, and find the drivers. Moss was still sticking resolutely to Rob Walker for Formula 1 – his manager worked for him, after all, not the other way around – but there were plenty of luminaries still about apart from Stirling.

To lead the team, Gregory chose Harry Schell, a Franco-Irish-American rakehell in his 39th year of life, and 13th of racing. Harry O'Reilly Schell had been born in Paris in 1921. He was one of two brothers who had discovered 500cc racing at the same time as Ken Gregory, Stirling Moss and Peter Collins. Some six feet four inches tall, with appetites to match, Schell had been more or less a fixture in racing since its reinvention after the war.

If Harry Schell had not existed it would have almost been necessary to invent him. He was cast in the 'mad, bad, and dangerous to know' mould, rather like a friend of his, Portago. While Hawthorn and Collins had been the quintessential 'mon ami mates', Schell had enjoyed a similar relationship with the Marquis de Portago until the latter's death in the final Mille Miglia. The pair, Schell and Portago, shared a common bond, that of Irish ancestry on their mothers' sides, and between them they defined a particular exemplar of the ruthless pursuit of self indulgence which left mere observers breathtaken.

They were different characters, though. Schell was totally committed to enjoying himself and, aside from a tendency toward a slightly theatrical mien, had few pretensions.

Portago cast himself in the mean and moody role and one is struck by the possibility that he never quite recovered from seeing James Dean films for the first time. By some accounts he was a most unpleasant man, by others, merely insufferably arrogant – this in a sport which seldom lacks examples. Schell's life was marked out by small episodes of good-natured outrageousness which left their mark on all who witnessed them.

It wasn't always Harry's fault, though. The reason that Schell's Goggomobil ended up on the first floor of the Lion d'Or hotel at Reims was nothing to do with his own exuberance, for that evening he had other plans. He merely had the temerity to check into the place with a girl on his arm so jaw-droppingly lovely (and suspiciously young) that the assembled racing folk decided to teach him a lesson, stripping the couple's room of every vestige of furnishing for good measure and carrying the little car up the stairs. There's sportsmanship for you.

Schell and Portago had met professionally in Argentina in 1954, sharing a Ferrari in the 1000 kilometre sports car race. It belonged to Portago, but he could not drive it, until Schell showed him how to heel and toe. They, or rather Schell, came second. Within 18 months, Portago was a works Ferrari driver – as an amateur, of course – and Schell was with Vanwall. The two were inseparable until Portago's death and, although neither man ever won a World Championship Grand Prix, both left their mark in other ways. Among his other interests, Schell owned a bar in Paris – 'L'Action Automobile'. Not quite the RAC, nor 'Le Chanteclair' in New York, over which Schell's friend René Dreyfus presided, this establishment offered Schell a modest living which seemed to keep him going. He was, at the time of Gregory's approach to him, planning to campaign his own Cooper under the Ecurie Bleu banner, and indeed was to retire on the 63rd lap of the Argentinian Grand Prix driving that very vehicle. He had a long history with Cooper cars, not always particularly amicable, and had in fact been the first entrant of a Cooper car in a Grand Prix – that of Monaco in 1950. His Grand Prix debut, and Cooper's, lasted less than two laps, as he and eight other drivers collided with each other at Tabac.

What Schell was to bring to the Yeoman Credit team was, in the first place, experience, and in the second, steadiness. If this sounds inconsistent with what is known of him, then it should be borne in mind that since the death of Portago, Schell had matured hugely. His time at Vanwall, Ferrari and BRM had leavened his exuberance to the point that he was quite simply one of the most seasoned of drivers and a man who inspired a following, even if it was sometimes one generated merely out of curiosity. His huge stature, slightly staring eyes and Franco-theatrical demeanour proved to be a magnet for the younger generation. 1960 was to be Harry Schell's last season.

Chapter 14

1960 · A TEST TO DESTRUCTION

'But bear me to that chamber, there I'll lie:
In that Jerusalem shall Harry die.'
HENRY IV, PART II

There was every reason to think that the Yeoman Credit organisation was faced with the prospect of early success in 1960. Certainly, the works teams of Lotus, Cooper and BRM thought so, as the amounts of money put up by the Samengo-Turners were sufficient to ensure that Gregory had a fat chequebook. That he probably had the best cars – three of them – and the best engineers, led by Robinson, to prepare them, did not help. Most other firms, despite the clear sea change which the various British efforts had wrought upon the sport, were functionally bust when compared with the reinvented BRP. An exception was BRM, still funded by the loyal Owen organisation. To both Chapman and the Coopers, the awful example of what can happen, the disaster of Connaught which had folded under the sheer weight of independence three years before, was clear to see.

BRM, with their new rear-engined P48, was not the only other team with money in its pocket, though. Aston Martin had reinvented the Maserati 250F in 1957 and had put into production their own version of it, although not quite as elegant and barely as quick. They had not raced it in 1958, fruitlessly preoccupied as they were with the World Sports Car Championship, but they had reintroduced the car for 1959, yet with scant success. Its 1960 successor, the DBR5, was a slightly modified effort, outdated before it began. Like the Vanwall, the architecture of its power unit was inspired by a motorcycle engine, but an AJS rather than a Norton. It was joined by the Scarab, a venture by Lance Reventlow of California. Reventlow had had much success in SCCA events in America with his Scarab sports cars which were Lister-like firebreathers and, rather like the Aston, the car was a development of a sports car chassis. It was a lemon, but a noble effort.

Lotus had finally produced a rear-engined car, too – the Type 18. Rob Walker bought one to hedge his bets, as it were, complementing the Cooper T51 from the previous season. Ferrari, yet to be fully committed to what the British manufacturers had already proved beyond doubt – that their pattern of building, however light and cheap it might appear, was the way forward – was late to develop the rear-engined layout; but when he did, employing the services of Mauro Forghieri, it was brilliant. That was not to be until 1961, though, and 1960 would be another rough season for Ferrari; but there were delayed dividends to be enjoyed from the emphasis he had given to 1500cc Formula 2, the basis for the 1961 Formula 1.

By now, Stirling himself was taking rather more of an interest in BRP. He was not at that point a shareholder, and was not even interested in the business side of the sport: 'I left all that side of things to Ken – I just wanted to get on with racing; I never really became interested in business until I retired.'

But he had begun to see the virtue of the sponsored approach, and despite his own apparent and totally mis-leading indifference to pounds, shillings and pence, except as they directly affected him, he knew full well that Alfred would not dream of being involved in BRP unless it was a winning proposition. He had, by 1960, started to make mental notes to investigate it further.

217A. *Cliff Allison. (Ken Gregory).*
217B. *Trevor Taylor. (Ken Gregory).*
217C. *Stuart Lewis-Evans, Morocco, 1958. (Bernard Cahier).*

218. *Olivier Gendebien chatting with Ken Gregory, Reims, 1960. (Ken Gregory).*
219A. *'This is your Life' with Eamonn Andrews, 27 April 1959. L-R: Tommy Wisdom, Ken Gregory, Don Müller, Katie Moss, Stirling Moss, Aileen Moss, Alfred Moss, Stirling's form teacher, Alf Francis.*
219B. *Alfred, Aileen and Pat Moss admiring the first issue of Cars Illustrated, March 1962. This magazine later evolved into Car and Car conversions. (Ken Gregory).*

220A. *The annual Ferrari awards lunch, Modena 1958. Seated from left: Wolfgang von Trips, Jesse Alexander, Ken Gregory, Mike Hawthorn, Bernard Cahier, Piero Taruffi. Bottom left; Olivier Gendebien and Luigi Musso. (Bernard Cahier).*

220B. *Innes Ireland in the Ferrari 156 'Sharknose' which had been intended for Stirling Moss. Silverstone, 1962. (T.C. March).*

221A. A rear view of the U.D.T. Laystall Lotus 18, with body removed. (Pembroke Stevens).
221B. Innes Ireland leading Roy Salvadori through the chicane at Goodwood, 1961.

222A. *Stirling talking to Tony Robinson and Stan Collier before his last race at Goodwood, Easter Monday, 1962.(John Fry).*
222B. *The start. Lofty England (arms folded) is standing behind Stirling's car.*
223. *The accident. (Daily Express)*

MANAGING A LEGEND

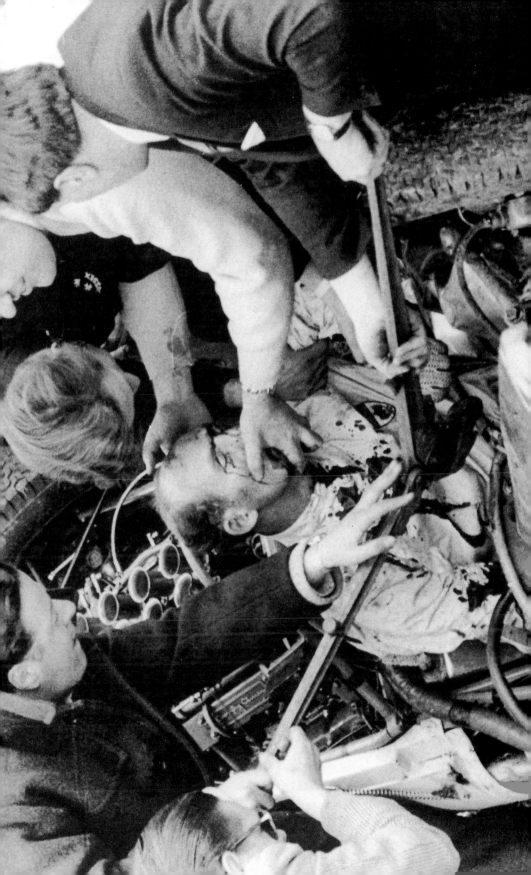

224. A year later, Stirling tests a Lotus 19, wearing his lucky number 7 at Goodwood, all to no avail. (Peter Downie).

Meanwhile, though, he pounded on through a racing schedule that would probably poleaxe most men, then and now. There is little doubt that he could not have achieved his extraordinary level of activity without the structure which Gregory had evolved around him. Despite his self-absorption in racing, one important Moss credo had, by now, become thoroughly established, the doctrine of value for money, both giving it and, perhaps more familiarly, receiving it. In this particular, he and Gregory were of one mind, despite the fierce protests which had come their way from BRM the previous year over the cost of their services.

The Samengo-Turners had no such reservations – not yet anyway – but their relationship with BRP and particularly with Ken Gregory was to deteriorate into a stormy one, which was to come to a bitter conclusion late in the season, and would expose both sides of the argument to some unpleasant scrutiny, and would drag on and on to end in an exhausted draw. Oddly, it was to have absolutely nothing to do with racing.

The core of the problem was growing at Lots Road. Robert Thornton, the opportunistic charmer who was managing Gregory's repair business, Express Coachcraft, was, in effect, cooking the books. To what degree had yet to emerge, but his activities were to expose Gregory to appalling financial risks with both his new sponsors and others.

The BRP had decided, as a matter of strategy that the Yeoman Credit team would not be totally international. The purpose of the venture as far as the sponsors were concerned was to sell the services of the Yeoman Credit company, rather than to win the World Championship. It was understood by all, though, that drivers of the first rank would only sign up with the team on the basis that the full calendar would be attempted.

This did not stop them entering the traditional (almost) series of warm-up races in South Africa and New Zealand, held early in the year and preceding Sebring and the Argentinian Grand Prix. For South Africa, Moss and Bristow entered the two Cooper Borgwards from the previous year, which were still in stock, and for New Zealand, Moss took a BRP Formula 1 Cooper T51 and did well until the transmission failed.

There were also plenty of events to choose from in Britain for that season – the International Trophy Race, the Gold Cup at Oulton Park, the Glover Trophy at Goodwood, the Lombard Trophy, the Silver City Airways Trophy, and so on – all of which were well organised and well attended, with worthwhile prize money .

The second of these non-Championship races of the UK season was the Glover Trophy Race at Goodwood. Bristow was astonishing, qualifying ahead of the Coopers of both Stirling and Schell, but the race was won by Innes Ireland in a works Lotus 18, which revealed that Colin Chapman had not been idle over the winter, and had produced, in the 18, a car which set brains working very hard indeed. The new Cooper chassis would be ready soon, but Ireland's performance at Goodwood had startled everyone.

The fourth event of the season, held a fortnight before the European Grand Prix at Monaco, was the *Daily Express* International Trophy at Silverstone, an important shakedown for the season. Held on a damp weekend in the middle of May, it was to be the second and last appearance of Harry Schell as the team leader of the Yeoman Credit Formula 1 effort, and was to set the tone for the season. Schell had shelved his ambitions for Ecurie Bleu after the Argentinian Grand Prix, and committed himself to building on the excellent work he had done for Vanwall and BRM.

He was practising on the Saturday, getting used to the car and doing rather well. Ken Gregory was watching. The track was drenched after a downpour, and at Abbey curve Schell aquaplaned on a puddle and clipped a low retaining wall at the corner. The car flipped and Schell, half thrown out, caught his helmet on the corner of it. His neck was broken and he died instantly. The car looked just as if it had been casually parked. Had he been wearing a harness, of course, he would have been shaken but not stirred, but the habit was not to catch on for some time yet. The newer, lower, rear-engined cars were hard enough to enter and exit as it was, particularly if the driver was Schell's size.

As team manager, Gregory was taken by the police to identify his friend. Schell's body was transferred from the circuit hospital to the mortuary at Buckingham, which had in earlier times served as a prison. As the shroud was lifted, a flurry of thoughts went through a stunned Ken Gregory's mind:

'There was this great, barrel-chested man, not a mark on him, lying on the slab. The oddest thing, though, apart from the fact that I had never been close to a dead body before, never even seen one, was that I could absolutely swear that he was smiling. I can still see him now.'

With the death of Harry Schell, something more than the man himself left the sport. The immediacy of the experience for Gregory was to have a profound effect on him, though, which would be pounded home again within two short months.

Obviously, Schell had to be replaced, and quickly. Gregory's choice fell upon Henry Taylor, who had sparkled in Formula 2, but the Samengo-Turner brothers felt that a higher profile driver could be found. They knew Tony Brooks might be persuaded, because they had already asked him. Any policy conflict between team owner and manager was resolved by their decision to finance an extra car for Brooks. The Samengo-Turners' view was that all-British drivers would make all the difference as well as restoring some of the lost morale, and a Brooks/Bristow/Taylor team would catch the public imagination, given that Stirling was clearly unavailable, driving as he was for Walker. So keen were the Samengo-Turners to have Brooks that they offered to pay a £400 premium per race for him. And rightly, as he was something of a catch. Swiftly, he was enrolled.

Charles Anthony Standish Brooks, born on 25 February 1932 at Dukinfield in Cheshire, had already achieved national hero status with his groundbreaking effort, driving a Connaught in the Syracuse Grand Prix, while still a dental student. Had Syracuse been a Championship event, Brooks would have taken Giancarlo Baghetti's record of winning first time out in a Grand Prix, for it was his first Formula 1 drive. That had been in 1955. Since then, he had figured prominently in the World Drivers' Championship, figuring a close second to Jack Brabham in 1959. Stirling Moss rated him – still does rate him – highly, as one of the top half dozen – ever.

Brooks lacked many of Schell's personal qualities, being quiet, studious and scrupulously polite, but made up for that in terms of a surgical precision in his driving, which Schell himself had famously lacked. Charming, slightly diffident perhaps, and possessed of the sort of self-discipline which had allowed him to revise calmly for his final exams while en route for his first Grand Prix, he was, in the eyes of some, the only other British driver around who could be considered in the same category as Moss. Bristow, naturally coming up fast, was perhaps callow by comparison. Innes Ireland, over at Lotus and starting his second season with

Colin Chapman and his first with a rear-engined car, was something of an unknown quantity, but his victory in the Glover Trophy had clearly produced a man to beat.

At the sharp end, Brooks managed fourth place at Monaco in what was one of Stirling's finest races for Rob Walker (or anyone), but Bristow retired with gearbox trouble, always a feature of a race with 1,500 gear changes. Bristow qualified at Monaco with an identical time to Brooks, and had done so earlier. He thus deserved a front row place on the grid which, at Monaco, would have given him a decent chance of winning, but he was persuaded by Gregory that he should give his place to the more seasoned Brooks. The timekeepers, clearly not paying attention, had failed to notice the young Londoner's performance in his distinctive chequered helmet (Brooks wore a white one) and agreed readily to the swapping of positions, assuming that they had confused the car numbers; Brooks was No. 18, Bristow 16. It was naughty in the extreme, but Bristow was good-natured and enough of a team player to put up with it.

Two BRP cars retired at Zandvoort, with Henry Taylor finishing seventh, and the attention turned to the Belgian Grand Prix at Spa-Francorchamps on 19 June. It was to be a tragic fiasco; another benighted chapter in the sad history of the Ardennes circuit.

Spa was a circuit well-known for monumental and particularly dangerous accidents. It suffered from being both very long, at nearly nine miles, which made marshalling difficult if not impossible, and hazard-strewn, being laid out using public roads. It was very fast, with lap speeds of 133 mph quite possible, even despite the modifications carried out in late 1958. Richard Seaman and Archie Scott Brown had both died after crashing there and this race was to up the total by two, and very nearly more. The Lotus entries would be the worst affected, but there would be one tragedy which was to affect BRP profoundly.

It was a practice accident which befell Moss and which really drew attention to the standard of preparation of the entire Lotus effort. Quite simply, his off-side rear wheel fell off at 135 mph while going through the Burnenville curve. There were four other Lotus entries, three from the works and one from Mike Taylor, which had been an old mount of Ireland's, which Chapman had sold to him. Chapman, unsettled by the Moss accident, instructed that the Lotuses should be parked and inspected. The team was looking for Mike Taylor and couldn't find him anywhere. After a search of the track the marshals discovered that he had left the road, too, and had been lying trapped in the car with broken bones and a wrenched neck for over half an hour. His steering column had snapped clean through at the same speed as Stirling had had his misfortune.

Stirling was grievously hurt, with nose and both legs broken and serious damage to his back, including both broken vertebrae and torn muscles. It was his first bad accident at Formula 1 and very nearly his last. Only his phenomenal reaction speeds, permitting him to whip the now three-wheeled car around and slide it backwards into the bank, saved him from the full shock of a frontal impact at well over 120 mph, which, as he wore no racing harness, would in all probability have killed him. Typically for Spa, the medical attention was scanty and he had to wait for nearly half an hour for an ambulance. He would race again after only a month.

When the Lotuses of Ireland, Jim Clark and Alan Stacey were inspected, it was found that the hubs on two of the cars were cracked, having been machined wrongly. They were, of course, replaced with components from a different batch with stronger, more radiused profiles, but the episode filled no-one with particular enthusiasm. Morale was low enough because of Stirling's crash, let alone the prospect of driving in exactly the same type of car. The Chapman philosophy regarding components – that if it breaks, it's too light, and if it doesn't break, it's too heavy – was neat, if Oscarish, but in this case the experimental nature of the cars was clearly revealed. The steering columns were not replaced, as the cause of Taylor's moment was only revealed later. Stacey, though, had also experienced directional problems, traced to a defective bolt in the steering mechanism.

The race itself started, for the Lotus drivers at least, with some circumspection. Jack Brabham led in his Cooper all the way, in fact, to win the race. Ireland had a huge spin at Seaman corner on lap 13, which put him out, and on lap 19, Chris Bristow left the road near the same spot which had seen Stirling's accident. He had re-passed Willy Mairesse's Ferrari and was contesting position with him when, apparently, although there were no eye-witnesses, he simply lost it. He careered off the circuit and was decapitated by a low fence. His body was thrown out on to the circuit for all to see, and a horrified Jim Clark, who hated the Spa circuit anyway, recalled:

'I came bustling down behind them and no-one had any flags out to warn me of what was round the corner. I saw a marshal suddenly dash out on to the road, waving his arms and trying to stop me and the next thing I saw was another marshal run from the far side of the road. I remember thinking 'where is he going?' and then he bent down and grabbed this thing by the side of the road. It looked just like a rag doll. It was horrible and I'll never forget the sight of his mangled body being dragged to the side. I was almost sick on the spot. I remember at the end of the race finding that my car was spattered with blood, and this put me off completely.'

Small wonder. As for any involvement of Willy Mairesse in Bristow's fatal accident, there is often confusion with the incident almost exactly two years later in the 1962 Spa Grand Prix when he nearly killed Trevor Taylor by hitting Taylor's Lotus on its rear-mounted gearbox and knocking it out of gear, both cars crashing. In the case of the Bristow accident, there seems no doubt that the pair were fighting tooth and nail for their place, but no evidence has ever been produced to show that Mairesse actually caused the crash.

Guillaume 'Wild Willy' Mairesse was one of two handi-capped drivers on the circuit that day. Mairesse had a with-ered arm and was also rather small. He has been described elsewhere as 'mildly deranged' and was certainly trying very hard on that day, making his Ferrari début at his home Grand Prix. He, as a local, had more experience of the track than Bristow, who like most other young British drivers, was more used to the airfield circuits of Britain, notwithstanding his success at Monaco, which is a much slower circuit. Mairesse was never a regular Ferrari driver, rather more of an occasional feature, which was unsurprising given his com-petition for a place with Phil Hill, Taffy von Trips and Ritchie Ginther, but all seem to agree that he was as much a danger to his fellow drivers as he was to himself. He com-mitted suicide in Ostend on 2 September 1969, after many other attempts, by shooting himself.

The other handicapped driver was Ireland's and Clark's Lotus team-mate Alan Stacey, from Chelmsford in Essex, who had an artificial leg as a result of a motorbike accident when much younger. There was always some confusion as to whether he would pass a medical, particularly overseas (at home, his condition was well-known) as the rules were always inexact concerning disabilities. The rudimentary medical examinations, which usually contained a knee-jerk reflex test, were circumvented by a neat collusion between the other drivers, particularly Ireland and Moss, who thought it immensely funny, and would distract the doctor's attention while Stacey re-presented his sound knee for a second test. Stacey could not operate a foot throttle, so used a motorcycle type mounted on the gearlever. He was No. 2 in the Lotus team.

Five laps after Bristow's dreadful crash, Stacey disappeared off the circuit. Apparently, he had been hit in the face by a rising pheasant and his Lotus left the road at high speed, rolled over and caught fire. Mercifully, Stacey, like Bristow, died instantly.

The end of the race was a relief to everyone. Olivier Gendebien, making his BRP début and standing in for the indisposed Henry Taylor, finished a useful third behind Bruce McLaren and Jack Brabham. Tony Brooks, by now a master at Spa, had retired on the second lap. Ken Gregory, beside himself, was obviously spared the ordeal of identifying poor Bristow's remains, as it would have been impossible. Weary and depressed, he gathered up the lad's belongings from his hotel room. In doing so, he could not help but leaf through some of Bristow's private papers. He noted a coolness in some of the correspondence there with home and family, and he later speculated that had Bristow had a happier home life, perhaps everything might have been different. He was almost irrational with grief at Bristow's death and Stirling's narrow escape, so much so that Gendebien's brilliant performance cheered him little. After the deaths of so many close to him, Ken Gregory was starting to view motor racing with something less than one hundred per cent enthusiasm. As he packed Chris Bristow's personal effects, he attempted to push such unworthy thoughts aside and, like many others who had been at that awful race, went off in search of a large drink. He found that Ireland, who had been carrying out a similarly dismal task in Alan Stacey's room, felt exactly the same way; Stacey had been his best friend in the sport. Tony Robinson had the sorry task of ferrying Bristow's Jaguar and belongings back to England. Gregory, tired and depressed, flew home.

Out of five Lotuses booked to start, only one, Clark's, finished. Clark, himself a kindly and humane fellow, recalled that he nearly stopped racing there and then, a thought which had occurred to him almost exactly two years before at the same circuit after Archie Scott Brown's accident, which he had also witnessed. As for Ireland, he felt the same. After the death of his friend Stacey, he too was minded to give up. He later claimed that his driving style, as well as his attitude to life, was always different after that day; but more vitally for his career, his faith in Lotus was deeply rattled. That he continued to drive the cars at all was remarkable. Chapman, with a single-mindedness for which he would become famous, merely pressed on regardless.

There was still no great safety lobby, though. Ironically, Spa was one of the few circuits which had actually appointed a director of safety, Pierre Stasse, in the light of the appalling accident which had befallen Scott Brown in 1958. Stasse, as a motoring publisher and principal of the Ecurie Nationale Belge, was rightly respected in the sport, but lacked a budget meaningful enough to make any difference. Armco barriers, for example, had yet to be invented, and fireproof clothing, developed later by Les Leston, was also a thing of the future. The man who really turned the tide of complacency on the subject of safety was Jackie Stewart, six years later. No wonder, really. At the 1966 Spa Grand Prix he was rescued from his wrecked BRM, soaked in high-octane petrol, not by marshals, of whom there were none available at the end of one of the fastest straights in Grand Prix racing, but by Graham Hill and Bob Bondurant, who sensibly stripped his clothes off and waited while a troop of nuns appeared to look after him. An ambulance appeared 45 minutes later! From the safety point of view, motor racing was really more like a war-zone until campaigners like Stewart managed to make themselves heard above the clamour made when stringent economy and simple old-fashioned tightfistedness disguise themselves as traditionalist machismo.

Gregory had been shaken by the horrors at Spa. The racer in him knew full well that such events were all too commonplace, but the businessman in him told him to do something to ameliorate the effects of such injuries as Stirling had received upon his commercial career. He resolved to harden up Stirling's commercial arrangements. He agreed a long-term contract with a form of words with the now separate British Petroleum Company that they would provide sponsorship arrangements for Stirling which would continue even if he were unable to drive as a result of a racing accident, but ceasing in the event of his death. This was not a life insurance policy, but merely a contingency arrangement should a freak accident like Spa take place again. Moss would continue to receive payments for his services even if it was not as a racing driver. Significantly, this arrangement was to stand for 13 years. Similar contracts would be negotiated with Dunlop tyres, Lodge sparkplugs and Ferodo brake linings over the ensuing six months. Stirling's earlier backer, Castrol, were keen to match the terms of the BP contract, including a directorship of Castrol

Oils, but the exposure which the BP deal was to give Stirling Moss would ensure that while he was contracted to them, he would be in the public eye like no other member of his profession ever had been.

The reason for this was the break-up of the marketing cartel of Shell Mex & BP. It had been decided to separate the identities of the two firms the previous year but, to BP's dismay, the operators of the new solus sites, when offered the choice of being BP or Shell stations, seemed overwhelmingly in favour of Shell. A campaign was organised whereby Stirling Moss, under the terms of the remarkable deal, was to be effectively the public face of British Petroleum. It was clever. The campaign was hugely expensive, at over £1m, but one result of it was that Moss's face became familiar to millions. He was on the back of buses (a great opportunity to tease, this; 'a face like the back of a bus' took on a whole new meaning), in local newspapers when helicoptering in to open a new BP station, and in the Press endorsing the products. It was a far cry from obscure dashboard accessories. This activity was to continue into the 1970s.

Moss became quite good at it. Always quick on the uptake, his natural sense of self-publicity which expressed itself on the track as waving at the crowds as he raced past translated quite easily into the kind of photo-opportunities which BP needed now that they were in open competition with their erstwhile bedfellows. The campaign was to be a great success for all concerned, and the biggest beneficiary was Moss himself. The relationship with BP kept him in the public eye for rather longer than any of his contemporaries would ever be, and it was to provide him with the grounding of his second career, which in many ways has been more successful than his first; being, simply, Stirling Moss.

Olivier Gendebien, a guest local at Spa, was offered his

seat again for the French Grand Prix at Reims and, less than three seconds ahead of Bruce McLaren, and second from Jack Brabham, with the doughty Henry Taylor in fourth place, and Bruce Halford in eighth, gave the wilting BRP their best finish of the season, with three out of three at the chequered flag. It was a small lift after the nightmare of Spa and, superstitious as racing folk always are, perhaps presaged a change of fortunes. It was too soon to put the deaths of Bristow, Schell and even Bueb behind them, but the Samengo-Turner brothers, not as directly involved, were delighted. These results were doubly impressive when it is remembered that the Cooper T51s which the BRP were entering were 1959 models.

The British Grand Prix resulted in a fifth place for Brooks, eighth for Taylor and ninth for Gendebien. Not as pleasing as Reims, but not bad to finish with all three cars at a home circuit, even if only one point was scored. Tellingly, no Lotuses actually retired, although Clark was 10 laps adrift with suspension problems and Ireland eased off with a hint of hub trouble to lose second place to John Surtees, drafted in, as his motorcycle commitments allowed, to replace Stacey.

All the doubts about Lotus build quality was bullish news for Coopers, for obvious commercial reasons, but as Stirling came out of hospital in time for the Portuguese Grand Prix, he surprised some by entering in Walker's new Lotus 18, bought to replace the car which had so nearly killed him at Spa. There was a new Cooper as reserve, though, just in case Moss had a change of mind. He didn't, and raced the Lotus. He was disqualified on the 50th lap, for driving in the wrong direction after a spin, giving fifth place to Brooks again. Gendebien came in seventh, nine laps adrift and poor Henry Taylor had a big accident which hurt both him and the car. It was surprising that there were not more accidents on a circuit as badly prepared as this one, covered with cobblestones and bisected by tramlines as it was – a situation happily unthinkable today.

The Italian Grand Prix threatened to be a replay of the previous year's Avus race, with the Monza authorities proudly unveiling their new banking. As one man, all the British teams, aside from a few curious privateers (the Brooklands tradition being a thing of the past) decided to stay away, which was a pity, if a potential lifesaver. Willy Mairesse finished third behind Phil Hill and Ritchie Ginther in a Ferrari parade, at which the *Tifosi*, as ever remembering with advantage, swooned.

Now, after a dreadful roller-coaster of a season, with the BRP losing two key drivers in quick and tragic succession, but as a business delivering an extremely pleasing result, some serious trouble was brewing at home. While Gregory had been taking care of and grieving over BRP business, Robert Thornton had been extremely naughty, taking his role as Ken's locum rather too literally and making free with the business. It seemed that Thornton had set himself up as a car dealer to the trade in his own right, and had – ahem – undertaken more than one transaction for a large number of vehicles, in order to fund what further investigation revealed to be a somewhat lavish and fun-filled lifestyle, part of which sadly involved Mrs Ken Gregory. It was worse than that, though, because one of the losers in this rather primitive but neatly-executed Ponzi scheme was one of the major providers of credit to the wholesale and retail motor trade, who were also the BRP's sponsor, Yeoman Credit. The Samengo-Turners were not amused, although, it later turned out, they had no reason to be surprised.

No less amused, of course, was Gregory. Faced with the

loss of a wife and a business, a rational man will attempt to save one or the other. Faced with the loss of a wife and two businesses, particularly for the same reason, a businessman will take a professional, cool(ish) cut-your-losses look at the situation and decide what is best to be done, particularly if the creditors of one business also support his other one. As any stress engineer will tell you, the rules of physics, like the rules of finance, are brutally simple. Plenty of stress here.

This was a sentiment shared by Yeoman Credit and one of Express Coachcraft's more vociferous creditors, one Bernie Ecclestone, then a car dealer. He was angry; very angry. He has probably never been angrier in his life. The two men knew each other well, of course, their common link being that they had both employed Stuart Lewis-Evans – Ecclestone as owner of the rump of the Connaught operation and Gregory through BRP – which naturally made the whole thing even more embarrassing, if that were possible.

Tellingly, Yeoman Credit seemed to be familiar with this bad egg in Gregory's larder. They were to respond, as the whole thing later went to law, that they had merely assumed that Gregory knew it too.

This was, upon analysis, disingenuous of them. They had, unbenownst to Gregory, summoned Thornton to their offices near Marble Arch and faced him with their intelligence about his dodgy past. He had confirmed that Ken Gregory did not know about it and would they please not tell him? He had, after all, paid the penalty for previous mistakes, and so on. The Samengo-Turners agreed to keep quiet about it. This decision, which neatly dropped Gregory in it, was to rather spoil his relationship with them, to say the least.

The implicit assumption outside this little group, that Ken Gregory had been, as owner of the firm and employer of Thornton, acting in bad faith, seemed, superficially at least, a hard charge to answer. It was, in the short term, only the undisputed nature of Thornton's other betrayal which, ironically, saved Gregory's reputation, at the price of many a snide remark. The whole matter would eventually be dealt with in the Queen's Bench Division of the High Court and, naturally, any further support of the BRP by Yeoman Credit was quite out of the question. Basically, by the time the last race of the season was over, Gregory would have six weeks to find a new backer, or that, as they say, would be that.

The core of the problem, financially at least, was that Gregory, as proprietor of the firm, was seen to have a duty of care to ensure that the providers of credit for the buyers of the cars actually got paid. These bills of exchange, effectively securitised loans which financed the transactions, were the means by which Thornton had been propping up his cash flow, and Gregory, as principal of the firm, was in practice the sole guarantor of the loans. Thornton, as merely an officer of the company, was never in any danger of being called upon to stump up any money.

Chapter 15

DIFFERENT COLOURS

*'And still the less they understand, the more
they admire his sleight of hand.'*
SAMUEL BUTLER, HUDIBRAS, 1664

Gregory greeted this situation with an admirable sang-froid. Stirling's marriage was also going somewhat less than perfectly, for altogether different reasons, and the pair, relieved at the prospect of each other's company, decided to share a house again. It was a statement of support by Moss in the face of a tide of gossip, and Gregory was grateful for it. It enabled him to stabilise a situation which was threatening, without some nifty footwork on his part, to go, in the modern vernacular, pear-shaped. There was speculation, of a uniquely tabloid, kite-flying nature, that Moss was somehow involved in the issue of Gregory's separation from his wife. Gregory informed the *News of the World* in his best deadpan manner that they had it all wrong; that his wife was the one who was suing for divorce, and that Stirling was the guilty party, which was why the two men were now living together. After a few moments of thought, the reporter, who realised full well that both men were about as gay as the average tomcat, worked out what was happening and no more mention of Ken's marital state was made.

Now, Gregory knew full well that his had not been the only sponsored motor-racing programme of recent years, although it was far and away the most prominent, the only one in Formula 1 and had clearly paid dividends on all sides. This last he knew because it was an open secret that Yeoman Credit were already in conversations with Reg

Parnell. Parnell, like Alfred Moss and Charles Cooper was a pig farmer, but that was the least of his claims to fame. He had been a successful driver since before the war and, along with such figures as Leslie Johnson and Jock Horsfall, had been a doyen of the racing scene immediately after the war. A far-sighted move of his had been to buy up a vast number of pre-war racing cars during the conflict, when they were more or less valueless, and store them in his various barns until they were needed again. He had recently retired from Aston Martin, where he had been racing manager from 1957-60 and had set up a works in Hounslow. He was eminently well-respected and well-qualified for the job.

Gregory, if he wanted to avoid reinventing the whole concept, had to act fast. He made a proposition (over an extremely costly lunch at the Boulestin restaurant in Covent Garden) to Bob Gibson-Jarvie of the UDT finance house, which also owned Laystall engineering, one of the main props of the British motor industry, supplying as it did most of the crankshafts and major forgings which went towards building cars from Jaguar to Austin.

The proposal was simple; the same deal as had been in place with Yeoman, to the penny, but quickly. Gibson-Jarvie, seeing the urgency, bravely took it upon himself to agree the deal and sell it to the board later. UDT had dabbled in supporting smaller formulae and sports car racing already and, in Gibson-Jarvie's view, whatever had gone on with Express Coachcraft, the firm naturally being the subject of a winding-up order, was no concern of his.

However, there were to be more important changes to the BRP apart from its new sponsor. There was, in fact, a new formula altogether. Well not quite, as it bore a remarkable resemblance to the current Formula 2 category of 1500cc unsupercharged. Several new British power plants were on the way, notably from BRM and Coventry Climax, and they would be of a V8 configuration with pistons the size of cotton reels, but they were as yet an unknown quantity. The faithful Coventry Climax four-cylinder engine, by now relatively long in the tooth, was one option, and one which most British teams went for, with the odd Maserati unit scattered about in Cooper chassis.

The Italian private entrants were denied anything but Coopers or Lotuses to enter. The combined efforts of Cooper and Chapman had rammed the point home, comprehensively and with no great subtlety, that the era of the red cars had finally come to an end, and the prevailing colour of the future winners was to be green, which just goes to show how wrong you can be.

Enzo Ferrari, on the other hand had played a very canny game indeed. While the 2½-litre formula had been running, he had resigned himself, more or less, to letting his Formula 1 effort fend for itself, for he had finally been persuaded that the Cooper school of design was the way forward. His Formula 2 cars, rear-engined and svelte, had been doing extremely well and he saw the change of formula as the perfect opportunity to wreak his revenge.

He was, for once, entirely right. The delays suffered by the BRM and Coventry-Climax factories allowed Ferrari to release his own new car, the delectable 156 – honed in the second-string events of 1960 – on to a startled public. The engine, a V6 which howled out 125 bhp per litre, was an aural and visual delight. His drivers, Phil Hill, Taffy von Trips and Ritchie Ginther, were supported by the staring-eyed Mairesse and the newcomer Giancarlo Baghetti. Ferrari would, with one or two exceptions, throw British ears to the crowd in 1961.

As for Tony Brooks, he gritted his teeth and opted for

BRM, to join Graham Hill. Hill had had a struggle in 1960, and 1961 would be little better. Brooks had, of course, worked for BRM before, and had not found it an edifying experience. It was a pity that 1961 would be his last season in Formula 1. In 1962 Graham Hill would win the Championship, the first British driver since Hawthorn to do so, and only the second ever.

There were two drivers whom Ken Gregory had been quietly stalking for some time – Jim Clark and Bruce McLaren. Clark, at Lotus with Innes Ireland, had discussed the possibility of a drive for BRP the previous year, but nothing was settled, whereas McLaren, at Cooper, had not been approached, and was not to be, as the Yeoman Credit fiasco prevented it. So, for the coming season, Gregory fell back on well-tried support. Henry Taylor was back in the fold, accompanied by Cliff Allison. Allison, from Westmorland, had driven for Ferrari the two previous seasons and Lotus before that. With his robust north country view of life, he was very practical. Henry Taylor, an agreeable Battle of Britain type, had little to prove. A sports car driver of great renown and famously skilled in the wet, he looked upon racing primarily as fun, despite all he had seen. Olivier Gendebien stepped in as an occasional. A gent through and through, he owed his freedom to race to a patent owned by his family on caustic soda, still in production today. He would also drive for Ferrari and the Ecurie Nationale Belge that year. Certainly a mixed bunch, this, but probably no more so than those involved in any other venture.

Well, having obtained the money and the drivers, Gregory, faced with a new formula, made his by now usual trip to Surbiton to order up some new cars. He had come to enjoy his visits to see Charlie Cooper, so was stopped in his tracks by his old friend when he was uncharacteristically shifty about the firm's ability to supply him. Ostensibly, the problem was a bottleneck in gearbox supplies, but Gregory was sceptical about this, and was therefore lowered by his old friend's inexplicable reluctance to do his usual trick and pull out the stops to fill the order of a valued client. It seemed that Cooper was rather embarrassed about it, too.

To make things even worse, the new Yeoman Credit operation, as managed by Parnell, had obtained Coopers with no difficulty whatsoever, which made Gregory even more suspicious. He became convinced that he was being 'got at' and, given that there were really only three manufacturers in Britain – Cooper, BRM and Lotus – he really didn't have a lot of choice. BRM were not selling cars anyway, so Gregory followed Rob Walker's example, went to Colin Chapman and bought three Lotus 18s, three Lotus 19s and an Elite, which was a nice little order. Much as he would have preferred to stay with Coopers as a supplier, that choice was not open to him.

However, another interpretation of events is possible. Given that Parnell's new team was contracted to Esso, as was Coopers' own works effort, it is not inconceivable that Esso was the source of the pressure, given that the UDT effort was a BP sponsored one. Whatever the truth of the matter, Charlie Cooper was not a happy man.

Nor was Ken Gregory. He may have misinterpreted the situation, but he was in something of a state by then. Despite his apparent coolness about the situation at Express Coachcraft and the way he handled both the break-up of his marriage, by now a foregone conclusion, and the sudden terminal decline of his relationship with Yeoman Credit, he was struggling somewhat. The news that his wife was expecting a child not his own added further to his worries. The singular irony was that Express Coachcraft was not really worth it anyway, and had he listened to the rest of his shareholders in the first place, who had left him to it, he could have avoided the whole situation.

Another spin-off, of course, was that the BRP had to move. As well as a new sponsor, Gregory had found a building in Highgate, at Duke's Head Yard, and installed Tony Robinson and his team there. There was a usefully-equipped workshop and rather more machinery than there had been at Lots Road.

So, as Moss and Gregory came to terms with their new roles as reinvented bachelors, the plans for 1961 were laid. It was clear that Parnell had ambitious plans for his new team, adopting a wider scope altogether, and BRP was determined to match them. In fact, the UDT-Laystall racing team, as it was called, was to prove to be a very happy association and was to leave no sour taste in anyone's mouth. Perhaps because Gibson-Jarvie and his company had more motor racing connections than Yeoman, and also had manufacturing interests of their own, their learning curve was shorter, but Yeoman were to complete only one more season with Parnell's team, while UDT/BRP were to press on for longer than that.

One of Ken Gregory's most pressing priorities for 1961, then, was to get divorced. His decree nisi came through on 2 January, with a decree absolute on 10 February. A week after that, he remarried, in a small private ceremony at Caxton Hall, his second wife Nem, and established a new Gregory household in Earl's Court. Without meaning offence, but nevertheless showing an untypical insensitivity, Gregory neglected to invite Stirling, which miffed Moss more than a little. The only witnesses were Mike McKee, Nem's brother-in-law, who would later drive sports cars for UDT/Laystall, and his wife Shireen.

The year 1961 was a hard and grinding one for British cars in Formula 1. Ferrari were to win all but three races, and Lotus were to claim the rest. Stirling, on top of his form with Rob Walker, won at Monaco and the Nürburgring, while Innes Ireland took victory at Watkins Glen to give Team Lotus its first Grand Prix win. Sadly, Ferrari were absent. They were assured of the Constructor's Championship after Phil Hill's win at Monza in September but, depressed by the death of the popular Taffy von Trips in the same race, withdrew their entry.

The BRP had a relatively poor season. The new V8 engines from Climax and BRM were not ready in time, indeed BRM themselves ran with Climax four-cylinder units as a stopgap, but compared to the 1960 season, the lack of Formula 1 results was amply offset by the fact that all the BRP drivers came through without a scratch, which cheered Gregory. There was a disaster, though. The crash at Monza on the first lap of the Italian Grand Prix which claimed the life of Taffy von Trips had also killed 14 spectators. True to form, the Italian authorities discussed charges against Jim Clark, who was involved in the crash.

UDT were quite satisfied with their new team, so much so that they augmented it with a new car at the end of the season – a Ferrari 250 GTO. These cars, then as now, are probably the ultimate in road/race machines, possessed of startling beauty and a performance which still causes jaws to drop. As Gregory looked back on the year, he totted up what the UDT investment had acquired – three Formula 1 Lotuses with engines and spares; three Lotus 19 sports cars, also with engines and spares, a minute Lotus Elite and a Ferrari GTO, complete with bespoke transporters and a vast tonnage of engines, transmissions, spares and tools. The total cost? A bargain at £80,000.

The relationship between the BRP and Rob Walker's effort was moving ever closer. For some time, Gregory had looked after the details of the R. R. C. Walker Racing Team entries and there was a free flow of information, spares and mutual assistance. The two teams had agreed that they would, as soon as they were available, use the Climax V8 engines which were finally ready, although proving troublesome with overheating problems.

Gregory, Alfred and Stirling had taken a strategic decision to diversify the activities of Stirling Moss Ltd. The first fruit of this policy, a magazine called *Sports Cars Illustrated*, was scheduled for launch in the Spring of 1962. There had been other business activities already, of course, including a fruitful bout of share trading which Gregory undertook. Alfred looked a little askance at this; he preferred real estate and high cash flow businesses.

Two of these, the 'Beefburger' restaurant and a small chain of three Laundrettes, were fulfilling that role admirably and Gregory had invested the results very successfully, including taking a stake in a travel agency. So, at the end of 1961, when the opportunity came to acquire *Motor Racing* magazine, the official magazine of the BRSCC, Alfred, Stirling, Gregory and Rob Walker set up a company, Speed and Sports Publications Ltd, to buy it. However, the negotiations fell through at the last minute and another journal was bought instead. It seemed a shame to waste the effort which had gone into forming the company.

Called *Sports Illustrated*, and totally unconnected with the US journal of that name, it was put up for sale by Hultons, who had never had much luck with it. Having spent so much on legal fees and attendant expenses, Gregory decided to buy it. The strategy was simple; change the name, put Stirling's face on the front, repackage it and re-launch it on an ecstatic public.

Stirling, like his father, was a fan of bricks and mortar. He had found a bombsite plot on which he was planning a house, a few yards from his own front door. One of the very few freeholds available in Mayfair, it was close to Park Lane and in the best area of the *Monopoly* board, even if the precise location was one which enjoyed a certain raffish reputation – Shepherd's Market. He still lives in it.

Gregory had also rediscovered the joys of flying. He had bought a Piper Commanche, which he kept at Denham in Buckinghamshire. It was the recommencement of a love affair with flight which had started in the Army during his time as a glider pilot, and which has never left him. It was to offer him his second career when the events of Easter 1962 ensured that the nature of his relationship with Moss was to change forever. Gregory had also moved house, to Kingston Hill, with his new wife and baby son, Christopher, which was to prove soon to be particularly convenient, but for the worst of all possible reasons.

In order to defray the costs of running a plane, Gregory engaged a pilot and incorporated Gregory Air Taxis late in 1961. When he was not using the plane, it would be hired out. Aircraft were and are so costly that they are expensive even when standing still. Events were to ensure that this was a smart move, and gradually Gregory started to build the business. Straightaway he realised that to operate an aeroplane for profit, or 'hire and reward' as the Department of Trade quaintly called it, the aircraft had to be at least twin-engined if it were to be flown over stretches of water across which the plane could not be glided, which ruled out Continental hops. Inexorably, the expansionist in Gregory started to take over.

The best news of all, though, was that Enzo Ferrari had attempted a reconciliation with Moss. The two men had not spoken since the Bari episode 10 years before, and Ferrari realised that if he was to have a chance to compete with the British teams and their new engines, he would need help. His team leader and 1961 World Champion, Phil Hill, was supremely skilled, but his experience was unmatched by his colleagues. Ferrari was openly courting Moss by the end of the 1961 season. He was not destined to catch him. Stirling consulted his old friend Juan Fangio and the advice was unequivocal – by all means drive a Ferrari, but don't, under any circumstances, sign up for the works team. Fangio's own experiences at Modena in 1956 had led him to believe that the Commendatore was totally incapable of anything which remotely resembled plain dealing.

For the UDT-Laystall Racing Team, the prospects were mixed. Stirling had become a director and equal sharehold-er of BRP along with his father and Gregory, on a very advantageous basis (buying in at the original par price after three profitable years) and there was some hope that he would drive in rather more races for them now. He still had a close relationship with Rob Walker, of course, but events over at Lotus were to offer the team the services of a new driver, Innes Ireland.

Ireland had given Chapman his first Grand Prix win at Watkins Glen in 1961, and was fired barely a month later in circumstances which would upset him for the rest of his life. Gregory had snapped him up as soon as he heard the news and only beat BRM, who were looking to replace Tony Brooks (who had announced his retirement), by one day. Obviously, the BRM offer was a more tempting one, but as Ireland had given his word, typically he stuck to it. As Gregory was to discover, Robert McGregor Innes Ireland was one of the most loyal people he could have ever hoped to have hired, and Ireland was to stay with BRP until the very end. For Formula 1 events he would be supported in 1962 by Masten Gregory, who, despite his success in sports cars, was something of a jobbing driver in single-seaters.

Ireland, whose reminiscences, entitled *All Arms and Elbows* are compulsory reading for students of the period, had served Colin Chapman faithfully and well, for very little reward, for three seasons. He had started racing with a Riley which he had exchanged for a kit car Lotus XI which he built up himself, drawing on his considerable engineering experience as a Rolls-Royce apprentice to do so. He was a fierce driver as well as being a technically well-informed one, but his career, like Masten Gregory's, would always be more productive in sports cars than in Grands Prix. His win at Watkins Glen in October 1961 was his first and only Championship victory out of 50 Grands Prix entered. The statistic conveys nothing of the man.

Chapter 16

END GAME · GOODWOOD 1962

*'A poem is never finished; it's always an
accident that puts a stop to it – that is to say,
gives it to the public.'*
PAUL VALERY, 1930

As the start of the 1962 season approached, Moss appeared
to be at the top of his form. He had, superficially at least,
recovered from the trauma of his marriage break-up and
looked forward to the opening up of his expanding business
interests. The new magazine was ready to go and his
Mayfair house-building project was underway. In conjunc-
tion with the architects, he was supervising the plans himself and, as an ardent DIY enthusiast, a man of his hands
like his father, he was keen to participate. The last house he
had built, at Nassau in the Bahamas, had been a similar project.

Two weeks before the Easter Monday Goodwood meeting, after returning from Sebring and Daytona, he had
flown to Modena to discuss with Enzo Ferrari the prospect
of driving both a Formula 1 car and a sports car in the 1962
season. They agreed that Rob Walker would enter the cars,
in his colours, but the factory would own and maintain
them. In this we see the hand of Ken Gregory at work; it was
more or less the same deal as he had conducted with BRM
in 1959. For Ferrari, whether he entered the cars or not, the
points they scored would still count towards the
Constructor's Championship – and if they didn't perform, it
would hardly be his fault. Driving a Ferrari, Moss would perhaps have a serious chance at the title. Unlikely, though,

MANAGING A LEGEND

given the way the 1962 season actually developed, but the Ferraris were at least well-made.

For there was some concern about the Lotus marque. Ever since Innes Ireland had found 14 separate cracks in his chassis at the Italian Grand Prix in 1959, not to mention the hub problems at Spa the next year, there had been a feeling that the cars were simply too flimsy, and under certain circumstances not fit to race. In the competition with Cooper to keep weight down, many commentators have noticed that Chapman could minimise design tolerances to the extreme. BRP, though, would stick with Lotus for the 1962 season.

The Glover Trophy for Formula 1 cars at Goodwood, which Stirling Moss had won before, was a popular opener to the UK season and was held on Easter Monday. The 1962 event promised to be an exciting one after the rather uninspiring Formula 1 races of the previous season. The BRM and Climax engines were at last available and all were anxious to see them perform. This would be the first time many would have the chance to see them. Perhaps this season the British cars could reassert themselves and stomp on the Italian opposition.

Goodwood had never attempted to host a full Grand Prix. The circuit is relatively small at 2.4 miles and crowd facilities were rather restricted. It had been the site of Moss's first proper motor race, though, and it would now be the occasion of his last. As a seasoned Goodwood veteran, he always drew a big crowd and expectations were high. It was one of the last events before the Monaco Grand Prix, where he had also always shone.

The car, though, was a hybrid. It was a Lotus 18, wearing Lotus 21 bodywork, into which had been fitted the latest Coventry-Climax V8, which had only just come into production. The car had been attended to by both Alf Francis and Claude Hill, the latter an employee of Walker's old friend Tony Rolt at Ferguson. Hill was a fine engineer. His experience went back as far as Aston Martin's pre-war days and he had designed the 'Atom', the first Aston Martin road car after the war. The modifications to the Lotus hybrid, though, had been troublesome and Stirling had struggled with a sticking throttle at Snetterton the previous weekend. As is often the case with a new engine, unless a car is specifically designed for it, adaptation can be tricky. In effect, the privateer Lotus customers like Walker were doing a lot of the development work themselves. Lotus had more customers in Formula 1 than any other team by now, which reflects the staggering pace (and human cost) of Chapman's development programme.

Although both the car and engine were Walker's, the Lotus had been entered as a BRP machine at both Snetterton and Goodwood. Walker reasoned that as the BRP mechanics had prepared it, it should enter the lists in the familiar light green. Walker himself was engaged to attend a race at Pau with Maurice Trantignant, and so was to miss the drama which unfolded.

That Easter Monday was to be a traumatic day. The crowd were to witness something which they really hadn't thought possible as the racing career of Stirling Moss finally ended in a crash which will be talked about until everyone who was there is gone. There have been more theories about this accident than just about any other in the history of the sport, Le Mans 1955 or Imola 1994, excepted. This is what Ken Gregory, after considerable research, believes actually happened.

The race had, for, Moss, been disappointing, despite the fact that the car bore his lucky number seven, and he was plagued by gearbox trouble. By lap 33, following a pit stop, he had overcome these problems enough to break the lap record, but he was two laps behind the leader Graham Hill with little chance of making any impression. The accident happened on lap 34 at St Mary's. Moss was, as ever, driving more or less flat out as he approached the rear of Hill's BRM to overtake. It seemed that a Marshall had given Hill a flag signal and Hill raised his hand to acknowledge it. Moss thinks now that he misinterpreted Hill's wave as a signal to pass and started to overtake, assuming Hill would brake and let him through. Hill's point of view, that it was a strange place to overtake, led him to assume that Moss would not attempt it and so both drivers took their lines into the corner, which is narrow. Moss was forced on to the grass, which was wet, and the car careered towards a high earth bank.

At St Mary's, there is a drainage gully on the outside of the circuit at nearly ninety degrees to the traffic. As the Lotus dropped its front wheels into it and bounced Moss out of his seat, he lost all control of the steering and pedals. This effectively prevented him from attempting to take any action to spin the car round, as he had done at Spa, where he had hit the bank with the rear of the car; this time, it collided head on. Evidence that he was bounced out of reach of the pedals is provided by the way the steering wheel is distorted, and from close inspection of a contemporary picture, it is clear that he pulled back upon it while hanging on for dear life. The wheel hangs on the wall of Moss's house to this day, looking for all the world like a large red pretzel.

The announcement over the Tannoy, in the clipped tones of James Tilling, was terse, uninformative and inaccurate in assuming that the brakes had failed. Gregory, running the BRP pit, stayed as cool as he could. He could not see the crash from where he was keeping the lap chart and, as soon as possible, he headed over to St Mary's with a concerned Alfred.

What he found appalled him. Moss was totally unconscious and clearly dreadfully injured. His helmet was split open and he was trapped in the remains of the car, which had doubled back like a hairpin. He was choking on a piece of chewing gum, which a doctor carefully removed as Stirling's unresponsive hand was held by a young St John Ambulance Association nurse, Ann Strudwick.

The word spread quickly as to the severity of the crash. Tony Robinson was running the pit in Gregory's absence and was startled when Reg Parnell came over and told him that Moss was still in the car and that efforts to free him were proving useless. He and Stan Collier hastily grabbed some tools and drove over to St Mary's while the race was still running. They found a distraught Alfred watching as the marshals attempted to cut the car up around Moss, using bolt-cutters. They had removed the bodywork and discovered that between Moss's knees was the battery, over them was an empty fuel tank and he was sitting between the other two side tanks, which, although nearly dry, were still dangerous. The tanks were in one piece, although fuel was leaking from broken pipework. Robinson and Collier eased the top tank out of the way and gingerly disconnected the battery. One spark from a grating terminal and the whole car could have gone up.

The two men found it very trying to proceed with a fire extinguisher being aimed point-blank at them, but started to saw up the tubes which trapped Stirling. There was only a small risk of sparks from the mild steel, but they were very, very careful nonetheless, eventually cutting the whole car in half at the hips. The operation took 40 minutes. Robinson tried to be as cheery as he could, to bolster

257A. Masten Gregory in the UDT-Laystall Lotus 24. (Bruce McIntosh).
257B. Innes Ireland taking the chequered flag in the UDT-Laystall Lotus 24.

258A. It is often hot at Reims. Here, Tony Robinson finds his own way of keeping cool. Stan Collier and Rod Gueran look on. (BP).

258B. Innes Ireland and Tony Robinson.

259A. *The UDT-Laystall transporter. L-R; Rod Gueran, Bruce McIntosh, Jim Chapman. Rouen, 1962. (Ken Gregory).*
259B. *The UDT-Laystall Ferrari 250GTO, Le Mans, 1962. (Ken Gregory).*

260A. *Tony Robinson testing his new creation, the 1963 monocoque BRP-BRM. Silverstone, 1963. (Peter Roberts).*
260B. *A pleasing portrait of Innes Ireland in the same car at the Silverstone test session. (Tony Robinson).*

261A. A rear view of BRP 2/64. Note the BRM 6-speed gearbox and longer
exhausts. Oulton Park, April 1964. (Francis Penn, Autosport).
261B. Innes heading out onto the track at Oulton Park. (Francis Penn, Autosport).

262A. A close-up of the BRM V-8 engine of BRP 2/64.
262B. Innes testing BRP 2/64. Oulton Park. (Autosport).

263A. Bruce McIntosh working on one of the 1965 Indycars at Highgate, early 1965. (Bruce McIntosh).

263B. The finished product. Masten Gregory is seated in the car. L-R; Jim Chapman, George Woodward, Tony Robinson, Stan Collier, Bruce McIntosh, Peter Downie. Highgate, 1965. (David Phipps).

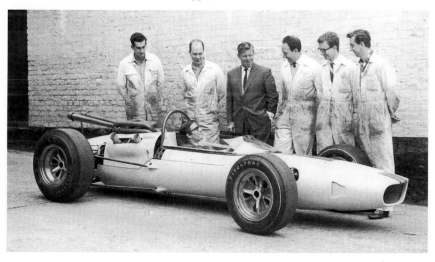

252. *Indianapolis, Memorial day, 1965. Masten Gregory in the car. Standing, L-R: Whiley Paddock, Donald Rose, George Bryant, George Salih, George Woodward, Jim Chapman, Jack Venture. The car qualified at 154.54 mph, but retired when lying fifth; the ZF gearbox failed.*

Alfred's fragile morale. He could see that Stirling's legs were clearly hurt and he could see the blood, but he knew little else. A photographer, Michael Cooper, was watching the procedure and said in an interview later that the doctor present said that if the car had caught fire, all he could have done would be to make sure Stirling was unconscious. Well, as the Duke of Wellington famously said: 'If you believe that, you'll believe anything.'

When the lighter front end was lifted away, all could see that the injuries were massive. His left arm was broken, the left leg was broken in two places, his cheekbone crushed, the eye socket displaced, he was badly cut about the head and there was some apparent evidence of a fractured skull but those were minor when compared to the main problem which emerged later; his brain was massively bruised. It had literally become detached from the skull on one side. Stirling was paralysed and comatose. He was not to wake up for some time. The BBC World Service, itself beset by enquiries from a concerned public, started to release hourly reports on his condition.

At midnight he was transferred from Chichester to the Atkinson Morley Hospital in Wimbledon – only two miles from Gregory's house – which specialised in brain injuries. The head surgeon was most concerned that a familiar face should be instantly recognised by Moss when he emerged from the coma, so Alfred, Aileen and Pat Moss, along with Gregory and Valerie Pirie, Stirling's secretary, all took turns at keeping a 24-hour vigil in the ward, awaiting signs that he was coming to. They were joined by Rob Walker and David Haynes, who shared the vigil. They waited for 38 days, and the whole country waited with them.

When he did come round, he was different. There was more to it than the ravages of the brain injuries, total paralysis on his left side and his slurred speech; the man who woke up in the Atkinson Morley Hospital did not, to Gregory, seem to be the same man who had climbed into the car at Goodwood over five weeks before. He could remember nothing at all, still cannot, save for a few blurred details, many of which have in fact been suggested to him.

As soon as Moss had worked out what had happened to him, he attempted to force the pace of his own recovery. As he was extremely fit, he was at an advantage and the broken bones started to heal relatively quickly, but the frustration at immobility and the sheer effort that small tasks took, as well as the lingering effects of paralysis were frustrating to him. His concentration, always a major asset, was gone.

One predictably upset by Moss's accident was Enzo Ferrari, for he felt that with Stirling's absence his chances of consolidating his success of the previous year, albeit against feeble opposition, were terminally degraded. However, now that he had actually built the car he gave some thought as to who might drive it.

UDT-Laystall had already had a brief but happy relationship with Col. Ronnie Hoare, Ferrari's UK distributor, and had already purchased a 250 GTO to enter in sports and GT events. The thought occurred that even though Moss could not drive, perhaps Innes Ireland might. The event chosen was the Silverstone International, the same race at which Harry Schell had died two years before. Ireland, Gregory and Hoare flew to Modena and were royally received. They arrived at Milan airport to be met by a Ferrari test driver who chauffeured them to the Ferrari works in a brand new 250 GT with prototype plates and slave wheels, seldom driving at less than 130 mph. Gregory and Ireland sat in the rear. Innes, like many race drivers, was never a great passenger.

While Ireland was 'fitted' with the car which Stirling was to have driven, Gregory was shown round the Modena service department. A poignant moment was the sight of a little Fiat saloon sitting forlorn under a tarpaulin. It had been there for years, and had been the property of Enzo's son Dino, who had died in 1956. Rumour has it that it was not moved until Enzo Ferrari's own death in 1988.

This was clearly an opportunity of some importance for the BRP. The possibility that UDT Laystall, as opposed to Rob Walker, might enter works-supported Ferrari cars for 1962 was a juicy one, and it was canny for Ferrari, too, as he knew that should Moss recover, he could deal with either Gregory or Walker should the need arise.

Walker, though, as a wealthy private entrant, was more concerned with the state of Stirling's health than anything else. He recalled Maurice Trintignant as a stand-in for Stirling and waited to see the outcome of his friend's treatment.

Stirling was coming up fast, at least as far as the informed observer was concerned. Others were less certain. After each visit Gregory made to the hospital, he was besieged by reporters as the Press interest in his condition was vast. Money was offered. Alarmed by the prospect of the worst excesses of the Press resulting in an unauthorised photograph, Gregory phoned Basil Cardew of the *Daily Express* to discuss the possibility of a picture and interview session. When asked how much such an opportunity would cost, Gregory blandly named a figure which caused Cardew's jaw to drop. Ten thousand pounds was quite simply outside his, or his editor's authority to spend.

Gregory, though, knew full well that Moss's racing days were, in all probability, at an end. Even if he were to recover it would take a long time and his job as manager was to maximize his friend's income – it may have seemed to be mere greed, but actually, the *Express* management completely understood Gregory's attitude. By way of contrast, at the time of writing, it was revealed in the sports press that Michael Schumacher had, in 1997, requested a similar amount merely to be photographed with Mickey Mouse at a Disney promotional event.

Following a meeting with Tom Blackburn, the then General Manager of Express Newspapers, who gave his permission to spend this vast sum, Cardew and Gregory made a private visit to Wimbledon. Gregory, by now used to the incoherence and frightening physical appearance of Moss, neglected to warn Cardew of what he might expect.

What the *Express* journalist saw shocked him. The resulting interview was a shambles and basically unprintable, so the pair retired privately to 'edit' it. Gregory had been Moss's spokesman on several occasions before and the pair produced a feasible piece, using Moss's few intelligible moments with interpretations by Gregory. Cardew submitted the article, optimistically titled 'Moss will race again this season', and while those who read it had every reason to believe that Moss was fine, Cardew, who was honourably economical with the facts with his paymasters about the true circumstances, was convinced that Stirling was basically going to be left a gibbering vegetable.

As the weeks dragged on, it became clear that there was no question of Moss even considering resuming his racing career at this time. Even as his semi-paralysis eased, so, almost terminally bored by the restrictions placed upon him, he started to turn his attention to business, a subject which had only interested him peripherally before. The development made Gregory uneasy, however much it pleased Cardew. Not only was Gregory trying to run the

BRP/UDT concern, he was closely involved with Stirling Moss Ltd and all the other ventures with Alfred and Walker. The new publishing business had just printed the first run of *Cars Illustrated*, ironically with Stirling on the cover. He was also running about trying to keep an eye on Moss's Mayfair house, by now well under construction, and his duties took on those of general factotum as much as anything, which was, he recalled, not only undignified, but, more important, inefficient. There was also a vast amount of post, up to 500 pieces a day. Merely opening the mail was a day-long task.

Stirling, unfortunately, didn't care about that overmuch. The ferocious mood swings which started to dominate his behaviour and which were to last for some time longer, as his brain fought to repair the massive bruising which had befallen it, made him very difficult indeed.

The reassurance of the tone in Cardew's article damped down the flow of messages of goodwill, which created a valuable breathing space for Gregory and Valerie Pirie. This was just as well, since as soon as anyone had the time to look at the true situation of the new magazine venture it was revealed as parlous. An inability to concentrate on the business had allowed serious overprinting, so that an unedifying backlog of unsold copies was building up everywhere, but which had to be paid for. The company was basically insolvent, having run up a debt to the printers which sales would not support, and which gobbled up the equity like a starving orphan. It had been a distribution and promotional problem just as much as it was one of quality; simple benign neglect.

The other shareholders were sceptical that anything could be salvaged from this and were minded to cut their losses. To be fair, they, Alfred and Rob Walker, were rather more concerned about Stirling than anything else, so perhaps they were hasty. Gregory, similarly distracted, but aware that above all, this was his deal, took the same view that he had taken with Express Coachcraft; he could save it, run it, and make it profitable, provided the other shareholders gave him control. They took the view that their equity was more or less worthless anyway, so handed it over. Unlike his efforts at Express Coachcraft, this time he was right, but not without some fairly fierce and perforce uncompromising negotiations with the printers who were owed the money. He pointed out that a company which is liquid and solvent is a better counterparty than one which could slip into receivership (his call, actually) at any time. It was really up to the printers, who were the single biggest creditor. The printers, over a barrel, agreed to take a fairly serious haircut about enforcing the debts, the company survived and so Ken Gregory became a publisher. Eventually, the printers were paid out in full, as in fact were the shareholders.

Chapter 17

WHEN FRIENDS FALL OUT

*'Friendship is not always
the sequel of obligation.'*
SAMUEL JOHNSON, 1781

The plight in which Stirling Moss found himself, in that late spring and early summer of 1962, placed upon him, and his friends, an almost intolerable strain.

To reach the top of one's form, to finally be relaxed in one's own company, to have a private deal with such as Enzo Ferrari, all after 14 years of trying, and trying very hard, whatever one has been paid for it, is a fine thing. To have it all taken away, particularly at a place like Goodwood, the site of so many triumphs, is a personal disaster, whoever you are, and nothing – not the support of friends, the letters of well-wishers or the praise of the Press – can assuage it. And Stirling was no different.

As his manager, Ken Gregory was as supportive as he could be, but this was a different Moss; a man, whom Gregory came to realise over the ensuing months, he barely knew. The realisation lowered him.

It wasn't as if there was a 'back from the dead' element in Stirling's behaviour, it was more as if he had been away a long time. The state of near-serenity which had existed during the best of his moments of success was gone, to be replaced by a sense of minor paranoia and an intense focusing on whatever was nearest to hand. Unfortunately for Gregory, what fell nearest to hand were the affairs of Stirling Moss Ltd, an enterprise which had run more or less faultlessly for eight years. Well, it wasn't faultless enough.

Not unsurprisingly, the affairs of the British Racing Partnership also came under early scrutiny, and particularly the ambition which both Gregory and Tony Robinson entertained to become constructors. Moss, by now a shareholder, was out of the loop, but Alfred, as usual, supported Gregory – his initial investment had, after all, been paid back many times and he trusted Ken's judgement completely.

The premises at Duke's Head Yard had seen, through the summer, a slight change of interest. Strategy decisions at UDT-Laystall decreed that the full sponsorship of racing would not continue; the exercise had served its purpose and all were agreed that an amicable parting of the ways was best achieved by not renewing the agreement at the end of the 1962 season. In fact, UDT were quite happy to carry on, but Laystall – whose core business was, after all, manufacturing – had upwards of £45,000 tied up in the various cars, spares and transporters. They felt that they had a better use for the capital. In the event, BRP bought most of it from them.

The simple fact was, though, that a new generation of cars, led by Lotus, were starting to exploit the merits of monocoque construction. This meant that if the BRP were to re-enter the 1962 Lotus 24s, having seen what the Lotus works were already making, then the exercise would simply not be competitive.

To our eyes, this seems obvious; but, at the time, it was not. A monocoque, a type of construction which eschews the use of a formal chassis, was one which owed much to design developments in the aircraft industry. It was an exoskeleton, in biological terms, whereby the construction of the body of the car was strong enough to support the weights of engine and suspension without recourse to a rigid frame. Malcolm Sayer had accomplished this state of grace with the D-type Jaguar, a form which Jaguar had followed in order to produce their groundbreaking series of Mk I, II and latterly S-type saloons, and ultimately the XJ6. For Grand Prix racing cars, though, this was new territory, apart from a few speculative one-offs, and while Colin Chapman was to emerge as its Messiah, there were to be a host of disciples, one of which was to be BRM, and another, Ferrari.

If the BRP was to remain competitive as a team, then it would have to make its own cars. There was no question that they couldn't, as they were possessed of formidable expertise in the form of Tony Robinson and his staff. All that was required was that there should be resources – money. UDT had given notice, by the time that Moss was on the road to recovery, that they would, regretfully, no longer be the source of it. If the BRP wished to carry on racing, then they would either have to find a new sponsor or fund it themselves. They chose the latter course.

The team's experience in running cars in competitions also entered by the manufacturers of the cars themselves had led all to realise that the works efforts would always have an edge. As it had been with Maserati and Cooper, so it would continue to be with Lotus. Despite the experimental and prescient work done by Robinson in the way of improvements to both car and engine (they had even tried using titanium cranks and rods in the engines – a very modern touch, and one aided by Imperial Metal Industries, an ICI subsidiary), it was fair to assume that, particularly when dealing with Lotus, they would always be at a disadvantage, whatever the assurances given by Chapman. Promising though the situation with Ferrari had looked, it came to nothing and seems to have been little more than a slightly speculative approach from Modena, although it was also a clear, if late, effort to make amends for previous hostilities to Moss.

Stirling was pushing himself in physiotherapy as hard as he could. He was to recover his mobility relatively quickly, and itched to get straight back in a racing car; but the specialists at Atkinson Morley were not so sure. In response and initiative tests – a kind of psychometric evaluation, set by Berenice Krikler, a noted psychologist of the day – he performed very badly, particularly when compared to Hill, Brabham, McLaren, Ireland and Clark, all of whom volunteered to act as a control for her tests. This upset him, not unnaturally, and although he threw himself back into the appearance of full recovery, he knew that the damage to his brain was still not fully repaired. But, he rationalised, they were just tests, not the real thing. On the strength of them, though, Dr Krikler advised him to give up.

In turning inward towards his business interests, he did little to actually assist Gregory, despite his impressions to the contrary. Part of the reason for the existence of Stirling Moss Ltd, tax planning aside, was to provide a cut-out between him and his market, a deniability by fellow directors 'Pa' Moss and Gregory, whereby a bad deal proposed to Stirling could be left unratified, or stupid ones turned down. His burgeoning enthusiasm for business, in the light of Dr Krikler's opinion, however depressing he found it, did not make life remotely easier for Gregory and Alfred, since Stirling knew very little about commerce, which was why he had given them discretion over his affairs in the first place. Further, the fact that his son was now becoming involved more and more put pressure on Alfred. While he had always looked after Stirling's best interests, as any father would, he started to find it emotionally difficult to side with Ken against his son, with the result that Ken was forced into extreme positions from time to time. The affair of Speed and Sports publications is a good example of this. Although Gregory made a great success of it, he did so only at the price of some considerable personal risk. But, then again, he has never been afraid of that, more's the pity.

So, by the autumn of 1962, both Stirling Moss Ltd and the BRP were facing something of an upheaval. In terms of racing, Innes Ireland and Masten Gregory had had a poor season in Formula 1, but Innes shone in the Lotus 19 sports car and was doing very well at Le Mans in the BRP Ferrari GTO, lying fifth and leading the GT class until the dynamo failed. The sports car victories were encouraging but, already, it was clear that Formula 1 was where the money was, in terms of both starting money and prizes, never mind sponsorship. Although the team had made a reasonable profit, none of the partners was in a position to rejoice much.

Gregory, though, was being subjected to an extra amount of stress. He was being pursued through the courts by Yeoman Credit over the small matter of £13,855, the sum total which had been removed so crudely from Express Coachcraft by the activities of Thornton. The case came before Judge Megaw in the Queen's Bench Division during the third week of November 1962. There was a lot of money at stake, in fact, since at that time a decent house could be bought for significantly less.

Ken was the only defendant. The case was both simple and complex, and revolved around the fact that as the bills of exchange, as they were called, issued by Yeoman Credit for the account of Express Coachcraft in order to finance the acquisition and repairing of various cars, were presented for payment at Coachcraft's banks as they fell due. It was clear that there were not sufficient funds to meet them, as the money which should have been there from the sale of the cars had been – ahem – diverted.

A nasty accusation, in fact. Yeoman Credit held that Ken Gregory, as the proprietor of the business which owed the money, was responsible for paying off the principal and interest on the bills, to wit, almost £14,000. At the time of the crisis, the winter of 1959-60, he had no knowledge of the holes in the firm's bank accounts, but as both a director of the firm and an endorser of the bills, he could still be liable for the money. Happily for Gregory, the ruling of the court was that the failure to pay the bills was not notified in time for him to act. (In fact, he had no knowledge of their being dishonoured. Thornton was attempting to juggle with the firm's dwindling bank balances on the telephone.) The outcome was that Gregory was ordered liable for only one of 14 bills, amounting to £900. So, in the end, he both won and lost the case.

Lighter by £900 plus his legal expenses, he turned his attention back to the business of racing cars. Against opposition, albeit very mild, Gregory and Tony Robinson, now a director of the firm, pushed to go ahead with the BRP's first car of its own manufacture. It would, of course, be a monocoque – and a proper one. The prototype Lotus 25, driven by Jim Clark in the 1962 season had, despite some transmission problems, showed extremely well, propelling him to a close second in the World Championship behind Graham Hill in the BRM, who were also working on their own monocoque design; as were Ferrari. Hill's victories, which also provided the Constructor's Championship for BRM marked, after the rather midfield results of 1961, a period of ascendancy for the Lincolnshire firm which was to last until 1966, after which they declined rapidly. It had taken Mays and Berthon 12 years since their cars' first entry into the lists. It took Tony Rudd, the new chief designer, only one year to improve the marque to competitive levels.

Building anything from scratch is hard. Building a racing car is a task to be undertaken by only the mad, the very rich or the extremely competent. Tony Robinson was of the latter persuasion. He had a well-equipped works in Highgate, but money was always going to be a potential problem without a sponsor, so there were no financial heroics. It is a nice coincidence that the source of his materials for the core jig on which the monocoque was built came from a sawn-up Morrison air raid shelter. If Alfred Moss, the designer of that, ever knew this, he never let on, at least not to Stirling, and certainly not to Innes Ireland, who was to drive the thing. Robinson was a master improviser. As Gregory recollected: 'I never told Tony how to build the cars; he never told me how to find the money.'

Things had undergone a sea-change from the early days of British racing car building, when fervently loyal artisans, slaving for pennies, had worked suicidal hours under 40-watt bulbs. The Formula 1 specification for which he was building, which would last until 1965, was fairly straightforward by comparison with modern parameters – 1500cc unsupercharged and a minimum weight of 992 lb (450kg). While there were more details, that was about it, and Robinson considered his options. What he came up with reflected, but did not copy, contemporary thinking. The car was cigar-shaped, of course, but so were everyone else's – even Cooper's, although that firm eschewed monocoque construction for the moment as being too complicated.

The tub designed by Tony Robinson weighed in at only 80 lb and was identical in weight to the frame of the 1962 Lotus 24 which the BRP had used. But that car, of course, had been a tubular-framed car, not a monocoque type. As he was somewhat in the dark about stress loadings, he rather over-engineered the car, using thick 16-gauge alloy and vast amounts of rivets. He knew little of rivets, but much about welding after attending a British Oxygen course on the subject. The way to find out is to experiment, so a multitude of small sections were assembled and riveted together in a variety of combinations, and then tested – twisting and bending them until they displayed signs of distress. Those which creaked were discarded; those which did not were put on one side for further development. Mushroom rivets were the favoured choice – they did not burr under installation and therefore would not become slack, a lesson which BRM would later learn.

The suspension and steering of the new car was fabricated mainly by Bruce McIntosh, and Lotus front suspension uprights were used, as the BRP had a few lying about the place. But, apart from that, the structure of the rolling shell was made in-house. Obviously, in common with other designer/constructors, many other items, such as tanks, brake parts and wheels were bought in, as was and is normal practice, but, significantly, little else was not of BRP manufacture. Bearing in mind what happened later, this is worth noting.

The engine, though, was by BRM, and the transmission by Valerio Colotti, who had gone into business with Alf Francis. Colotti had started Studio Tecnica Meccanica in 1959, and rather naïvely hoped to develop both transmissions and the Maserati 250F, which he had had a hand in designing. The 'Tec Mec' never did any good, but it is revealing that two of the most seasoned mechanic/engineers in the business could even conceive that the front-engined 250F layout could succeed against the new school. Clearly, for some, the rear engined vogue was but an aberration in a general trend. Even today, most road cars have their engines in the front, although the frequency with which front-wheel-drive is found underlines the development of complex but compact transmissions which were first developed by firms such as Cooper.

The question was, would Stirling be one of its drivers? It had been a year, more or less to the day, since the Goodwood accident, and while Stirling was, to Basil Cardew's amazement, roaring about in his little Mini-Cooper and generally behaving more like his old self, the big decision, whether or not to enter racing, had still to be taken. It would not be enough to merely get round a track, he had to feel that he was competitive, by which Moss meant the following, in a bemusingly eloquent stream-of-consciousness statement he made in *All But My Life*, the writing of which, by Ken Purdy, had ironically straddled his accident:

'You go through a corner absolutely flat out, right on the ragged edge, but absolutely in control, on your own line to an inch, the car just hanging there, the tyres as good as geared to the road, locked to it, and yet you know that if you ask one more mile an hour out of the car, if you put another five pounds of sidethrust on it, you'll lose the whole flaming vehicle as surely as if someone had smeared the road with six inches of grease; so you stay just this side of that fraction of extra speed, that fraction of extra weight that could ruin everything, and perhaps kill you to boot, you're on top of it all, and the exhilaration, the thrill is tremendous, you say to yourself, 'All right, you bastards, top that one, match it, even,' and you feel like a painter who has put the last brush stroke on a canvas, after years of trying to catch a certain expression.'

Not exactly tiddlywinks, is it? In that book, Moss also

described that he could, in all probability, walk on water if he set his mind to it and sacrificed everything else. An interesting allusion, and one which may shed some light upon his mental state. As to whether Moss could still paint a da Vinci or would need the numbers to help him do it, he found out on May Day 1963. Gregory hired Goodwood for the day and sent, in total secrecy, a BRP Lotus 19 sports car down there with Tony Robinson. It was wet, but it had stopped raining. A small group was assembled there, with no Press, but one photographer friend, and probably a few watchers on the hill. It was a Wednesday.

Moss had been forewarned by Dr Krikler's uncompromising conclusions that this effort would not be easy. He perhaps even thought, more in hope than real expectation, that merely being at Goodwood might help him recover the total amnesia about the crash which has dogged him ever since. Not a chance.

He drove the car for just over an hour and a half, and discovered that Berenice Krikler had been absolutely right. He put it this way:

'I had to think. I had to give orders to myself; here I'll brake, here I must change down, and so on ... and another thing, I used to be able to look at the rev counter without taking my eyes off the road; not only that, I could see the rev counter and the road and a friend waving to me, all at the same time ... I've lost that, that's gone.'

Thirty five years later, Moss said almost those same words to me when we met. It is a moment imprinted vividly on his mind, that instant when he realised that he could no longer be a part of the sport which he had done so much to popularise. He also thought, and still does, that he should have waited, perhaps a year longer.

Naturally, he was physiologically different. Not the broken legs or other injuries, those were relatively trivial, but his eyes. Denis Jenkinson recalled that Moss, in 1955, could identify miles ahead on a dusty road the driver of a car, when Jenks himself could not even divine its make or colour. Moss had, by that May Day, undergone major surgery to put his left eye back where it should be, the socket having been comprehensively shattered. It had been a masterpiece of reconstructive surgery, using slivers of bone from his hip, but the sensation, learned over a lifetime and 494 races, of looking at near and far objects from just such a perspective, is irretrievably changed once the left and right eye are in positions subtly different from each other. But you can get used to it. Perhaps, in his haste to remount and earn a living, not that he was exactly broke, Moss had let his own impatience get in the way of practicality. That is now his view, anyway, and one certainly shared by Gregory, both at the time and now.

Although it was half-expected, his decision, as transmitted through Gregory's Press Release: 'I have decided to retire; I will not drive again', caused a predictable reaction in Fleet Street, and not purely because it was a quiet news week. It was considered to be a national tragedy, although a number of insiders in the sport breathed a sigh of relief at the news. Some, like Peter Garnier, of the *Autocar*, went so far as to say so in print:

'He had nothing whatever to gain by making a dramatic return. He had inherited world supremacy on Fangio's retirement at the end of 1957, and had held it unchallenged ever since. He had, however, a great deal to lose by continuing with the sport if there was the slightest chance that he had not fully recovered from his injuries – at best his great reputation, and at worst his life.'

There were also sound economic reasons to stop,

though. The BP and other support contracts included a form of words, supplied by Gregory, which continued BP's financial support in the event that Moss, by reason of an accident, was unable to continue racing. It was this clause which was triggered by not only Dr Krikler's opinion, but the opinion of Moss himself, who was, by that time, acknowledged as being Mister Motor Racing. Further, Stirling Moss Ltd held an insurance policy for £10,000 with Lloyds. One of the provisions under which payment would be made on it was that if the insured suffered injury through any accident which prevented him from pursuing his normal occupation. Clearly, the evidence was that Moss could not carry on as a racing driver.

*   *   *

The transmission of the new BRP car, which Innes Ireland first drove at Spa in the Belgian Grand Prix in early June 1963, had five forward speeds which, he recalled, started to select themselves, and he wisely retired on lap 9. Robinson tore down the gearbox and the car was ready for the Dutch Grand Prix later in the month. He came fourth, which was, on the face of it, an astounding result. A ninth place at Reims and a retirement at Silverstone in the British Grand Prix were disappointing, but at the Nürburgring in August he was doing rather well in practice until he hit oil and went off, which bent the steering and suspension somewhat. He entered the old Lotus 24 in the actual race and was shunted off at the Karussel by Lorenzo Bandini. Jim Hall managed a fifth place in one of the pair of ex-UDT Lotuses.

In September, Innes Ireland was back in the BRP-BRM and he came fourth as the engine was expiring at Monza – and that was the last Formula 1 appearance of Innes that season, for he had a frightful crash at Seattle while racing in a sports car event in an ex-UDT Laystall Lotus 19 for Rosebud racing, his US employer. Ireland was left in plaster for the rest of the season.

Jim Hall, later to design and develop the Chaparral marque, had shown well during the season and, while he never improved upon his German result, learned much about racing, sufficient that he decided quite soon to concentrate on sports cars, taking up rather more successfully where Lance Reventlow's Scarab sports car had left off.

As Gregory, Robinson and the Mosses reviewed the season, it was clear that the gap between competitive and merely good was widening. When the numbers were calculated, the BRP was in deficit for Formula 1, the first time it had ever happened. The main reason was the double whammy of the cost of developing the BRP-BRM, minus a sponsor, and the simple expense of running a team on a new formula of starting money, FOCA's Paris Agreement. It was sobering.

BRP resolved to press on and make an improved and lighter car. Reinforcing failure, perhaps, but the loss was relatively small and Ireland had shown that the car could be competitive, and there was still the prospect of starting money for sports car races, at which the team had shown well.

Through the winter of 1963-64 Robinson undertook the task of a thorough analysis and critique of the 1963 car and to produce another version of it, clearly a development but possessed of some modification. For a start, it was clear that the materials used could be lighter, so 18- and 20-gauge alloy was now used to make the monocoque, with no apparent loss of rigidity. In the transmission department, the main evidence of change was the presence of a BRM six-speed gearbox. The new cars, there were to be two of them, the other to be driven by Trevor Taylor, were not ready in time for the domestic warm-up races, and Ireland, by now fully recovered, managed to win a very wet race at Snetterton in March in the 1963 car. That was his best Formula 1 result of the season, albeit not in a Grand Prix.

In his memoirs, Ireland is convinced that the BRM engines as supplied to the BRP were down on power from those of the previous season. That may well have been true, but it was a risk which every user of other people's engines took. He was disarmingly frank about his own shortcomings, though, and resolutely supportive of Gregory, Taylor, Robinson, et al. His sense of underachievement comes out well in an account he gives of what took place at the Mexican Grand Prix in October 1964. It is a classic of misunderstanding. Stirling Moss, who, unbeknownst to Ireland, is working as a reporter for live television, but who is, first and foremost, also a director of the BRP, approaches Innes to question him about the poor performance of the light green car. Expletives, are deleted. It went like this:

Moss: 'What's the matter, Innes?'
Innes: 'Oh, I don't ****** well know, except the ******* car is as rough as a bear's arse.'
Moss: (flinching but regrouping): 'Well, why have you retired, Innes?'
Innes: 'Oh, the bloody thing was wandering all over the ******* road. It's like a bag of ****.'

Manfully, Moss tried to cover up, or at best ignore the expletives. He failed, as stopping Innes in full flow was a task for only the most resolute, and thus brought to an end what might have been a fulltime career in broadcasting. It was the last race which Ireland drove for the BRP, but not because of his full use of his native tongue. There were other events taking place which would ensure the end of the firm.

The first of these was Ken Gregory's decision to resign as Stirling's manager. While he remained a director of Stirling Moss Ltd, he rationalised that as Stirling was no longer racing, he could spend more time running his own affairs, as there was certainly not enough room for both of them to do so, as the intervening period had proved.

At the beginning of 1964, the Formula 1 Constructors Association came into being. FOCA, as it is now commonly known, was set up by Cooper, Brabham, BRM and Lotus. It was the 'Paris agreement', cooked up by the British-based car makers which pointedly and very effectively ended any aspirations which the BRP had of being a serious racing-car manufacturer. After the slump in numbers of manufacturers in 1957, Lotus, Cooper, Brabham and BRM were now well to the forefront, with the only serious foreign opposition coming from Ferrari and a few specials builders. The agreement was an attempt to carve up the sport among the main manufacturers. Applications for membership were announced at the beginning of 1964. The main stipulations were that a candidate vehicle (for it was really a car club) should be built in the main by its entrant and that it should have at least a season of competition under its belt. Enzo Ferrari, splendidly grand, refused point-blank to join. Who were these Anglo-Saxon garagistas to write the rules? Cleverly, though, he realised that he could profit from the scheme without endorsing it. Unwittingly, by his refusal to co-operate with these arriviste proposals, Enzo Ferrari put the final piece of the jigsaw in place. He was both part of it by heritage and outside it, but now, Formula 1 was, commercially, a British sport, and has been ever since.

The BRP, except occasionally, had not exactly frightened anyone with their results, promising as they were, but the British constructors in effect formed a cartel in order to define such terms as starting and prize money and, given that attendances were now routinely as high as they had been pre-war, the pot was potentially huge. The plan was that there should be a first rank of manufacturers who would divide the cash between them. Technically, the BRP qualified for membership – and there really is no doubt about this – as they used only the same number of bought in parts as anyone else, and rather less than some. In the summer of 1964 the BRP informed the powers that be that they were ready to comply with the requirements and offered their cars for inspection. No-one came to see them, but they were declared ineligible for membership anyway and neatly partitioned off from the money. Blackballed.

It was not that long a time since Gregory had arrived on the scene with such a fat chequebook that Lotus and Cooper had come close to panic. All were aware of his ability to pull rabbits out of hats with a potential sponsor, after all, and that would have effectively broken the cartel as well as monopolising the drivers of his choice. Gregory and the BRP had to go. There had been attempts to block them before, at the birth of the UDT effort, but now the group of Cooper, Lotus, Brabham and BRM had a structure by which they could actually do it.

This was hypocrisy of a high order. It was not a matter of public record at the time that the BRP had actually been approached by Jack Brabham in the winter of 1963-64 to construct a run of monocoque chassis for his own team, and that Reg Parnell, Gregory's successor as manager of the Yeoman Credit team, had also shown an interest in the same idea. The fact that Tony Robinson would be later headhunted by both Cooper and Brabham to develop their own monocoque car was adequate testimony to what the generally held opinion of the BRP operation really was – a threat, particularly if it were to become well-funded again.

It was a clear signal and a hard one to ignore. Alfred, Ken and Stirling, between them, had done more than anyone else, the latter by sheer effort, the others by business acumen, to attract money to the sport. Colin Chapman was to follow the Yeoman Credit/UDT example quite soon with his groundbreaking deal with Player's cigarettes, and shortly after that the whole sport was at it, with the honourable exception of Cooper and Ferrari. But, with the Paris agreement, an effective lockout, the sport changed. Lives would still be lost, tragedies would persist, and the politics at Ferrari would never change, but any claim made now that the activity of Formula 1 racing is anything more than, in Stirling Moss's own words, 'a great occasion, but not a sport' would seem relatively hollow. The world of the private entrant – the organiser, the trier – had been swept aside. It was now a business. The greatest irony, though, was that Ken Gregory, Alfred and Stirling had done more to transform the activity of motor racing from sport to business than anyone had, and there was no room in the new structure for their organisation. The BRP had been given the cold shoulder.

The classic Gregory manoeuvre, the one of which the cartel were most apprehensive, would have been to find a sponsor and bypass the whole process, following the example set by Enzo Ferrari, who was being quietly supported by Fiat. Why did he not contest the issue? He was a better businessman than any of the opposition; of this there can be little doubt. The reason he acquiesced to this crude move – which effectively sent him to Coventry – by those whose customer he had been was rather more straightforward. He was simply exhausted.

He had been, in effect, running the BRP more or less single-handed. Stirling, despite his commercial interest in the business, was not fired with enthusiasm at sharing the stage and indeed had rather snippily started his own venture, the Stirling Moss Automobile Racing Team (SMART), which campaigned a weird-looking Lotus Elan with improvements by Frank Costin. Hardly, one may think, a particular vote of confidence in the BRP. A cynic might think that Moss was anxious to prove that he could manage a team as well as Gregory could.

The toll, for Ken Gregory, had been heavy. The losses of Bueb, Lewis-Evans, Bristow, Collins, Schell and a host of others, some obscure now but many famous then – Mike Keen, Archie Scott Brown, Luigi Musso, Alan Stacey, Eugenio Castellotti, Taffy von Trips, Ricardo Rodriguez, Jean Behra, Carel de Beaufort, Fon de Portago – had left him wondering whether all the effort was really worth it. The near loss of Moss probably acted as much as a catalyst as anything else to make him consider his options, so it was ironic that Stirling seemed so disinterested. Perhaps a united front on the matter of the future of the BRP would have made a difference.

Anyway, this apparent betrayal of the BRP rather worked to focus Gregory's mind. The out and out declaration that the business of motor racing at the highest level was now the subject of an unseemly sprint for position which was clearly creating its own bureaucracy of self-interest may have deterred him from pressing on as a thing of itself. Despite the part of regulator which he had played at senior club level, he was and is not much of a corporate soul, unless, of course, it is his corporation. Team player, certainly, but teams need captains and Colin Chapman rather seemed to have reserved that role for himself.

Was there a sense of schadenfreude at Gregory's rather unseemly exit from motor sport? Probably. He had, in a comparatively short time, done as much as anyone (and more than many) to promote the interests of the sport and its participants. Of course, he had made money out of it and, eventually, lived well, which is more than some had, but he had also put a lot back. He had made few enemies, although one detects a faint resentment from some about the way he managed Stirling, at the expense of those who wanted his services for nothing. He would, though, come to understand exactly what Gore Vidal meant when he said, in a 1973 interview in *The Sunday Times*, 'Whenever a friend succeeds, a little something in me dies.' The timing of that remark was coincidental, given what the secondary banking crisis would do to Gregory's carefully amassed fortune. Meanwhile, though, he resolved to focus more of his attention on the aircraft business.

Poor Innes Ireland was in Switzerland when the news came through, in December 1964, that the BRP was no longer involved in Formula 1. He was miffed at not being informed, but he had been told by a journalist before Gregory could contact him. To his dying day, he felt that the BRP had been treated shabbily, and that Robinson's design, which was much better that anyone has ever given it credit for, would have stood up to the competition given an engine which was powerful enough.

But Innes' attitude to the sport was already antediluvian. He raced purely for the fun of it and, while he certainly paid a high price for his involvement, including some hair-raising accidents, he never stopped enjoying it, except perhaps when his best friend Stacey was killed. Innes was not the last of the Harry Schell school of race driver, for that honour rightly belongs to the late great James Hunt, but he was a man totally at odds with the changes which he witnessed in the organisation of the sport. The collapse of the BRP, which Ken Gregory today freely admits was more his fault than anyone else's, marginalised Innes Ireland to a degree with which he was to become uncomfortable. The absolute contempt which he always had for money, which is probably why he spent it so freely, had put him at odds with the new trend, but his frank and total admiration for Gregory and the Moss family, who could all be more than a little beady-eyed about the prospect of valuta at times, comes through clearly in everything he wrote of those years. He finally retired from racing, with some relief, in the winter of 1966-67, ironically after collecting the 'Rookie of the Year' award after his engine blew up in the Daytona 500-miler. Later, he went to work for the *Autocar* and his last truly commercial assignment was as a consultant to Aston Martin Lagonda once Walter Hayes, the Ford Motor Company's own Mr Motor Racing, had taken the helm there. Innes did achieve a very high recognition late in his life; he was elected President of the British Racing Drivers' Club, at a very difficult time for it, and by all accounts did a splendid job. He died on 22 October 1993. His last public appearance, before cancer finally carried him off, was to deliver Rudyard Kipling's poem 'If' at the memorial service for James Hunt a month before his own early death. One resolutely committed public school plunger seeing another on his way.

*　　*　　*

The BRP was not quite history yet, though. There was unfinished business as a manufacturer which was happily tangential to Formula 1 entries. In November 1964 Masten Gregory contacted his old employers with a very simple proposal. Would Tony Robinson, Rod Guerin and the rest of the crew care to build two cars for the upcoming Indianapolis 500 to be held, as ever, on Memorial Day weekend – May 1965? Ken, Alfred and Tony barely hesitated. The boys needed the work and the BRP needed the money. Alfred, who had run in the 1924 and 1925 events, was particularly tickled. In the event, the whole exercise more or less broke even.

The Indy 500, run since 1911, has, since inception, gone in and out of fashion. It had not been a World Championship event since 1960, by which time it had been realised that not only did it clash with Monaco, but the qualities required in the cars were radically different. By the time Stirling Moss had won the 1958 Argentinian Grand Prix in his ridiculous Cooper, at 83 mph, the fastest lap speed at Indianapolis was already 149 mph, set by Tony Bettenhausen in a front-engined Epperly-Offenhauser – on a brick surface. The track was not actually Tarmacked until 1961. The 2.5 mile circuit has only four 90 degree corners, which blur into two, and is a geometrically perfect rectangle. There was, and is, no race to match Indy for pure speed.

Indianapolis cars need to be beefy. The pounding of a 500-mile race, over a track faced with 3,200,000 ten pound bricks, even when covered by a thin skim of blacktop, would wreck a delicate Grand Prix car and, conversely, the complexity of a Grand Prix circuit would completely overwhelm an Indy car. By comparison to Formula 1, Indianapolis cars had been slow to change. The race had been dominated for years by Offenhauser-powered front-engined 'roadsters' producing 400 bhp on a volatile cocktail of methanol and oxygen-bearing nitromethane. Transmissions, typically, were two-speed, slow and fast. Then in 1962, Ford took an interest. It was clear to the Ford Motor Company that this extraordinary event – in its way as unique as the Mille Miglia, attracting as it did some 500,000 spectators, all total fans and more than a little blue-collar – could be turned to their advantage, if they could win. Dan Gurney had brought Colin Chapman together with Lee Iacocca to discuss a Lotus-Ford entry for the Greatest Motor Race in the World. The nod was given, and a design loosely based upon the block of the production Fairlane V8 engine was laid down. It was to have two cams per bank, four valves and be of 4.2 litres displacement, but, vitally, it would run on gasoline fuel, not methanol. Gurney and Chapman knew that the cornering power of a Lotus Formula 1 design, albeit a heavy one, would simply blindside the opposition. They were right. The advantage of the better fuel consumption of the new Ford should obviate the necessity for the numerous fuel stops which the very powerful but prodigiously greedy Offys would need. They were right. Only a little rule-bending on the part of the locals had cost Jim Clark the race in 1963. The new Ford engines were to cost a staggering $31,500 each at inception. By the time Masten Gregory became interested, the bean counters from Dearborn had managed to shave $10,000 off that.

Masten, though, was more or less broke and had been for years. He relied upon the good offices of his new stepfather, George Bryant. Bryant had accumulated a large fortune on the back of a mail order business and had recently married Masten's widowed mother. Masten's own father had died at an early age after making a fortune in insurance, and Masten had inherited around $500,000 in 1951. Now, 13 years later, it was all gone.

Bryant was not messing about; he had hired the services

of George Salih, a veteran mechanic/engineer from earlier days. He was America's Alf Francis in many ways and he made sure that there was adequate funding. Bryant was no piker, after all, and it was a proper effort.

And so was Robinson's. He had never even seen Indianapolis but, armed with the liberal rule book, embarked upon a chunkier, longer wheelbase version of the 1964 Grand Prix car, complete with adjustable suspension offsets, a characteristic of brickyard cars, which only ever really need to turn left. Masten sent over a dummy engine and transmission so that the dimensions would be known, and work began just as Innes was receiving the news in Switzerland that his Formula 1 career was over with the BRP.

Just like the 1964 Formula 1 car, more or less everything structural on the Indycars was of BRP manufacture. All the suspension uprights, for example, were fabricated by them. Wheels were by Halibrand, the gearbox by ZF, the fuel tanks by an ICI subsidiary. These flexible bag tanks were vastly expensive, almost the same amount which had been budgeted for the cars themselves. Tony Robinson, keenly aware as a BRP director that money was tight, appealed to the better nature of the managing director of the makers, one John Harvey-Jones, who assented to a reduction of the cost. It is nice to think that the famous trouble-shooter played such a key role in furthering the ambitions of Masten Gregory to join the ranks of Abner Jenkins, Wilbur Shaw, Frank Lockhart and Jimmy Murphy. Immortality in American racing is only assured by winning the Indianapolis 500. Nothing else will do it.

The cars were finished by March 1965, a bare four months from inception. They arrived at Speedway, Indiana as rolling chassis, with Jim Chapman and George Woodward escorting them as mechanics, for fitting up and testing more than six weeks before qualifying began. George Salih, who had famously high standards, rather liked the look of the cars. He had been the first man to tip, heretically, an Offenhauser motor on its side in order to lower the frontal area of the car which it powered; that had helped Troy Ruttman's Kurtis win the 1951 race at 128 mph. Since then Salih had built two more winners, and was therefore a great man in his way. The second BRP-made car was to be driven by Jimmy Lloyd. Both Lloyd and Gregory qualified their cars at speeds in the order of 150 mph and were well satisfied. The BRP had clearly delivered the goods without ever having seen the circuit and there was further encouragement – Stirling Moss, sporting a piratical beard, went along to manage the pit.

Jim Clark won the race, famously, but although Lloyd came nowhere, Masten Gregory was running a respectable fifth when the gearbox gave out. It was a vast disappointment, of course, but 1965 had other compensations for Masten, for later that summer, he won the Le Mans 24 hour race, partnered, albeit reluctantly, by Jochen Rindt, driving a privately-entered Ferrari.

The quality of the work done by the BRP had always been the envy of its competitors, and was perhaps ultimately the indirect cause of its downfall. Sundry other entrants, over the few years of its existence as a manufacturer, had suggested that perhaps the BRP could build chassis for them, as all appreciated the thoroughness and attention to detail which was one of the firm's most salient characteristics. Perhaps the thought of that prompted a rather tongue-in-cheek announcement in March 1965, as the Indianapolis cars were made ready, that anyone else who wanted one should simply produce £8,000 and they could be a happy owner. Sadly, by then there were no takers.

Consider, though, the magnitude of Robinson's achievement, to design and build a car in a matter of months, for an engine he did not know, to race on the toughest circuit in the world which he had never seen. To have that car even qualify is nothing short of extraordinary. To have it running a competitive fifth and to be let down by the transmission was galling, but the BRP Indycar confirmed that Tony Robinson was really of the first rank of designer/builders.

With hindsight it is far too easy to say that building Formula 1 cars was perhaps a step too far for the BRP – not that they were uncompetitive, for they were beautifully made, well thought out and clearly potential winners, but merely that after the UDT period, the team hit a pocket of resentment in the sport at the prospect of their success, coupled with a brief absence of sponsors. The birth of FOCA triggered the start of a period of tooth-grinding inflation in the business of motor racing as the doctrine of only – only – spending other people's money took hold. Several generations of sponsors have learned that the risible cost of building, entering and managing the weird thing that is a modern motor racing team is not for the faint-hearted. Up to that point, winning motor races was a matter of power, handling, design, courage and flair. Suddenly, it had become a matter of money. That Gregory had been instrumental in starting all this is an irony that was, and is, not lost upon him.

So, within a few years, cars – which up to now had, with a few exceptions, been more or less designed on the back of a cigarette packet – would grow to resemble those very cartons, as tobacco advertising, progressively banned from television, started to find its way on to the track. In many ways the BRP was ejected from the elevator right at the ground floor. It had been accomplished sneakily – of that there is no doubt – and caught the BRP at a weak moment. Had this crude spivvery been tried even a scant year earlier, then there can be little doubt that Gregory would have swatted it out of the air and stamped on it without even breaking stride as he charged about the place, and in all likelihood would have ended up running the whole thing. The man who effectively did, who later replaced Gregory in the sport, Bernie Ecclestone, owes much of his own success to the blueprint laid down by Ken Gregory as the original Formula 1 entrepreneur.

Despite that, though, the BRP was over. The Highgate works were sold to Charles Lucas who planned to use the premises for maintenance of his own vehicles, which included a Maserati 250F and, later, for the production of Titan single-seater Formula 3 and Formula Ford racing cars. The three remaining BRM-engined Formula 1 cars were despatched to Gregory's garage at Higher Denham, Bucks, where he had moved in order to be nearer to both his aircraft and publishing businesses. They did not stay there long.

The popularity which Formula 1 now enjoyed spawned two major (and probably several minor) film projects in 1965. The first on the scene was Steve McQueen, who planned a big budget drama set in the world of Formula 1, and hired Stirling Moss as a consultant to the project. The second proposal, which found more favour from the financiers, was to be directed by John Frankenheimer, who had recently directed *The Birdman of Alcatraz* and *The Manchurian Candidate*. There could only be one winner and ultimately it turned out to be Frankenheimer, with *Grand Prix*. But before that transpired, Stirling requested that SMART took delivery of the three cars. Knowing his involvement in McQueen's project, Ken readily handed them over.

297A. Ken Gregory with his second wife, Nem, at a Zoological society reception at Regent's Park. They seem at risk of sharing their dinner with a local resident. (Ken Gregory).

297B. Michelle, Sophia and Christopher Gregory, Dickfield House, Denham, c.1976. (Ken Gregory).

296A. Ken Gregory and Cyril Audrey in front of Ken's first aircraft, a Piper Commanche 250. (Ken Gregory).
296B. Gregory Air Taxis' Piper Aztec. Denham. (Ken Gregory).

MANAGING A LEGEND

299A. On a visit to EMAP, Gregory causes some concern by parking his Hughes 300 helicopter in the office car park... (Ken Gregory).
299B. Sultan bin Ladin's HS125 after return to the UK. (Ken Gregory).

300A. *Ken Gregory, front row right, during flying training, RAF Booker, July 1945.*
(Ken Gregory).
300B. *The Gregory Air Services DC3 Dakota in front of the Gregory Air Engineering works at Newcastle. This aircraft was used for one of the UK's first package holiday operations. (Ken Gregory).*

MANAGING A LEGEND

301A. *Ken and Julie Gregory at their wedding. (Ken Gregory).*
301B. *The Juan Manuel Fangio memorial service at Farm Street, Mayfair on Oct 17, 1995. L-R, Stirling Moss, Ken Gregory, Cliff Allison, Tony Robinson. (Eoin Young).*

302. The UDT-Laystall pit at Goodwood. L-R; Tony Robinson, Doreen Audrey, Celia Ercolani, Ken Gregory, Maria Robinson, Mike McKee, Bob Gibson-Jarvie, two unknowns and John Ball. (John Fry).
303. The UDT-Laystall team lined up for the sportscar race at Goodwood, Easter 1961. All the UDT cars are Lotus 19s. (John Brierley).
304 (overleaf). Ken Gregory with one of the Gregory Air Taxis' Piper Aztecs, Denham, 1965. (Ken Gregory).

He was under the impression that Stirling might prepare them for racing or for use in the forthcoming film. There was even a thought that one might appear at the Monaco Grand Prix in 1966. Frankly, he didn't care much.†

When it was decided in Hollywood to abandon the McQueen project in favour of Frankenheimer's, Gregory was barely interested. He was at that stage planning the acquisition of his first jet aircraft, which was much more exciting than motor racing, and he really thought no more about it. He was, he reasoned, finally out of racing and was no longer depressed and distracted by the sight of the cars sitting in his garage. It was time to get on. If he thought that the process of disengagement was going to be easy, or stress-free, or entirely without regret, he was wrong.

†McQueen did, in fact, go on to make a motor racing film; *Le Mans*, in 1971. Filmed largely at the 1970 24-hour race, it was short on plot and long on action. By and large, it had a gloomy, introspective tone. Opinions vary about the merits of *Grand Prix*. One of the reasons it appears so dated now is the portrayal of the behaviour of the drivers, which many agree was reasonably accurate. Many of the then current stars, such as Graham Hill, played cameo roles, but Stirling Moss, to his irritation, was not involved in it.

Chapter 18

DECREE NISI

*'It is true that around every man a fatal circle
is traced, beyond which he cannot pass; but
within the wide verge of that circle he is
powerful and free.'*
ALEXIS DE TOCQUEVILLE, 1841

Gregory's total and final separation from Moss was neither
a quick nor particularly pleasant process. A decree absolute,
as it were, would never be granted, but the partnership,
worn out by the crisis over the sudden end of Stirling's racing career, and burdened by a whole series of petty and
unnecessary squabbles over business policy – not made any
easier by the issue of Speed and Sports Publications – was
itself in something of a qualitative crisis. From being a
focused business enterprise, capable of generating relatively
vast amounts of cash, Stirling Moss Ltd, and all it represented, 13 years of hard work, was now riven by animosity.

Basically, Moss was not only bored, but still severely
injured, and Gregory was both rather busy and extremely
distressed. That Moss had always had a passion for detail
outside his raw drive Gregory knew very well. The evidence
was clear enough, anyway, and if Gregory had had the time
to read Parkinson's Law, published in 1958 – in which the
old cynic had stated that 'Work expands so as to fill the time
available for its completion.' – he would have known that
after the Goodwood accident, nothing would be the same
for either of them and he could (and should) have braced
himself for the deluge which was now about to descend,
from a great height, upon his well-barbered head.

Clearly, he hadn't read it, probably because he was too distracted, and when both men looked at the situation calmly, they came to a realisation, at first unspoken, that the basic differences between them which had hitherto been subsumed by a common goal, were now exposed to the full force of Moss's sense of frustration at being unable to carry on racing, and Gregory's sense of frustration at being unable to carry out his job properly. Sharing a flat was one thing; and that had not worked out well at all. Sharing a life was hardly going to be any better.

But this was by no means Ken Gregory's only job by now. Not only had he taken Speed and Sports Publications forward, which gave him both a great deal of satisfaction (overlaid by a slight sense of relief), but he had also started to build Gregory Air Taxis into something of a serious and thriving business which he was starting to find totally absorbing. Wisely, he had diversified his own activities almost as much as Stirling's, even before that first shiver of doubt had gone through him when the BRP became a triumvirate. Even though he was no longer Stirling's manager, he was a director of both Stirling Moss Ltd and the BRP and, frankly, the level of petty conflicts over commercial issues within both concerns was rather wearing him down.

These developments alarmed Alfred, who was rather caught in the middle. Ever conscious of advancing age (he may even have known he was ill then), he tried inordinately hard to referee the squabble and keep the pair functioning as a unit. They had, he reasoned, both seen each other through traumatic separations from other people, by either divorce, or, professionally, death – both of which events had brought with them the kind of emotional baggage with which neither man was really equipped to deal, and he feared the onset of a sense of abandonment on the part of his son. On top of this, he was distressed at the prospect of losing Ken as a surrogate second son. Ken's resignation as Stirling's professional manager had clearly been a straw in the wind. As it became clear that the glue which had held the pair together was losing its strength, he tried one more approach which smacks of desperation, but at the time seemed logical, to Alfred at least. Ken would receive 10 per cent of Stirling's earnings for life. On top of this, he would also receive 10 per cent of Stirling's inheritance. In return, he would invest one hundred per cent of his own assets into this hurriedly thought out merged joint venture. As a ratio, it may well have been realistic and equitable; as a proposal, it was certainly not. Alfred tried very hard, but all in vain.

Gregory was adamant. The role of factotum for life in exchange for financial security was most definitely not for him. He had already become very cross indeed at the prospect of lobbying on Stirling's behalf so that Stirling's new house could be finished and fitted out below budget, and he knew full well that the main reason that he had dealt so well with Stirling in the past was that the man's character simply required confrontation and discussion in order to arrive at decisions. Sadly, the approach by Alfred, however generous its terms, was very wide of the mark so far as Ken was concerned.

So, a depressing process of disengagement had begun. The correspondence between the two men at this time, and for some time to come, reveals a total change of emphasis – not so much master/slave, although there is rather more than just a touch of that, but a deep coolness which is all the chillier, given that the reader is acutely aware of a basic loneliness, or at least a sense of it, on the part of Moss which is only partly to do with a lack of company. Gregory felt it, too. There is a clear reluctance on the part of both men to revisit events which had previously defined their lives, trivia excepted. It is lowering reading.

The divorce image is a compelling one. As every sit-com which touches the subject thrives upon the truisms of separation – is this yours or mine? – so the Moss/Gregory alliance descended into mild vituperation, formally expressed, although not without regret. Arguments about money, never easy to sort out and seldom a comedy theme, were eventually settled by November 1965, although a slight mystery remains, for this writer at least, concerning the division of the British Racing Partnership assets.

By the beginning of 1966, all formal business commitments between the two were terminated. But, to Stirling, who had, with an untypically charming diplomacy, drawn a line under the pair's squabbles, Ken Gregory seemed to have more or less disappeared off the face of the earth.

The reason was Air Gregory, which had started to grow exponentially since the acquisition of the first Piper Commanche in 1960, which he had wisely hired out while not using it himself. In expanding the business, he had bought aircraft engineering and repair facilities at Denham, Birmingham and Newcastle, as well as building up the aircraft fleet. Eventually it would reach a total of 27, the strength of a small airline, which is what, in effect, it was to become. It was starting to become a big enterprise, and was therefore absorbing all his time. He delegated the management of the publishing business to one Julian Berrisford and focused his considerable energies upon turning his back on motor racing, in all its manifestations, and becoming a full-time aircraft operator.

The lessons which Gregory had learned from motor racing at all its levels were certainly useful in running an airline, although the parallels were rather far apart. Thorough preparation and maintenance, coupled with attention to detail, were part of his soul anyway, but the prospect of technical failure, merely catastrophic in a racing car but truly disastrous in an aircraft, was always at the back of his mind. He developed something of a fetish for safety, which naturally cost money and reduced margins, but he made up for it in volume of business. He could not afford, he reasoned, to be the man whose aeroplane fell apart and killed the Beatles, or Frank Sinatra, or a television crew, or indeed anyone.

Gregory's client list was, to say the least, comprehensive. From industry barons, musicians, entertainers and movie stars to the merely indulgent, Gregory Air flew them all, famous or infamous. John Bloom, the owner of the Rolls Razor company, which went the way of all flesh in 1965, had to be more or less smuggled in under the eyes of the Press; John Lennon and Yoko Ono offered different sets of problems as they were flown to Gibraltar for their wedding.

However, there was rather more to it than that. The operation was split into four separate areas – Gregory Air Taxis, Gregory Air Services, Gregory Air Engineering, and Gregory Flying Training. Gregory Air Services, for example, gained a fine reputation for aerial camera work; covering news assignments such as the Torrey Canyon disaster and feature film work such as *Oh! What a Lovely War!* The flying training school, with locations at both Denham and Birmingham, was, at one stage, training and qualifying over three hundred pilots a year. He had also acquired selling and repairing agencies for Piper and Cessna aircraft, as well as Hughes helicopters, through Gregory Air Engineering.

It was, though, a very tough business, and Gregory's insistence upon Grand Prix levels of attention to detail did not make it cheap to do. The Air Taxi business also had one other undesirable, but built-in characteristic – appalling cash flow. All the running costs, particularly fuel, and of course spares, had to be paid for on demand, whereas the clients were offered languid credit accounts, which many of them abused. One who did not was Cilla Black, who took one look at a Piper twin Commanche and absolutely refused to even get in it.

Gregory's reinvestment strategy had threatened to put a strain upon the resources of the firm more than once, but he kept debt levels relatively low, with management contracts on as many expensive aircraft as he could (shades of the BRP), but he, like others, had discovered the secret of running an aeroplane – it costs almost as much when it is sitting still in finance and depreciation as it does when flying; so keep it flying. The idea of managing aircraft the way he had managed racing cars was a sound one, as everybody made money. To this day, Gregory articulates a similar view – the only good deal is one in which everyone is happy to be involved.

One pair of adventurous Yorkshire businessmen to whom this seemed a good idea was James Hanson and Gordon White, who were progressing far enough up the ladder running a small conglomerate, the Wiles Group, that they reasoned that a Hawker-Siddeley HS125 executive jet, the 300SLR of the aircraft business, was a sensible purchase. With good management, it would surely make a fine corporate asset. Gordon White had contacted Gregory, originally in an attempt to buy Gregory Air Services, in fact, but it was not for sale, so they countered with an offer which was hard to refuse. They would buy the jet, and GAS would operate it for hire and reward. The management contract would offer a decent return to both sides and everyone would be happy. A splendid idea, sign here.

By the end of June 1967, however, the three entrepreneurs were not quite so sure. In what was probably the first hijack of a British commercial jet, their HS125, carrying the exiled former Katangan and Congo President Moise Tshombe on a jaunt around the Balearics, was seized by an agent of the Congo regime and diverted to Algeria. The drama was, of course, wholly unexpected. The pilots, David Taylor and Trevor Coplestone, were, like all Gregory's pilots, ex-RAF and very experienced, and their first idea when they heard a shot from the passenger compartment and turned to see the hijacker with a pistol in his hand was to invert the plane and drop him on his head. They knew that the cabin pressure had not been compromised but were unaware of the nature of any injuries. In the event, they decided that a wait-and-see strategy was best. They obeyed instructions from the hijacker and headed across the Mediterranean to Algeria. With all the reasonableness which characterises third world regimes then, as now, they were immediately locked up.

Taylor had been a Vulcan bomber pilot and Coplestone an instructor on Hawker Hunters at RAF Chivenor. The hijacker, an adventurer (although 'poor sap' would be a better appellation in the light of later events), by the name of François Bodenan, claimed to be a representative of the Kinshasa government, but this cut no ice with the Algerians, so they locked him up, too. Gregory's crew were released after three hard months in an Algerian prison, and the aircraft came back three months after that. It took a fair amount of lobbying to secure the crew's freedom. Gregory recalls a series of ludicrous meetings with the bovine Foreign Office minister, Fred Mulley, and it was only an energetic Press campaign orchestrated by Gordon White through the good offices of Chapman Pincher of the *Daily*

Express, as well as a huge effort by the International Red Cross, which generated enough embarrassment in Whitehall for the pressure to be brought to bear on the Algerians. While he was at it, Gregory organised an exclusive interview with the *Sunday Express* for the pilots' stories. As a result, they received enough, upon their return, to each buy a decent house with the proceeds. One reason for the governmental inactivity was nervousness about the implications of the recent Six Day War. To pressurise a North African government which had so clearly supported the aggressors against a western ally, Israel, and whose side had been so comprehensively thrashed was a diplomatic initiative quite beyond the Foreign Office.

The pilots had had a terrible time. The fact that they both had passport stamps from Israel's Ben Gurion airport did not make their plight any easier, despite the fact that they were clearly commercial pilots, and they were denied even the most basic facilities. It was a hard three months for them, victims as they were of the child-like analysis which is often the reaction of third-world regimes to international events outside their control. They survived, however, but they easily might not have done. Moise Tshombe was not so fortunate. He died under house arrest in Algiers almost exactly two years after his abduction.

This was all very irritating, to say the least. Insurance money due as a result of the force majeure – but short of war – nature of the event, prevented deep financial damage to both Gregory Air Services and the burgeoning Hanson-White concern, but only just. The jet was the property of Air Hanson, the special purpose subsidiary set up under the Wiles group banner, and the counterparty to Gregory's management contract. Naturally, Gregory carried on paying Taylor and Coplestone during their incarceration.

Having rather got used to the idea of being a jet operator, Gregory set about replacing it. As an interim measure, he leased one from the manufacturer at a modest £4,000 per month. In order to help pay for it, he undertook to deliver Hawker-Siddeley product to their buyers in North America. This part was easy, as he had trained and secured the services of no less than six qualified HS125 pilots, who, like the aircraft themselves, also ate their heads off whether working or not.

But this was merely a stopgap. Leasing a brand-new plane – paying the other man's price, as it were – is very costly. What Gregory needed was a good used machine, to which he could add value. His chance came in the autumn of 1967, when he received a telex from the Lockheed Aircraft Corporation in Georgia, who knew of his interest, which proposed a deal. They were attempting to sell the Saudis a brace of Jetstar aircraft, and the Saudis had agreed in principle to accept, but there was a problem – they had insisted that Lockheed had to sell an HS125 first (I cannot imagine this happening today, I must say). Was GAS prepared to break this apparent deadlock? Certainly.

The story of the HS125 was rather a sad one, though. The plane was actually part of the estate of the late Sheikh bin Ladin, owner of the Kingdom's largest construction company. The company was the customer for no less than four per cent of American Caterpillar's overseas sales, in fact, and bin Ladin had been building roads, airstrips, bridges and other civil engineering firsts all over the Kingdom since the war. The poor man had died in an air crash while site surveying in the interior and his will was being executed by a committee set up by the Saudi Royal family, on which served several worthies – the head of the Saudi Air Force, the head of the Saudi Aviation Authority, the Head of the Saudi

Monetary Agency and, last but not least, a Lockheed executive. Hence the telex. If this seems a formidable array of executives, it should be borne in mind that the purpose was to obtain a good deal for the Sheikh's grieving family. Insurance is, after all, a dubious concept under Islamic Law.

The asking price for the jet was £225,000 – a snip, in fact, as it had only 200 hours flying time. Gregory, though, could not afford it. The strain which this acquisition would put on the already creaking cash flow could imperil the company. If Gregory wanted to remain a jet operator, then he would have to have a co-investor apart from his wife Nem, who had already supported him to the hilt. Well, he had pulled irons as hot as this from the fire before, as he had shown with the BRP, and there was an advantage here. The true value of the plane was closer to £325,000, so there was instant equity as well as operating profits on the plate for whoever would dig out their cutlery and sit down with him.

David Wickens, Chairman of British Car Auctions, found Gregory his white knight in the form of the Bristol Street Group, the national firm of car dealers based in Birmingham, who also had subsidiary interests in aviation as manufacturers of aircraft seats. The deal was simple. A new company, Air Gregory, would be formed, of which Gregory himself would own 40 per cent, with Bristol Street owning 60 per cent, for cash. Ken had surrendered control, so keen was he to run jets, but the new firm would at least have adequate capital. He was appointed Deputy Chairman and Managing Director, and given a service agreement to run the business. So, armed with a draft, he happily returned to Jeddah to collect the jet, which was a five-day bureaucratic nightmare. Externally, at least, the HS125 was in fine condition.

Inside, it was slightly different. Maintaining the in-flight loo had clearly been a problem for the crew, so a little memory of the poor Sheikh accompanied the ferry crew all the way back to England. Actually, the olfactory upset was quite unnecessary. Gregory had, more out of habit than anything else, secured the aircraft doors as soon as he had title which, of course, in Saudi Arabia is ridiculous, for larceny was and is almost non-existent. The penalties under Islamic law for theft transcend Draconian. The price paid, though, for sealing up the HS125, as opposed to allowing it to ventilate, was truly appalling.

Ken was well-pleased, though. He was back in the jet business with at least a share of his own freehold. He knew that the 125 would form the core of a good enterprise, a cash cow. Some of his own equity had been released by the Bristol Street deal and he could, he thought, relax a little. He was quite wrong.

He had made one fatal miscalculation, but not one which he could have foreseen. It was an event totally unassociated with either aviation or cars, but which would totally banjax not only his, but virtually every other businessman's plans for years. It was called Selective Employment Tax.

As a piece of economic incompetence, SET has few peers, even in a period not short of examples. Perhaps the only thing to match it was the salt tax in pre-revolutionary France, or perhaps the window tax of eighteenth century Britain. It has been said by some wag that the Wilson Labour government did more damage to the economic infrastructure of Britain than the Luftwaffe had. If that were true, and it may have been, then Selective Employment Tax was its Heinkel 111 and Harold Wilson was the pilot.

Broadly, this iniquitous measure was a crude effort to milk the economy of Britain of even more money than the stultifyingly short-sighted Labour government was already doing by taxing the very act of hiring labour, particularly skilled labour, so that the economy could be levelled down to its lowest common denominator and planned into chaotic state control. The government document laying out this strategy was a less than scholarly piece of work entitled 'The National Plan' and clearly designed to justify the recent currency devaluation.

Obviously, both Bristol Street and Air Gregory employed more than their fair share of clever people. The prospects were suddenly less than rosy. They were not the only ones in the glue. Stirling Moss's old employer, David Brown, was forced to lower the price of his flagship Aston Martin by 20 per cent; but still he could not sell them. Hardly a national economic disaster, but symptomatic of the state of affairs. Jobs were threatened in a way which had not been seen since the 1930s. The stock market took one look at the state of affairs and proceeded to dive like a wounded Messerschmitt. It was to lose nearly half its value by 1970.

Bristol Street, were it to survive, had to retrench and raise cash to weather the coming storm. Sadly, the most obvious candidate was the poor Sheikh's HS125 – there was a quick £100,000 in that, given that it had the virtue of being portable. This was a uniquely British problem, they felt, and the aircraft could always be sold overseas, unlike, for example, a building. Gregory, of course, protested. Here was the core of his business about to be dumped, and he fought his corner hard. It was not Bristol Street's core business, though. Ken was out-voted at a very short-notice board meeting, and he furiously tore up his now irrelevant service agreement in front of an expressionless board before storming out. That was the beginning of the end of Air Gregory. Ken's devalued 40 per cent was bought back from him and the whole firm was closed down as a tax-loss. It was back to books and magazines.

The business to which Gregory now returned had, in his absence, been ably managed by Julian Berrisford. Having been bought out of a state of insolvency from Stirling Moss and others, Gregory had every reason to be pleased with it, particularly because he had effectively rescued the other investors' equity, which is always a good way to stay popular. It would be expanded, partly by choice, partly by expedient. By 1969 it encompassed book and magazine publishing, including the third oldest book publisher in the business, exhibition management and assorted stationery and gifts, to which was added magazine distribution. An integrated media group, in the modern parlance. In June 1970, Harold Wilson's government was weighed in the balance and found wanting, and Edward Heath entered 10 Downing Street. In the event, things would hardly be any better – indeed, far worse – but there seemed to be a new optimism abroad. The stock market stumbled about and started to move north by the end of the year. The economy was enjoying a small lift, aided by a new wave of clever and acquisitive financiers who were sniffing about and finding value.

One of the oddest transactions in Gregory's Curriculum Vitae, a document which is hardly short of them, was the acquisition of Wells, Gardner Darton, a magazine and journal distributor. He had little choice but to buy it, given that it owed him so much money – some £10,000. He received a tip-off from Robert Maxwell's Pergamon Press, who were owed rather more, that Wells, Gardner was about to go into receivership, for reasons of simple incompetence on the part of Wells, Gardners' owners, a family trust. Gregory took the rash step of acquiring it as a going concern in stages, while issuing at the same time a personal guarantee to

Robert Maxwell that the debt to Pergamon, some £26,000, would be honoured. Had he realised the nature of the man to whom he made this extravagant offer, he might have reconsidered, but Maxwell was in the throes of preparing Pergamon for sale to Saul Steinberg, so made little of it, except to put it in the books as an asset, which, properly, it was. When Gregory later read the DTI report on the man to whom he had undertaken to pay £26,000 in order to recover his own £10,000, he gave thanks to providence. It was an expensive way to recover money at the shortest possible odds, but it worked, and under his benign eye, and that of Ted Sperrin, the retained Managing Director, Wells Gardner flourished. He considered other acquisitions, but Paul Raymond beat him to it, although he gave Wells Gardner the distribution deal for *Men Only* and a few other choice titles. Not Ken Gregory, pornographer, but Ken Gregory, distributor of same, despite his more than slight surprise at the overhaul of these pedestrian titles which Raymond had put in train. By the end of 1971 the disparate net assets of Gregory's various holdings and enterprises were well over a million pounds. Result, Micawberish happiness.

Almost as pleasing was the fact that Gregory's relations with Moss were fully repaired and by now cordial. Stirling's bemused admiration for the way which Gregory's business had survived the hijack, the Bristol Street episode, as well as the success with which he had parlayed a busted magazine into a mini-empire worth so much, was total. He had not been idle since motor racing had stopped for him, either. His own businesses, which covered areas as diverse as gem trading (but not with Masten Gregory) and public relations, wrapped around a core of real estate speculation, were reaping benefits from the boom which was just starting. The two men started to meet more regularly and compare notes. It was clear to Gregory from these and other meetings that other people were having rather a lot more fun than he was. Figures like John Bentley, Jim Slater, Peter Walker and Christopher Selmes, not to mention his old chums Hanson and White, who were in the process of renaming the Wiles Group as Hanson Trust, were having the time of their lives and Ken was minded to change direction somewhat, to join in the fun. In doing so, he made an error which is second only to a military commander splitting his forces. He abandoned one of his core businesses.

He decided, upon approach from Link House publications, to unload some of his magazine businesses. He would keep Wells, Gardner, but sell *Car and Car Conversions*, the flagship title of Speed and Sports Publications Ltd. The sale took place in the first week of January, 1972. He received £300,000 for this title, and was well-pleased. He considered what was best to be done with the money and decided that, as the market was clearly steaming north, a little leverage might be in order. Leverage, to the investor, is the pledging of one asset, in this case Link House's cash, in exchange for loans with which to buy other assets. If the performance of those new assets outstrip the cost of funding, then there is a further Micawberish satisfaction about the process. If the reverse happens, it is worse – much worse. No matter, the bank rate was 5 per cent. What could go wrong?

He regrouped his assets into a holding company, Burke House Holdings Ltd. In the event, but only with hindsight, it was aptly named, for in 1972, Kenneth Albert Gregory, pilot, airline operator, racing driver, manager, businessman and publisher, discovered the economic phenomenon known as leverage. It was to be a mistake.

Chapter 19

EXIT, PURSUED BY A BEAR

*'All you need in this life is ignorance and
confidence; then success is sure.'*
MARK TWAIN, 1887

To say that Link House's money was burning a hole in Ken
Gregory's well-tailored pocket would, in the light of subsequent events, be something of an understatement. He head-
quartered his new holding company in an elegant seven-
teenth-century converted coach house in Beaconsfield,
Buckinghamshire. Then, he went shopping.

First, he called on some friendly bankers, Coutts and
Company, who happily loaned Burke House £300,000.
National Westminster, who were later to buy Coutts for reasons not unassociated with subsequent events, stumped up
£250,000. His old friends at UDT, pleased to see him after so
long, contributed another quarter million, an amount
which Slater Walker Finance, who had funded many of the
Gregory Air fleet, matched. In a matter of weeks, Gregory
accumulated over £1.25 million in debt. That, dear reader,
is leverage.

After its dump during the Wilson years, the market was
doing rather well. The *Financial Times* 30-share index had,
by the time Gregory had finished tapping his bankers,
already climbed from around 320 to 400. Clearly, it was a
bull market again. Real estate was doing even better. A more
seasoned operator than Gregory, when told proudly by
someone, possibly his stock broker at Tustain Lestrange,
that more than the entire GDP of the nation was now committed to real estate development, might have measured the

distance to the door and politely requested his hat and coat; but he was not a seasoned operator. The business he had conducted for Moss, through stockbrokers Vickers da Costa, who, it must be said, survived rather longer than Tustain's, was small beer compared to what he was doing now.

After such a volatile and prolonged decline in common stocks, most of the brains in the City were in the Bond market, not the equity market. There were operators in equities who knew as little about the workings of the real economy as plankton knows about the food chain. They understood weight of money, though, and this is what drove that extraordinary episode in British financial history which became known as the secondary banking crisis, or, if you were in it, the 1974 property crash.

Gregory's arrogance with his lenders was as breathtaking as their naïvety. He would pick the investments, he alone would vet them, and their security would be the value of the investments themselves; they accepted. They were doing it, too, with their depositor's money, and lending was their business. Besides, Gregory seemed to know as much as they did, as the market, and thus indirectly the economy, seemed to have come out of the shadows.

Everyone was at it. The febrile regulation of the City of London, which could well be summed up as 'I'm all right, Jack', almost ensured that speculative fevers, or 'fundamental repricings', as they are called, could be financed relatively easily by a host of secondary or tertiary banks who were not subject to scrutiny by the Bank of England. Many of these 'banks' were little more than leveraged share and real estate speculators like Gregory was about to become, who drew down their funds, for on-lending or proprietary speculation, from the major high street banks or a gullible public hooked by their high deposit rates. No-one thought overmuch about actually looking at their operations – the study of liquidity ratios, the broad definition of this being the ability of banks to pay out depositors should the need arise, was as an obsession, a thing of the future, as the City mandarins beamed down at the sight of so many of their boys doing so well. So did the government – the very thought of acting to cool this economy, for so long in the grip of fiscal illiterates, would surely consign the entire Treasury to the tumbrels. There was no obvious benefit of appealing to the property developers for restraint, either; better to ask a piranha fish to a hunger lunch. They sat back to watch the fun.

The Barber boom, so called after the Chancellor of the day, was in full swing. As tax exiles returned, fit, tanned and at long last solvent in their own country, they were greeted as the harbingers of finer weather to come by the twitchers on the financial pages. No Sunday supplement was considered editorially complete without a profile of some kipper-tie'd financial Solon holding forth from the back seat of his new Roller on the secrets of investment serenity. In the words of the man who tried to corner the Wolfram market on borrowed money, 'It all seemed like a frightfully good idea at the time.'

The key to the equity market was a technique which became known as asset stripping. It was very simple. The value of a given corporation was, upon close inspection, found to be far higher than the hammered stock market had stated it to be, so that a disparate group with a languishing stock price could be bought and broken up into its constituent parts and sold piecemeal, the purpose being to actually acquire the core business for as little as possible. The newly cleaned-up businesses would be amalgamated into a new conglomerate with little fat attached. The core of the strategy involved take-overs which utilised a high stock price which would obviate the use of cash when making an acquisition. It was and is a momentum-driven business, and relies upon a positive market rating for the shares of the aggressor company – a high price/earnings ratio. In breaking up the acquired corporation, obviously, job losses are involved, and the plundering and reinvestment of an over-funded pension scheme ('well, the market's up, isn't it, they won't need all that') was mandatory, which gave the practice a rather bad name. The bull market of 1970-72 did nothing less than introduce a startled British public to a set of attitudes which would later be called Thatcherism, but was really not invented by the Iron Lady, but rather by that group of people who for a few years, set the market on fire.

Every rheumy-eyed old dog, dozing by a fire stoked loyally by patient shareholders, suddenly became a potential bid target. Even today, tales are told of deals done on the back on a fag packet in Annabel's night-club, whereby whole city blocks, prised away from their unsuspecting owners, long depressed by the sluggish economy, were punted out within hours for twice as much, to be broken up and resold for twice as much again. It was, in short, new money chasing out old, and Slater Walker and their peers were the high priests of this new religion of efficiency.

Jim Slater had formed Slater Walker in 1964 by the acquisition of Productafoam Ltd. With this vehicle, he acquired control of H. Lotery and Co., which had one asset, an office block. He sold it at a huge premium to its tenants, P&O, and he was off. By 1972, Slater Walker's market capitalisation was £200,000,000 and its shares were trading on a Price/Earnings ratio of more that 25:1, or about double the average market levels. With such expensive and well-performing stock, Slater was able to effectively swap Slater

Walker stock for more languid performers, strip them out, take the cash and grow exponentially. It is fair to say that the activities of Jim Slater, Jimmy Goldsmith, John Bentley and others really prepared Britain for the 1980s. Corporations were slimmed down, efficiency grew, return on capital improved. Slater, a slightly diffident, rather suburban man with a mild fixation for alternative medicine, was, without doubt, one of the most inspired financiers of the century.

For a while, it was great fun. There seemed to be a levelling up which, properly, wealth and success provided while socialism had not. Ex-barrow boys were tolerated at, or even welcomed into, clubs which not three years before would have turned them out. Certifiable idiots were making more money that they had ever thought possible, as a whole economy, freed from the dead hand of thinly-disguised central planning, as an insect from its cocoon, woke up, blinked, stretched, roared and bought stocks. But timing is all.

Ken Gregory, his pockets bulging with money, considered his investment strategy. It had three prongs – real estate, stocks and works of art. He bought some marvellous paintings, mainly through the offices of Bill Patterson, an Albermarle Street dealer, and David Mason of Duke Street.

In the City it had not gone unnoticed that monetary policy was being tightened in response to the credit boom and attendant asset price inflation, and the smart money was leaving as the bull market lost momentum. Jim Slater recalled turning cautiously bearish on the market in the first quarter of 1972, and Slater Walker started to unload its quoted investments on the stock market to revert to bricks and mortar. He was right to sell stocks, but as he disarmingly admits, he too failed to spot the overbought state of the property market. It was to be his undoing. Others were more forthright. Jimmy Goldsmith, displaying the same unerring sense of timing which was to save him in the summer of 1987, unloaded everything. By May 1972 the FT30 index had topped out at 543 and by the end of the year had shed 20 per cent of its value, which was uneasy news, but not as sad for Ken Gregory as the news that Alfred Moss, Gregory's surrogate father, had died of cancer in the autumn.

The market was finally hammered by the Yom Kippur War in October 1973. A concentrated Arab assault upon the state of Israel, which, just like the previous one, failed, produced an embargo from Arab oil exporters upon those states deemed to be pro-Israel. The price of oil, long languishing at an artificially low price, went vertically up, and another fundamental repricing took place at the expense of already wobbly asset values in the West.

Real estate, illiquid and unstoppable except by its own momentum, continued to fare well, though; but as the bank rate inexorably squeezed up towards its final level of 13 per cent to head off the inflation which oil inflation would surely bring, the stock market collapsed. By the last day of 1974, the FT30 had sunk to 146, far below the lowest level under Wilson's government and, by comparison, lower than it had been in 1940, as British troops were being evacuated by boat from Dunkirk. Using the same analysis, the FT30, at the time of writing, is now worth about 2500. The reason was that the property market, which had apparently been more resilient than most asset classes, had finally crashed. Leveraged investors, unable to sell in a nose-diving market, were wiped out for years. A curious trader at Ackroyd and Smithers, the stockjobbers, worked out on the back of an envelope that if this continued, the stock market could quite reasonably be expected to have negative value.

In fact, the real estate market had started to wobble as soon as the stock market had. However, whereas shares have a posted 'clearing' price at the close of business every day, a building does not. Valuing a building is the job of a surveyor, and a surveyor, unlike an auditor, is often in thrall to his customer, and reluctant to be pessimistic about real estate values even when it is clear that the market as a whole is in deep trouble. Only when tenants cannot pay their rent does the market really worry. Thus it was that the property crash was delayed, just as it was after the 1987 equity crash. It only became clear, when some of the smaller operators went into receivership, that there were, literally, no buyers. The real estate market was 'in denial' as the psychologists would have it. The suicide rate rose sharply. With that dreadful irony which is the characteristic of markets, the end of 1974 was, of course, the very low point. By Easter of 1975 the market had doubled. It was too late for most, including Slater and Gregory.

Huge bankruptcies had been created; the leveraged play had failed. Household names then, but long-forgotten now, were, in Slater's own words, dropping like flies. Vavasseur, Jessel, First National, Cannon Street Investments, Triumph Investment Trust – all dust. Investors were left holding assets which were worth a fraction of the debts which had been raised to buy them, and their gearing, loosely defined as the ratio of debt to equity on the balance sheet of UK Ltd had gone through the roof. The Bank of England was forced to act to support, not the secondary banks, but the big ones, all of whom suffered massively through their lending strategies. It was the end of nineteenth-century banking. Edward Heath, traumatised by these events, and really rather more concerned with his ambitions to join the Common Market, called a snap election in February 1974, and came predictably second. A Labour government returned, finger-wagging at the previous excesses of the City, and attempted to address the issues. They were to fail, which was unsurprising, and were later compelled to go to the IMF for emergency loans. The real estate market continued to plunge in money terms, but the emerging oil-driven inflation which was gripping the country appeared to protect the outright value of property. For those who could afford to hang on, the devaluation of money, particularly debts, offset against assets which were at best holding steady, seemed to be the only way out. Certainly it was for Gregory. He sat down at the beginning of 1974 and worked out his losses. They were horrendous, easily equal to his debts, which of course he still owed.

He owed the value of one hundred Aston Martins, and he had lost the value of one hundred more. From being in a position of some strength at the start of 1972, call it thirty Aston Martins, he was now well and truly in the glue. In today's money, using the Aston Martin as a currency, he owed something in the order of £30,000,000. He would work his way out of it, but not for 12 more years. More than once his skill as a deal-maker would save him from total oblivion, but it would be hard work.

The art collection had to go. He called Bill Patterson and the pair trudged off to Amsterdam in May 1974, where so many of the pictures had originated anyway. One glance at the denizens of the hotel bar, huddled together as they were like a covey of grouse in front of the beaters, convinced Patterson that this was going to be a copper-bottomed disaster. He had never seen the owners of so many pictures queuing up to sell in one place at the same time. Mentally, Patterson calculated his own financial position – there would be some bargains here. The quality and quantity of work on offer made the walls of the National Gallery look more like the railings on the Bayswater Road.

In Amsterdam, Ken ran into Masten Gregory, the buyer of BRP's last two racing cars. The two had not met since then and Masten, now based in Rome, had become a diamond dealer – perhaps a strange occupation for a Le Mans winner. For want of anything else about which to talk, they discussed motor racing. It was clear to both of them that it had changed, vastly, and while Masten Gregory clearly missed it, Ken Gregory did not. Racing had changed in one respect by the early seventies in that everyone now had sponsors and the cars were prepared to resemble advertising billboards rather than racers, with the exception of Ferrari, whose cars were still proudly scarlet. These two men with the same surname, from totally different ends of the sport, went on to discuss those who had come and gone since the end of the BRP. The list was as vast as the changes: Bonnier, Revson, Rindt, Rodriguez, Courage, Williamson, Spence, Cevert. Ken learned that Willy Mairesse had committed suicide in Ostend and that David Murray had died in a car crash in the Canaries, and he felt hardly a pang for the old days, despite the dire financial crisis in which he found himself now. Masten did not seem to be doing so well, either, particularly when the bill arrived, whereupon he performed the Kansas City pocket-slapping dance, having yet again apparently forgotten his wallet, so Ken paid for dinner, which he could ill afford to do, and the two men parted. Ken turned his attention to the upcoming sale.

Patterson, a leading expert in Dutch paintings knew his business and was absolutely right. The paintings which actually were sold went for decent prices, but that accounted for only two of them. As Gregory watched his fine collection of seventeenth- and eighteenth-century Dutch pictures go under the hammer to be 'bought in' he became more and more apprehensive. It was clear that this market, too, was in a state of collapse, at least against the reserve figures put upon them, and that his cash flow problems were not going to be eased at all. Ironically, the auctioneers, Mak van Waay, were conducting their last sale as an independent before they fell into British hands and had been keen to match their previous effort, at Christmas 1973, which had broken all records.

The time had come to be practical. On the advice of a friendly partner in Arthur Andersen's, the accountants, he consolidated the disparate borrowings into one loan, from Barclays Bank, and addressed the issue of putting Burke House Holdings back on its feet. It was to be an exhausting task.

The situation was not desperate, not yet. Certainly, both he and the firm were burdened with a vast amount of debt, which was costing in the region of 20 per cent per annum in interest alone, but this was easily matched by inflation as the buying power of money collapsed. Each part of Burke House had their own borrowings, secured on their own cash flows, and were mutually supportive. The net borrowing of all the members of the holding group was what the interest was charged upon. It was a perilous situation; if one went down, the rest would probably go, too. Prior to the consolidation, the disparate parts of Burke House Holdings had been servicing both principal and interest, but Gregory found to his consternation that Barclays viewed it rather differently – Burke House was but one borrower now that the rules had changed. This toughness on the part of the banks, albeit too late, and, of course, right at the bottom of the market, did for Jim Slater as well. In 1975 he was to be forced to resign from the firm which he had started, and his place was taken by James Goldsmith, whose market timing, considered by many to be insane in the heady days of 1972, was the making of him.

More sorrow came on Sunday, 30 November 1975. Gregory received a call from his old friend Peter Jopp, who told him that Graham Hill had died in an aeroplane crash near Elstree. He had been piloting his own Piper and had come down on a golf course at Arkeley in thick fog. With him died Tony Brise, Hill's upcoming driver, and four members of the Embassy/Hill Formula 1 team. They had been flying back from the Paul Ricard circuit in France after practice. Hill, who had won the World Championship twice, in 1962 for BRM, and 1968 for Lotus, and taken the mantle of Britain's Mr Motor Racing after the death of Jim Clark and the retirement of Jackie Stewart. His loss was to be seen as a national tragedy.

It was more of a tragedy for his wife and three children, of course, and when the information filtered out that all had not been as it should be concerning the insurance aspects of Hill's crash, their loss was compounded by the prospect of real financial hardship. Gregory invited Bette, Damon, Samantha and Brigitte to his villa on Menorca in the spring of 1976, so that they might have a chance to be on their own.

Now that the great crash was over, Gregory regrouped and concentrated. The businesses were going well, and the Thatcher victory in the 1979 election offered the possibility of a slightly better economy, even though BHH was still handicapped by its borrowings. He had finally sold the balance of the pictures, but the interest on the loans had effectively doubled their cost. Interest rates were starting to come down as inflation gradually receded, and although the popularity of the Tory government was as low as it could be, the business climate was undeniably better. Then Ted Sperrin, the skilled managing director of Wells Gardner, the cash cow, had a heart attack.

The hiring of his replacement was probably a mistake, in the light of what then happened. In order to boost sales, Wells Gardner started offering more generous payment terms to its clients, with disastrous consequences on the cash flow of not only Wells Gardner, but the rest of BHH as well. Within one year, the cash cow had started to dry up.

Barclays started getting seriously tough in 1983. Burke House still appeared to be trading its way toward solvency, but the borrowings were in reality going up again. Gregory was obliged to issue a £200,000 personal guarantee for any increase in the firm's borrowings over their limit, which had been firmly frozen. Eventually the bank decided to call in a receiver to Wells Gardner, which was holding the cash flow of Burke House Holdings together. To refuse to extend facilities further would destroy all the other businesses, but basically Barclays wanted its money back and there was nothing Gregory could do about it. It was a rather larger replay of the Air Gregory episode. The initial report on Wells Gardner, for which Gregory, as group chairman was not even interviewed, is not a learned piece of work by any means, as potential receivers often indulge in a sort of lip-smacking emphasis of the negative. However, the issue appears to have been a fait accompli, as receiverships often are, particularly when the trigger is pulled by the senior lender rather than the company itself. That, after all, is how receivers get business. A good parallel in the garage trade might be, accompanied by much sucking of teeth: 'Sorry, guv, the engine's had it.'

Of the eight companies in the Burke House Holdings Group, all bar one, Burke House Periodicals, were put into liquidation. Gregory, working for the receiver in running the only business left intact, was quick to point out that the value of the goodwill of the periodicals in the larger group balance sheet was a mere £40,000, whereas, he reasoned, the real figure was more like £500,000. The receivers, and the bank, were sceptical, as they often are in these situations, and maintained that it was worth nothing. Gregory was then asked to sign a three-year non-competition agreement by the receivers so that they could attempt sell the magazines, which were *Auto Accessory Retailer* and *Automotive & Commercial Refinisher*, and, not unnaturally, he refused. (The other main asset was the right to stage the well-known trade show Autopartac.) Gregory knew full well that the value which he put on the goodwill of the separate businesses was closer to the reality than the receivers could realise, because he had, in the past, been approached on several occasions to sell the titles. He had also already been approached by one of Burke House Periodicals' biggest rivals, *Car and Accessory Trader*, with an offer of employment, and to sign the non-competition agreement would have put him out of the business completely while 'his' company was knocked down at a fire sale price. There was an impasse.

He broke it by suggesting that the periodicals were sold to him. It was audacious, as he had less than no money, but it broke the deadlock over the non-competition clause and allowed him to make a substantial turn when he sold the business to Morgan Grampian in the summer of 1984. At the same meeting, Burke House periodicals was sold to him, and he sold it to Morgan Grampian, who were sitting across the table. The profit? Coincidentally, it was the exact amount which he had said the goodwill of merely one title was worth, £250,000. He was also offered, and accepted, a consultancy by the new owners. It was, he reasoned, the most significant piece of negotiating that he had ever done and it included securing the financial future of his printer for whom he negotiated a further twelve month contract with Morgan Grampian. It finally got him off the hook, for with the final disposal of the titles the liquidation was over. He was no longer obliged to maintain his personal guarantee to Barclays.

There were several trade creditors to be paid, including a large printers bill, and he paid it off with his personal profit from the deal with Morgan Grampian. After paying sundry other personal creditors, tailor's bills really, he was back to exactly the financial status which he had had in 1970.

His second marriage had collapsed under the strain of all this and he was once again faced with the prospect, at nearly 60, of rebuilding his life again. He had paid off every penny which he owed, and although Barclays were left with egg on their faces, that, he rationalised, was hardly his fault. He, after all, was personally left with very little. Perhaps, naïvely, Gregory was of the view that his repayment record merited better treatment than was meted out to him. Perhaps it did, but it was not a view shared by Stoy Hayward, the authors of the report which had triggered the bank's hard stance. Like almost everything else in life, it could all have turned out very differently.

The strain on him was so vast that for the first and only time in his life, he contemplated, albeit briefly, the way out which had been taken, after several attempts, by Willy Mairesse. But if in motor racing he had made rivals, even enemies, he was pleased to find that his career in publishing had left him with some fine friends. The agonising saga of Burke House was well-known within the trade and it was not long – a matter of days, in fact – before one of the biggest advertising accounts contacted him. Basically, he was offered the use of a free line of credit to use as he saw fit. But the moral support which he was offered was even more useful, for it literally brought him back from the edge.

One of the most supportive people was Keith Jeffrey of Creative Print and Design – the firm which has printed this book. Jeffrey, who had been under considerable pressure himself, not only offered Gregory financial assistance, but talked to him repeatedly into the wee small hours, encouraging, reviewing, supporting. Gregory, under Jeffrey's calm wing, realised that he had more markers out, both professionally and personally, in business than he had ever realised, and the willingness of his fellow businessmen, many of whom had struggled like him, to honour them unilaterally went a long way to restoring his faith in human nature, which had taken several hard knocks.

Stirling Moss rallied round as well, offering him a loan to tide him over. It was gratefully accepted and over a period of a few long weeks and months, Ken Gregory came back to normal; back to being organised, imaginative, and busy. Gradually, he rebuilt his life – he relocated to the north-east, remarried and eased back into publishing. He had met the editor of *The Sunday Sun* and, fortunately, he was short of a motoring correspondent. The previous incumbent had resigned to become director of Public Relations at Octav Bottner's Nissan UK, so Gregory took over the task. Soon, he was filling up to three pages a week. He launched the north-east annual Car of the Year awards, which, in the consumerist 1980s, became a huge success, the largest regional car award show in the country. A change of editor at *The Sunday Sun* brought with it a clash of personalities, which did not go unnoticed at the headquarters of Thomson

Regional Newspapers, and he was then offered the motoring correspondent's job at *The Journal*, the group's regional daily broadsheet. One of his most successful ventures was *Autofocus*, a quarterly supplement, also published by Thomson Regional Newspapers – edited by him, and carried by *The Scotsman, Scotland on Sunday, Aberdeen Press & Journal, The Belfast Telegraph, The Western Mail* and *The Journal* – which hit circulation approaching 600,000 by the middle of the 1990s. He was also offered, and accepted, the chairmanship of a London-based Public Relations company, Campaign Marketing Services Ltd. To no-one's surprise, it is flourishing.

As this book was being finished, we talked about the sport, its changes, its priorities, cast into sharp relief by the announcement that Bernie Ecclestone, in many ways Ken Gregory's successor, has put some of his commercial interests in Formula 1 up for sale.

Inevitably, the subject of the best drivers comes up. As a pivotal figure in the sport, perhaps his opinion is worth reading. While all lists are necessarily subjective, and this is not exclusively to do with Formula 1, Gregory's top ten, from 1950 to 1970, is in alphabetical order: Alberto Ascari, Jean Behra, Jim Clark, Juan Manuel Fangio, Froilan Gonzales, Phil Hill, Bruce McLaren, Stirling Moss, Jackie Stewart, John Surtees. Casting a wider net, Chris Bristow and Stuart Lewis-Evans would certainly be there, as would Tony Brooks, Peter Collins and, pleasingly for this writer, Archie Scott Brown. Bring it up to date, then Senna, Schumacher, Villeneuve and Damon Hill would obviously be there. But the best? Ever? By rather more than a short and bald head, Stirling Craufurd Moss.

Epilogue

This book has been about the meeting of motor sport and business and how that process came about. The parts played by Ken Gregory, Alfred and Stirling Moss, the Samengo-Turners, UDT, Reg Parnell, Colin Chapman and the fuel companies is a story of the democratisation of what had been, with a few exceptions, purely a gent's sport. Under the eye of Bernie Ecclestone and others, Formula 1 has, after that initial impetus, come a long way – not so much a sport, as Stirling Moss says, but a great occasion, none the less.

If you stroll round Goodwood circuit, near Chichester in West Sussex, which is rather difficult now that it is so busy, you can still feel with your foot the drainage gully which undid Stirling Moss so comprehensively that day in 1962 and literally bounced him out of racing. As Goodwood gradually emerges again as a racing circuit, an event only recently sanctioned, perhaps someone will have the presence of mind to fill the wretched thing in properly before some poor scribbler breaks an ankle.

If the ghosts of Schell, Bristow, Bueb, Collins, Lewis-Evans, Stacey and all the others are looking down, then it may be some comfort to them to know that they are not forgotten, certainly not by the people who helped me to write this book, and that the parts they played, willingly or not, laid the groundwork for the development of an industry which has no peer in history. It is, while the petrol (and the sponsorship money) lasts, simply the biggest spectator sport on the planet.

Abbey curve at Silverstone, where Harry Schell died, was removed in 1984, but the building in Buckingham where a traumatised Ken Gregory identified his body is still there.

Burneville, where Bristow died so horribly, and Stirling Moss nearly did, is no longer a part of the Spa circuit, and the Nürburgring, where Onofre Marimon, Peter Collins and many others met their ends, is no longer used in the form in which it appeared in this book. A smaller, safer track is now the site of the German Grand Prix. From time to time, motoring journalists take one or other of the great cars, usually a Mercedes, around the old Nürburgring and, rather predictably, mourn its passing. This writer is not so sure.

The Mille Miglia was banned, under pressure from the Vatican, after the 1957 race which killed Portago and all the others. It is still run as a rather pallid historic event, and Moss and Jenkinson's record is happily safe for ever. One by one the great races disappeared. The only one left in Europe now is Le Mans, which is altogether safer than it was in 1955.

Duke's Head Yard, in Highgate, where Tony Robinson built the marvellous monocoque BRP cars, is, appropriately enough the headquarters of a car dealer, Hexagon of Highgate. Tony lives not far away, as North London has always been his back yard; indeed, he strolls past it from time to time. To Tony Robinson, Ken Gregory is still 'The Boss'; to Ken Gregory, Tony Robinson is still a genius.

The room at Royal Victoria Hospital, East Grinstead, where Sir Archibald McIndoe worked so hard and poor Stuart Lewis-Evans died, so brave and uncomplaining, is still there and indeed is still a medical facility, although it is no longer a burns unit, but an orthodontic surgery. This writer's daughter has had treatment there.

Alf Francis died in 1980. His old employer, Rob Walker, still lives in Somerset, where he always has, and contributes regular columns to automotive journals. He and Moss are still the best of friends and treasure their association.

Stirling Moss is still Stirling Moss. The same quick, quiet voice, the same Flashman-like self-knowledge, the same house in Shepherd Street. 'Everywhere is a suburb of London,' he once airily declared, and he practises what he preaches. He is still ferociously busy 'flogging a fading image', as he puts it, and he still finds it hard to sit still. Stirling Moss also still drives a Mercedes. When I met Moss in the autumn of 1996, his first words were: 'You do realise, don't you, boy, that if Ken Gregory was still managing me, you'd be paying for this?' I did, indeed; maybe, after researching this book, rather more than he did.

Fading image? Nonsense. If you are stopped for speeding, an ever more likely event now that the motor car has made criminals of us all, the question you are still most likely to be asked is 'Who do you think you are, Stirling Moss?' This from a policeman who was probably not even born when these events took place. It has, as a truculent cop's challenge, passed into the language, and will probably stay there. I rather hope it does. One young chap was asked it in the north of England in 1992. He replied: 'No, actually, I'm Ayrton Senna.' He was, too. It meant nothing to the policeman, although Senna was actually World Champion at the time.

If you walk down Baker Street in London's West End, the branch of Barclays Bank which undid Ken Gregory so comprehensively and bounced him out of business is still there. It was an unavoidable episode, just commerce, but he is still a little cross about it.

Ken and Julie Gregory live in a delightful complex of converted farm buildings not far from Hadrian's Wall in Northumberland, much of which he restored himself. Despite the ravages of the property crash, he is still very good at real estate and, surprisingly, given what he has been through, experiences which would have broken some, and nearly broke him, has few misgivings about his extraordinary life. Those he has are exclusively about people. Only in a war does a man lose so many friends. He still misses Harry Schell, Chris Bristow, Stuart Lewis-Evans, Ivor Bueb, Peter Collins and the others, and will probably never really come to terms with their passing. He still finds motor racing pleasing, though, now that it is safer. He is a Damon Hill fan.

His hobbies now revolve around fly-fishing and field sports, at which he is a polished practitioner. He cooks the results quite superbly. He no longer actively collects oil paintings, but in his study, on the left as you go in, there are just a few, the most striking of which is by Roy Nockolds of Stirling Moss, blasting down the Thillois straight at Reims in the height of summer 1959, in the meadow-green British Racing Partnership BRM. You can almost hear it.

Appendix I

THE BRP RACING CARS

All in all, the British Racing Partnership designed and constructed a total of five single-seater racing cars, three for Formula 1 World Championship Grands Prix and two for the 1965 Indianapolis 500-mile race.

Chassis Histories

BRP 1/63. Completed May 1963, fitted with V8 BRM engine and five speed Colotti gearbox. First outing, driven by Innes Ireland, Belgian Grand Prix, Spa, 9 June 1963. Sold in 1966 to Tim Parnell, who sold it on in August to Alf Francis, who was by then working for Count Volpi's Scuderia Serenissima in Modena. Volpi had commissioned, from Albert Massimino, a 3-litre 4-cam V8 engine and transmission. The engine and transmission were fitted to BRP 1/63, which necessitated cutting the rear part of the monocoque away and substituting a relatively crude frame. Other modifications included the fitting of a divided de Dion rear suspension and extremely crude front wishbones. The car was painted bright yellow and never competed. It was sold, as a Serenissima Formula 1 car, to an Egon Hofer of Salzburg and was subsequently stolen. The car was rumoured to be in Scandinavia in the early 1980s, but, even if it should be found, it is no longer a BRP machine except for a handful of rivets.

BRP 2/64. Completed March 1964, fitted with V8 BRM engine and six-speed BRM gearbox. First outing, driven by Innes Ireland, BARC 200, Aintree, 18 April 1964. This car was distinctively narrower than BRP 1/63. Sold in 1966 to

John Willment Automobiles. It was fitted with a Coventry Climax V8 supplied by Paul Emery. Tony Robinson assisted in the conversion. The new set-up was tested at Silverstone on 13 September by Tony Dean and entered in the Oulton Park Gold Cup on 19 September driven by John Campbell Jones. From Willment, the car went to K. Griffiths, who fitted a Ford V8 engine for Formula 5000 events. Griffiths shipped it to New Zealand for the 1969 and 1970 Tasman series.

The car did not go back to the UK, possibly having been damaged, and was discovered in the 1980s on the back of a lorry by Ferris de Joux, a New Zealander, who undertook a full restoration of the car, which included re-uniting it with its original engine block. The car was brought back to the UK around 1990 and sold to the late collector, Anthony Mayman, for a sum not unadjacent to £100,000. At the sale of Mayman's cars in 1993 it passed to Hall and Fowler, of Lincolnshire. It seems that BRP 2/64 is the only complete example of the three BRP Formula 1 cars which can be traced.

BRP 3/64. Completed June 1964, fitted with V8 BRM engine and six-speed BRM transmission. First outing, driven by Trevor Taylor, practice for the Belgian Grand Prix, Spa, 14 June 1964. Did not start. First race, French Grand Prix, Rouen, 28 June 1964 (retired). SMART entered the car for the South African Grand Prix, 1 January 1966, driven by Ritchie Ginther and damaged. Brought back to England and repaired by SMART before being sold to Tim Parnell and delivered to Italy with BRP 1/63 in August 1966. The car was used in the John Frankenheimer film Grand Prix; possibly it was used in race sequences, but more likely it was cut in half, fitted with a tow bar and used as a reverse shot camera stand. It is known that the racing driver Jo Siffert bought many of the cars used in the film, but it is not known whether or not the remains of BRP 3/64 was one of them.

BRP 4/65 and *BRP 5/65* were the two 1965 Indianapolis 500 cars, built to the order of George Bryant. Completed in March 1965 and delivered to George Salih at Indianapolis. Fitted with 4.2-litre Ford V8 engines and 5-speed ZF transmissions. First outings, Indianapolis 500, 1965, driven by Masten Gregory and Jimmy Lloyd. Neither finished. It is known that they competed there again in 1966, although not, I think entered by Bryant, and were involved with the huge pile-up, but apart from that, little or nothing is known of their subsequent careers. One of them, at the time of writing, resides in the Speedway Museum at Indianapolis, Indiana. The other, it seems, is lost.

If it seems odd to contemporary eyes that such torture and abuse could be meted out to such fine cars, then it must be borne in mind that in the fast-changing world of racing in the 1960s, older or obsolete machinery was worth little, and often fell into the hands of the impecunious special-builder. It is only more recently that the importance of such vehicles has become appreciated, partly, of course, because of their rarity.

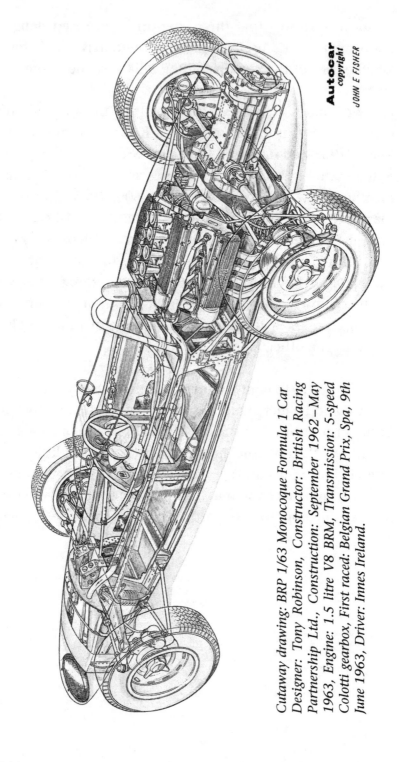

Cutaway drawing: BRP 1/63 Monocoque Formula 1 Car Designer: Tony Robinson, Constructor: British Racing Partnership Ltd., Construction: September 1962–May 1963, Engine: 1.5 litre V8 BRM, Transmission: 5-speed Colotti gearbox, First raced: Belgian Grand Prix, Spa, 9th June 1963, Driver: Innes Ireland.

Appendix II

RACING HISTORY

Schedule of events and results of the 278 cars entered by the British Racing Partnership in 160 races during the seven year period, 1958 to 1964.

Abbreviations Cra: Crashed Disq: Disqualified DNS: Did not start FL: Fastest lap FTQ: Failed to qualify
LR: Lap record NC: Finished but not classified OA: Overall position in a mixed class race
PP: Pole grid position Ret: Retired Wdr: Car withdrawn from race

1958 · BRITISH RACING PARTNERSHIP

Date	Event	Circuit	Driver	Car	Result
Apr 7th	Lavant Cup	Goodwood	Stuart Lewis-Evans	Cooper Climax	4th
Apr 7th	Glover Trophy	Goodwood	Tom Bridger	Cooper Climax	Cra
Apr 19th	Aintree 200	Aintree	Stuart Lewis-Evans	Cooper Climax F2 class	2nd/5th OA
May 3rd	International Trophy	Silverstone	Stuart Lewis-Evans	Cooper Climax F2 class	2nd/7th OA
May 18th	BRSCC F2 Race	Brands Hatch	Tom Bridger	Cooper Climax	5th
May 26th	Crystal Palace	Crystal Palace	Tom Bridger	Cooper Climax	2nd
Jun 8th	BRSCC F2 Race	Brands Hatch	Stuart Lewis-Evans	Cooper Climax	1st
Jul 6th	Coupe de Vitesse	Reims	Tom Bridger	Cooper Climax	8th
Jul 20th	Caen GP	Caen	Stuart Lewis-Evans	Cooper Climax F2 class	2nd/5th OA

Date	Event	Circuit	Driver	Car	Result
Jul 27th	Trophée D'Auvergne	Clermont Ferrand	Stuart Lewis-Evans	Cooper Climax	3rd
Aug 4th	Kent Trophy	Brands Hatch	Stuart Lewis-Evans	Cooper Climax	2nd
Aug 30th	Kentish 100	Brands Hatch	Stuart Lewis-Evans	Cooper Climax	3rd
Oct 19th	Morocco GP	Casablanca	Tom Bridger	Cooper Climax	Cra

1959 · BRITISH RACING PARTNERSHIP

Date	Event	Circuit	Driver	Car	Result
Mar 30th	Lavant Cup	Goodwood	Ivor Bueb George Wicken	Cooper Borgward Cooper Borgward	10th 12th
Apr 11th	Empire Trophy Race	Oulton Park	Ivor Bueb George Wicken	Cooper Borgward Cooper Borgward	3rd 15th
Apr 18th	BARC 200	Aintree	Ivor Bueb George Wicken	Cooper Borgward Cooper Borgward F2 class	Ret 4th/8th OA
Apr 25th	Syracuse GP	Syracuse	Ivor Bueb George Wicken	Cooper Borgward Cooper Borgward	5th 8th
May 2nd	International Trophy	Silverstone	Ivor Bueb	Cooper Borgward F2 class	2nd/8th OA
May 18th	London Trophy	Crystal Palace	Ivor Bueb George Wicken	Cooper Borgward Cooper Borgward	2nd 4th
May 5th	GP De L'ACF	Reims	Stirling Moss	BRM	Ret
Jul 5th	Coupe Int De Vitesse	Reims	Ivor Bueb Chris Bristow	Cooper Borgward Cooper Borgward	Ret Ret

Both drivers retired with heat exhaustion.

Date	Event	Circuit	Driver	Car	Result
Jul 12th	GP Rouen Les Essarts	Rouen	Ivor Bueb	Cooper Borgward	Ret
			Chris Bristow	Cooper Borgward	5th
Jul 18th	British GP	Aintree	Stirling Moss	BRM	2nd/Joint FL
			Ivor Bueb	Cooper Borgward F2 class	4th/14th OA
			Chris Bristow	Cooper Borgward F2 class	1st/10th OA
Jul 26th	Clermont Ferrand GP	Clermont Ferrand	Ivor Bueb	Cooper Borgward	Cra
			Chris Bristow	Cooper Borgward	Ret

Ivor Bueb crashed with fatal injuries.

Date	Event	Circuit	Driver	Car	Result
Aug 2nd	German GP	Berlin/Avus	Hans Herrmann	BRM	Cra
Aug 3rd	John Davy Trophy	Brands Hatch	Chris Bristow	Cooper Borgward	1st
Aug 29th	Kentish 100	Brands Hatch	Chris Bristow	Cooper Borgward	Ret
Sep 26th	Gold Cup Race	Oulton Park	Chris Bristow	Cooper Borgward	3rd
Oct 10th	Silver City Trophy	Snetterton	Chris Bristow	Cooper Borgward F2 class	1st/5th OA
Oct 18th	Libre GP	Watkins Glen, USA	Stirling Moss	Cooper Climax	1st/FL

1960 · YEOMAN CREDIT RACING TEAM

Date	Event	Circuit	Driver	Car	Result
Jan 1st	South African GP	East London	Chris Bristow	Cooper Climax	Ret

Date	Race	Circuit	Driver	Car	Result
Jan 1st	New Zealand GP Heat 1	Ardmore	Stirling Moss	Cooper Climax	1st/FL
	Heat 2		Stirling Moss	Cooper Climax	Ret/PP/FL
Jan 8th	False Bay 100	Cape Town	Chris Bristow	Cooper Borgward	1st/FL
Mar 19th	Syracuse GP	Syracuse	Harry Schell	Cooper Climax	7th
			Chris Bristow	Cooper Climax	Ret
Apr 2nd	Trophy Race	Oulton Park	Harry Schell	Cooper Climax	5th
			Chris Bristow	Cooper Climax	4th
Apr 8th	Brussels GP	Brussels	Harry Schell	Cooper Climax	4th
			Chris Bristow	Cooper Climax	Disq
Apr 18th	Lavant Cup	Goodwood	Harry Schell	Cooper Climax	8th
			Chris Bristow	Cooper Climax	4th
Apr 18th	Glover Trophy	Goodwood	Harry Schell	Cooper Climax	Ret
			Chris Bristow	Cooper Climax	3rd
Apr 30th	Aintree 200	Aintree	Harry Schell	Cooper Climax	8th
			Chris Bristow	Cooper Climax	6th
May 10th	Brusells GP	Brusells	Harry Schell	Cooper Climax	4th
			Chris Bristow	Cooper Climax	Disq
May 14th	Daily Express Trophy	Silverstone	Harry Schell	Cooper Climax	Cra
			Chris Bristow	Cooper Climax	Wdr

Harry Schell crashed in practice with fatal injuries. Cars withdrawn.

Date	Race	Circuit	Driver	Car	Result
May 29th	Monaco GP	Monte Carlo	Tony Brooks	Cooper Climax	4th
			Chris Bristow	Cooper Climax	Ret

MANAGING A LEGEND

Date	Event	Circuit	Driver	Car	Result
Jun 6th	Crystal Palace Trophy	Crystal Palace	Jack Sears	Cooper Climax	3rd/Joint FL
June 6th	Dutch GP	Zandvoort	Tony Brooks	Cooper Climax	Ret
			Chris Bristow	Cooper Climax	Ret
			Henry Taylor	Cooper Climax	7th
Jun 19th	Belgian GP	Spa	Olivier Gendebien	Cooper Climax	3rd
			Chris Bristow	Cooper Climax	Cra
			Tony Brooks	Cooper Climax	Ret

Chris Bristow crashed with fatal injuries.

Date	Event	Circuit	Driver	Car	Result
Jul 3rd	French GP	Reims	Olivier Gendebien	Cooper Climax	2nd
			Henry Taylor	Cooper Climax	4th
			Bruce Halford	Cooper Climax	8th
Jul 16th	British GP	Silverstone	Olivier Gendebien	Cooper Climax	9th
			Tony Brooks	Cooper Climax	5th
			Henry Taylor	Cooper Climax	8th
Aug 1st	Silver City Trophy	Brands Hatch	Tony Brooks	Cooper Climax	Ret
			Dan Gurney	Cooper Climax	7th
			Henry Taylor	Cooper Climax	5th
			Bruce Halford	Cooper Climax	8th
Aug 6th	Vanwall Trophy	Snetterton	Jack Sears	Cooper Climax	Ret
Aug 8th	Kannonloppet	Karlskoga, Sweden	Stirling Moss	Lotus Climax 19	1st/LR
Aug 14th	Portuguese GP	Oporto	Olivier Gendebien	Cooper Climax	7th
			Tony Brooks	Cooper Climax	5th
			Henry Taylor	Cooper Climax	Cra

Henry Taylor crashed in practice. Unable to start due to injuries received.

Date	Event	Location	Driver	Car	Result
Aug 28th	Kentish 100	Brands Hatch	Olivier Gendebien	Cooper Climax	Ret
Sep 17th	Lombank Trophy	Snetterton	Denny Hulme	Cooper Climax	5th
			Henry Taylor	Cooper Climax	10th

First ever F1 drive for Denny Hulme.

Date	Event	Location	Driver	Car	Result
Sep 24th	Int. Gold Cup	Oulton Park	Henry Taylor	Cooper Climax	7th
			Bruce Halford	Cooper Climax	8th
Oct 16th	LA Times GP	Riverside USA	Stirling Moss	Lotus 19 Climax	Ret/PP
Oct 23rd	Pacific GP	Laguna Seca USA	Stirling Moss	Lotus 19 Climax	1st/LR
Nov 11th	United States GP	Riverside	Olivier Gendebien	Cooper Climax	12th
			Tony Brooks	Cooper Climax	Ret
			Henry Taylor	Cooper Climax	14th
			Phil Hill	Cooper Climax	6th

1961 · UDT LAYSTALL RACING TEAM

Date	Event	Location	Driver	Car	Result
Mar 26th	Lombank Trophy	Snetterton	Henry Taylor	Lotus Climax	4th
			Cliff Allison	Lotus Climax	2nd
Apr 3rd	Glover Trophy	Goodwood	Henry Taylor	Lotus Climax	6th
			Cliff Allison	Lotus Climax	8th
	Sports Car Race	Goodwood	Stirling Moss	Lotus 19 Climax	1st
			Henry Taylor	Lotus 19 Climax	2nd/FL
			Cliff Allison	Lotus 19 Climax	Ret
	GT Race	Goodwood	Mike McKee	Lotus Elite	2nd 1300 Class

Date	Event	Location	Driver	Car	Result
Apr 9th	Brussels GP	Brussels	Henry Taylor	Lotus Climax	Ret
			Cliff Allison	Lotus Climax	5th
Apr 22nd	Aintree 200	Aintree	Henry Taylor	Lotus Climax	Ret
			Cliff Allison	Lotus Climax	15th
Apr 22nd	Sports Car Race	Aintree	Stirling Moss	Lotus 19 Climax	1st/FL/LR
			Henry Taylor	Lotus 19 Climax	3rd/PP
			Cliff Allison	Lotus 19 Climax	1st/5th OA/FL
				1500 class	
May 6th	International Trophy Race	Silverstone	Henry Taylor	Lotus Climax	4th
			Cliff Allison	Lotus Climax	NC
	Sports Car Race	Silverstone	Stirling Moss	Lotus 19 Climax	1st/PP/FL/LR
			Cliff Allison	Lotus 19 Climax	3rd
			Henry Taylor	Lotus 19 Climax	1st
				1500 Class	FL
May 14th	Monaco GP	Monte Carlo	Henry Taylor	Lotus Climax	FTQ
			Cliff Allison	Lotus Climax	8th
May 22nd	London Trophy Race	Crystal Palace	Henry Taylor	Lotus Climax	2nd
			Cliff Allison	Lotus Climax	8th
	Sports Car Race	Crystal Palace	Henry Taylor	Lotus 19 Climax	Ret
			Cliff Allison	Lotus 19 Climax	Ret
			Mike Parkes	Lotus 19 Climax	Ret
Jun 3rd	Silver City Trophy	Brands Hatch	Stirling Moss	Lotus Climax	1st/PP/FL
			Henry Taylor	Lotus Climax	8th
			Jo Bonnier	Lotus Climax	11th

New knock-on hubs were fitted for this event in preparation for the 1,000 Km Nürburgring race. The hubs proved to be faulty.

Date	Event	Circuit	Drivers	Car	Result
Jun 9/10	Le Mans 24 Hrs	Le Mans	Cliff Allison / Mike McKee	Lotus Elite 742cc	Ret

The car was forced to retire with a broken oil pump drive at 2am. At the time it was leading the Index of Performance by a handsome margin

Date	Event	Circuit	Drivers	Car	Result
Jun 18th	Belgian GP	Spa	Cliff Allison / Henry Taylor	Lotus Climax / Lotus Climax	DNS / DNS

Only one car was accepted for this event. As Allison crashed in practice, Taylor was unable to qualify.

Date	Event	Circuit	Drivers	Car	Result
Jun 19th	Players 200	Mosport Park	Stirling Moss	Lotus 19 Climax	1st/LR
Jul 2nd	French GP	Reims	Henry Taylor / Lucien Bianchi	Lotus Climax / Lotus Climax	10th / Ret

Fangio's protégé Juan Manuel Bordeo was given a trial run in practice. He equalled the lap times of the two team drivers. In a further trial at Goodwood with a Lotus Elite he was hospitalised as a result of an incident at St Mary's in which the car was written-off.

Date	Event	Circuit	Drivers	Car	Result
Jul 8th	British Empire Trophy	Silverstone	Henry Taylor / Bianchi/Taylor	Lotus Climax / Lotus Climax	Ret / 10th
Jul 15th	British GP	Silverstone	Henry Taylor / Lucien Bianchi	Lotus Climax / Lotus Climax	Cra / Ret
Jul 23rd	Solitude GP	Stuttgart	Stirling Moss	Lotus Climax	10th
Aug 7th	Guards Trophy Race	Brands Hatch	Masten Gregory / Dan Gurney	Lotus Climax / Lotus Climax	Cra / Ret
Aug 20th	Kanonloppet	Karlskoga, Sweden	Stirling Moss / G Hammerlund	Lotus Climax / Lotus Climax	1st / Cra

Date	Race	Location	Driver	Car	Result
Aug 26/27	Danish GP	Copenhagen	Stirling Moss	Lotus Climax	1st/PP/FL
			Masten Gregory	Lotus Climax	Ret
			Henry Taylor	Lotus Climax	5th
Sep 3rd	Modena GP	Modena	Masten Gregory	Lotus Climax	NC
			Henry Taylor	Lotus Climax	Ret
Sep 10th	Italian GP	Monza	Masten Gregory	Lotus Climax	Ret
			Henry Taylor	Lotus Climax	11th
Sep 23rd	Gold Cup Race	Oulton Park	Masten Gregory	Lotus Climax	5th
			Henry Taylor	Lotus Climax	8th
Oct 8th	United States GP	Watkins Glen	Masten Gregory	Lotus Climax	Ret
			Olivier Gendebien	Lotus Climax	11th
Oct 22nd	Pacific GP	Monterey, California	Stirling Moss	Lotus 19 Climax	1st
Dec 9th	Rand GP	Kyalami	Masten Gregory	Lotus Climax	Ret
Dec 17th	Natal GP	Durban	Stirling Moss	Lotus Climax	2nd/LR
			Masten Gregory	Lotus Climax	Ret
Dec 3/10	Nassau Speed Week	Nassau	Stirling Moss	Lotus 19 Climax	Ret
Dec 26th	South African GP	East London	Stirling Moss	Lotus Climax	2nd
			Masten Gregory	Lotus Climax	Ret

1962 · UDT LAYSTALL RACING TEAM

Date	Race	Location	Driver	Car	Result
Jan 2nd	Cape GP	Killarney, South Africa	Masten Gregory	Lotus Climax	4th

Date	Event	Location	Driver	Car	Result
Feb 11th	Daytona 3 Hours	Daytona, USA	Stirling Moss	Ferrari Berlinetta GT Class	1st/4th OA
			Innes Ireland	Ferrari Berlinetta	Ret

Combined GT & Sports Car event. Car entered by UDT Laystall/Luigi Chinetti North American Racing Team

Date	Event	Location	Driver	Car	Result
Mar 25th	GP D'Endurance	Sebring, Florida	Stirling Moss	Ferrari Berlinetta	Disq
			Innes Ireland		

After taking on fuel under the minimum permitted distance, the fuel tank seal was cut by an over-enthusiastic marshal during a pit stop and the car was disqualified.

Date	Event	Location	Driver	Car	Result
Apr 1st	European GP	Brussels	Innes Ireland	Lotus Climax	3rd
			Masten Gregory	Lotus Climax	Ret

Date	Event	Location	Driver	Car	Result
Apr 14th	Lombank Trophy	Snetterton	Stirling Moss	Lotus Climax	7th/PP/FL
			Innes Ireland	Lotus Climax	Ret
			Masten Gregory	Lotus Climax	Ret

Ireland & Gregory forced to retire after making contact on the first lap.

Date	Event	Location	Driver	Car	Result
Apr 23rd	International 100	Goodwood	Stirling Moss	Lotus Climax	Cra/PP/FL
			Innes Ireland	Lotus Climax	3rd
			Masten Gregory	Lotus Climax	5th

Stirling Moss crashed on the 36th lap. The cause of the accident has never been clearly established due to Moss having no memory of the actual incident, even to this day. Ken Gregory, UDT/Laystall team manager and Moss's manager provides the most likely answer to the cause in the text of this book.

Date	Race	Circuit	Driver	Car	Result
Apr 23rd	Sports GT Race	Goodwood	Stirling Moss	Ferrari GTO	Wdr

Car withdrawn due to Moss accident in previous event.

Date	Race	Circuit	Driver	Car	Result
Apr 23rd	Sussex Trophy	Goodwood	Innes Ireland	Lotus 19 Climax	1st/LR
Apr 28th	Aintree 200	Aintree	Innes Ireland	Lotus Climax	Ret
			Masten Gregory	Lotus Climax	Ret
Apr 28th	Sports Car Trophy Race	Aintree	Innes Ireland	Lotus 19 Climax	1st/FL/LR
May 12th	International Trophy Race	Silverstone	Innes Ireland	Ferrari Dino	4th
			Masten Gregory	Lotus Climax	8th

Enzo Ferrari personally loaned the Ferrari Dino 156/61 F1 team car to the British Racing Partnership for this event, prepared and supported by the Ferrari team mechanics.

Date	Race	Circuit	Driver	Car	Result
May 12th	Sports Car Race	Silverstone	Innes Ireland	Lotus Climax	1st/FL
May 20th	European GP	Zandvoort	Innes Ireland	Lotus Climax	Cra
			Masten Gregory	Lotus Climax	Ret
Jun 3rd	Monaco GP	Monte Carlo	Innes Ireland	Lotus Climax	Ret
			Masten Gregory	Lotus BRM	FTQ
Jun 9th	Players 200	Mosport Park, Canada	Masten Gregory	Lotus 19 Climax	1st
			Innes Ireland	Ferrari Dino246S	Ret

Works Ferrari Targa Florio winning car loaned to BRP.

Date	Race	Circuit	Driver	Car	Result
Jun 11th	2,000 Guineas	Mallory Park	Masten Gregory	Lotus Climax	5th
Jun 11th	Crystal Palace Trophy	Crystal Palace	Innes Ireland	Lotus BRM	1st/FL

Date	Event	Location	Driver	Car	Result
Jun 17th	Belgian GP	Spa	Innes Ireland	Lotus Climax	Wdr
			Masten Gregory	Lotus BRM	Wdr

Innes Ireland came in for an unscheduled pit stop on lap 8 complaining of poor handling. An inspection revealed cracked rear wishbone anchorage points. Both cars were immediately withdrawn as a safety measure.

Date	Event	Location	Driver	Car	Result
June 23/4	Le Mans 24 Hours	Le Mans	Innes Ireland	Ferrari	Ret
			Masten Gregory		

Retirement caused by dynamo failure after 10 hours. At the time it was leading the GT category.

| | | | Les Leston | Lotus 23 Climax | DNS |
| | | | Tony Shelley | 742cc | |

Scrutineers refused to allow the car to start. They alleged an infringement of the regulations relating to the wheel fixings. They also banned the works Lotus 23 2-litre entry on the same basis. Damages were subsequently paid to both teams.

Date	Event	Location	Driver	Car	Result
Jul 1st	Rheims GP	Rheims	Innes Ireland	Lotus Climax	3rd
			Masten Gregory	Lotus BRM	Ret
Jul 8th	French GP	Rouen	Innes Ireland	Lotus Climax	Ret
			Masten Gregory	Lotus BRM	Ret
Jul 14th	Scott-Brown Trophy Race	Snetterton	Graham Hill	Lotus 19 Climax	1st/LR

First 100mph lap by a sports car at Snetterton 1-36.8 secs 100.79 mph.

Date	Event	Location	Driver	Car	Result
Jul 21st	British GP	Aintree	Innes Ireland	Lotus Climax	NC
			Masten Gregory	Lotus BRM	7th
Jul 29th	Hoosier GP	Indianapolis	Innes Ireland	Lotus Climax	NC
Aug 5th	Guards Trophy	Brands Hatch	Innes Ireland	Lotus 19 Climax	2nd
	Peco Trophy	Brands Hatch	Innes Ireland	Ferrari GTO	3rd

Date	Race	Location	Driver	Car	Result
Aug 12th	Kannonloppet	Karlskoga, Sweden	Innes Ireland	Lotus Climax	4th/FL
			Masten Gregory	Lotus BRM	1st
Aug 18th	Tourist Trophy Race	Goodwood	Innes Ireland	Ferrari GTO	1st
Aug 26th	Danish GP	Copenhagen	Innes Ireland	Lotus Climax	3rd
			Masten Gregory	Lotus BRM	2nd
Sep 1st	International Trophy Race	Oulton Park	Innes Ireland	Lotus Climax	Ret
			Masten Gregory	Lotus BRM	6th
Sep 1st	Sports Car Race	Oulton Park	Innes Ireland	Lotus 19 Climax	1st
Sep 12th	Italian GP	Monza	Innes Ireland	Lotus Climax	Ret
			Masten Gregory	Lotus BRM	12th
Sep 22nd	Canadian GP Sports Cars	Mosport Park, Canada	Masten Gregory	Lotus 19 Climax	1st
Oct 7th	USA GP	Watkins Glen	Innes Ireland	Lotus Climax	8th
			Masten Gregory	Lotus BRM	6th
			Roger Penske	Lotus BRM	9th
Oct 14th	Sports Car GP	Riverside, California	Masten Gregory	Lotus 19 Climax	3rd
Oct 21st	Pacific GP	Laguna Seca, California	Masten Gregory	Lotus 19 Climax	6th
Nov 4th	Mexican GP	Mexico City	Innes Ireland	Lotus Climax	3rd
			Masten Gregory	Lotus BRM	5th
Dec 29th	S African GP	East London	Innes Ireland	Lotus Climax	5th

1963 · BRITISH RACING PARTNERSHIP

Date	Event	Location	Driver	Car	Result
Mar 30th	Lombank Trophy	Snetterton	Innes Ireland	Lotus BRM	3rd
			Jim Hall	Lotus BRM	6th
	Sports Car Race		Innes Ireland	Lotus 19 Climax	Ret
Apr 15th	Glover Trophy	Goodwood	Innes Ireland	Lotus BRM	1st
			Jim Hall	Lotus BRM	4th
Apr 15th	Lavant Cup	Goodwood	Innes Ireland	Lotus 19 Climax	4th OA/FL 3rd in class
Apr 27th	Aintree 200	Aintree	Innes Ireland	Lotus BRM	2nd
			Jim Hall	Lotus BRM	New F1 LR/FL Ret
Apr 27th	Sports Car Race		Innes Ireland	Lotus 19 Climax	2nd
May 5th	International Trophy Race	Silverstone	Innes Ireland	Lotus BRM	4th/PP/FL Ret
May 5th	Sports Car Race		Innes Ireland	Lotus 19 Climax	2nd
May 26th	Monaco GP	Monte Carlo	Innes Ireland	Lotus BRM	Ret
			Jim Hall	Lotus BRM	Ret
Jun 9th	Belgian GP	Spa	Innes Ireland	BRP/1 BRM	Ret
			Jim Hall	Lotus BRM	Ret
Jun 23rd	Dutch GP	Zandvoort	Innes Ireland	BRP/1 BRM	4th
			Jim Hall	Lotus BRM	8th
Jun 30th	French GP	Reims	Innes Ireland	BRP/1 BRM	9th
			Jim Hall	Lotus BRM	11th

Date	Event	Location	Driver	Car	Result
Jul 20th	British GP	Silverstone	Innes Ireland Jim Hall	BRP/1 BRM Lotus BRM	Disq 6th
Jul 28th	Solitude GP	Stuttgart	Innes Ireland Jim Hall	BRP/1 BRM Lotus BRM	3rd 6th
Aug 8th	German GP	Nürburgring	Innes Ireland Jim Hall	BRP/1 BRM Lotus BRM	Ret 5th

Innes Ireland's car damaged by Bandini making an overambitious overtaking attempt.

Date	Event	Location	Driver	Car	Result
Sep 1st	Austrian GP	Zeltweg	Innes Ireland Jim Hall	Lotus BRM Lotus BRM	8th Ret
Sep 8th	Italian GP	Monza	Innes Ireland Jim Hall	BRP/1 BRM Lotus BRM	4th 8th
Sep 21st	International Gold Cup	Oulton Park	Innes Ireland Mike Beckwith	Lotus BRM Lotus BRM	Ret Cra
Oct 6th	United States GP	Watkins Glen	Jim Hall	Lotus BRM	Ret
Oct 27th	Mexican GP	Mexico City	Jim Hall	Lotus BRM	8th

1964 · BRITISH RACING PARTNERSHIP

Date	Event	Location	Driver	Car	Result
Mar 14th	Daily Mirror Trophy	Snetterton	Innes Ireland Trevor Taylor	BRP/1 BRM Lotus BRM	1st Ret
Mar 30th	News Of The World Trophy	Goodwood	Innes Ireland Trevor Taylor	BRP/1 BRM Lotus BRM	Cra 3rd
Apr 18th	Aintree 200	Aintree	Innes Ireland Trevor Taylor	BRP/2 BRM BRP/1 BRM	Ret Ret

Date	Race	Venue	Driver	Car	Result
May 2nd	International Trophy	Silverstone	Innes Ireland	BRP/2 BRM	12th
			Trevor Taylor	BRP/1 BRM	Ret
May 10th	Monaco GP	Monte Carlo	Innes Ireland	Lotus BRM	DNS
			Trevor Taylor	BRP/1 BRM	Ret

Innes Ireland crashed two cars in practice, one being a write off. He was annoyed when the team would not give him Taylor's car for the race. He was then involved in a further crash in the Nice Airport tunnel with a hire car. It was neither his, nor BRP's week.

Date	Race	Venue	Driver	Car	Result
Jun 14th	Belgian GP	Spa	Innes Ireland	BRP/1 BRM	10th
			Trevor Taylor	BRP/2 BRM	7th

First appearance of BRP/3 BRM. Used in practice but not raced.

Date	Race	Venue	Driver	Car	Result
Jun 28th	French GP	Rouen Les Essarts	Innes Ireland	BRP/1 BRM	Cra
			Trevor Taylor	BRP/2 BRM	Ret
Jul 11th	British GP	Brands Hatch	Innes Ireland	BRP/2 BRM	10th
			Trevor Taylor	Lotus BRM	Ret
Jul 19th	Solitude GP	Stuttgart	Innes Ireland	BRP/2 BRM	Cra
			Trevor Taylor	Lotus BRM	6th

The race started with the track awash from heavy rain. Seven cars including Ireland were involved in incidents on the first lap caused by spinning cars.

Date	Race	Venue	Driver	Car	Result
Aug 16th	Mediterraneo GP	Pergusa	Innes Ireland	BRP/2 BRM	3rd
			Trevor Taylor	BRP/1 BRM	Ret
Aug 23rd	Austrian GP	Zeltweg	Innes Ireland	BRP/2 BRM	5th
			Trevor Taylor	BRP/1 BRM	Ret

Sep 6th	Italian GP	Innes Ireland	BRP/2 BRM	5th
		Trevor Taylor	BRP/1 BRM	DNQ
Oct 4th	United States GP	Innes Ireland	BRP/2 BRM	Ret
		Trevor Taylor	BRP/3 BRM	6th
Oct 25th	Mexican GP	Innes Ireland	BRP/2 BRM	12th
		Trevor Taylor	BRP/3 BRM	Ret

In the seven year period of 1958 to 1964, the following drivers in alphabetical order, were engaged to drive the team cars of the British Racing Partnership:

Cliff Allison · Mike Beckwith · Lucian Bianchi · Jo Bonnier · Juan Manuel Bordeo · Tommy Bridger · Chris Bristow Tony Brooks · Ivor Bueb · Olivier Gendebien · Masten Gregory · Dan Gurney · Bruce Halford · Jim Hall Hans Herrmann · Graham Hill (World Champion) · Phil Hill (World Champion) · Denny Hulme (World Champion) Gunnar Hammerlund · Innes Ireland · Les Leston · Stuart Lewis-Evans · Mike McKee · Stirling Moss · Michael Parkes Roger Penske · Harry Schell · Jack Sears · Tony Shelley · Henry Taylor · Trevor Taylor · George Wicken

Bibliography

There is a growing body of work which covers motor racing in the late 1950's and early 1960's and this is not really a place to evaluate it. Suffice to say that the contemporary accounts, as found in Autosport, Motor Sport, Motor Racing, The Autocar and Motor, are often the most reliable, at least in terms of statistical input. However, it is also fair to say that the business of reporting motor racing was different then; as I discovered when researching Archie and the Listers, there was present then an overlay of taste, of distance, which is perhaps sometimes absent now.

The reasons for this of course are money, product placement, marketing needs, sponsorship demands and so forth. Nothing wrong with this of course, save that there is a risk that the sheer effort, risk, courage and simple curiosity that makes motor racing so fascinating also brings with it the baggage of commercialism which, in many ways negates why people do it.

Here, though, is a list of sources; some of them contained simple fact which bellow acknowledgement, others merely provide simple matters of technical fact and still more offer a simpler, perhaps purer view of why people pursue this oddest of sports, this search for excellence, at the risk of everything.

Nye, D.
Cooper Cars. (Osprey, 1983) ✓

Ireland, I.
All Arms and Elbows. (Pelham Books, 1967) ✓

Nixon C.
Racing with the David Brown Aston Martins. ✓
(Transport Bookman, 1980)

[handwritten margin note:] PITY AUTHOR DIDN'T REA[D] THE BRM BOOK BY NYE — THERE WOULD BE LESS ERRO[R]

Hayhoe, D. & Holland, D.
The Grand Prix Data Book. *(D.H. Publications, 1995)*

Yates, B.
Enzo Ferrari. *(Doubleday, 1991)*

Jenkinson, D.
The Racing Driver. *(B. T. Batsford, 1962)*

Jenkinson, D. (& Others)
The Racing Car. *(B.T. Batsford, 1963)*

Purdey, K.
All But My Life. *(Pan, 1962)*

Posthumous, C.
Behind the Scenes of Motor Racing. *(William Kimber, 1959)*

Bamsey, I.
Vanwall 2.5 litre F1; a technical appraisal. *(Haynes, 1990)*

Hall, A.
Maserati 250F; a technical appraisal. *(Haynes, 1990)*

Pritchard, A. & Salvadori, R.
Roy Salvadori – Racing Driver. *(PSL, 1985)*

Ortenburger, D.
Flying on Four Wheels. *(PSL 1986)*

Johnson, C.
To Draw a Long Line. *(Bookmarque Publishing, 1989)*

Whyte, A.
Jaguar Sports, Racing & Competition Cars, vol I & II. *(Haynes, 1987)*.

Clark, J.
Jim Clark at the Wheel. *(Arthur Barker, 1964)*.

Slater, J.
Return to Go. *(Weidenfeld and Nicholson, 1977)*.

Wansell, G.
Tycoon. *(Grafton Books, 1987)*.

Index

Clarke, Rodney 170
Collier, Stan 256
Collins, Peter John 29, 39, 160-1, 163, 164, 165, 167, 172, 173, 187, 188, 189
Colombo, Gioacchino 77, 79, 84, 94
Colotti, Valerio 84-5, 200, 211, 278
Connaught Engineering (Send) 42, 78, 138, 168, 170, 176, 177
contract renegotiation 235-6
Cooper Car Company (Surbiton) 42, 45, 78, 80, 168, 197, 211
Cooper T45 178
Cooper T51 226, 237
Cooper, Charles 24-5, 30, 242, 244-5
Cooper, John 30, 182
Cooper, John A. (*Autocar*) 40, 73
Cooper, Michael 265
Cooper-Alta 74, 75, 78
Cooper-Borgward 198, 199, 205, 208, 226
Cooper-Climax 179, 184, 185
Cooper-JAP 47
Coplestone, Trevor 312
Costin, Frank 169, 288
Coventry Climax 78, 138, 178, 243, 248, 253
Craufurd, General Sir Robert 'Black Bob' 27
Creative Print and Design 335

Davis, Colin 163
Davis, S.C.H. 163
de Beaufort, Count Carel 116
de Gebert, Teddy 199
de Graffenried, Baron Emanuel 116
de Portago, Marquis 'Fon' 116, 163, 172, 212-13
Delamont, Dean 40
Denham (Bucks) 296, 310
Docker, Lady Norah 137
Duke's Head Yard (Highgate) 246, 272, 338
Dundrod TT 49-50, 56, 75

Ecclestone, Bernie 170, 176, 178, 179, 239, 296, 336, 337
England, F.R.W. 'Lofty' (Jaguar racing manager) 50, 51, 80, 192, 193
ERA 48, 49, 63
Esso 85, 245
Express Coachcraft 206, 225, 239, 242, 245, 270, 275

Fangio, Juan Manuel 54, 59, 80, 82, 87, 95, 99, 104, 114, 115, 120, 121, 122, 127, 128, 129, 135, 153, 154, 163, 164-5, 168, 172, 173, 180, 181, 250
Farina, Giuseppe 59, 62
Ferrari 156 243
Ferrari 250 GTO 247, 266, 275
Ferrari, Alfredo 'Dino' 165, 267
Ferrari, Enzo 52, 53, 54, 55, 56, 64, 77, 172, 184, 187, 193, 211, 243, 250, 252, 266, 285, 287
Ferrari politics 169, 216, 273, 285
Fitch, John 143, 154, 156
Flockhart, Ron 208
Florio, Vincenzo 161
FOCA 285, 295
Forghieri, Mauro 216
Francis, Alf 41, 42, 45, 52, 58, 73, 75, 78, 97, 100, 101, 104, 113, 114, 119, 120, 131, 165, 168, 181-2, 200, 254, 278, 338
Frankenheimer, John 296-7
Frère, Paul 163

Galvez, Oscar 113
Garnier, Peter (*Autocar*) 281
Gendebien, Olivier 163, 233, 244
Gibson-Jarvie, Bob 242, 246
Gilby Engineering 85, 87, 88
Ginther, Ritchie 232, 238, 243
Glenridding 22
Glider Pilot regiment 23
Godiva V8 engine 78, 138
Goldsmith, Jimmy 325, 326, 331
Gonzalez, Froilan 53, 54, 55, 59, 77, 87, 95, 96, 103, 104, 115, 135, 210
Goodwood (May Day 1963) 280
Greene, Syd 85, 86
Gregory Air 309-17
Gregory, Christopher 249, 291
Gregory, John 22, 178
Gregory, Julie 339
Gregory, Masten 116, 173, 251, 275, 292-4, 329
Gregory, Nem 246, 315
Guerin, Rod 291
Gurney, Dan 292

Halford, Bruce 176
Hall, Jim 282
Hamilton, Duncan 38

Sheikh bin Ladin 314
Shell Mex & BP 85, 117, 128, 132, 133
Shepherd Street 249, 252, 269, 308, 339
Simon, André 59, 154, 160
Slater Walker 324
Slater, Jim 320, 324, 325, 330
Smith, Bill 160
Speed and Sports Publications Ltd 248, 307, 320
Spencer, Derek 176, 178, 179, 187
Sperrin, Ted 319, 332
sponsorship 194
Stacey, Alan 177, 230, 231, 232-3
Stasse, Pierre 234
Steinberg, Saul 319
Stewart, Jackie 234-5, 331
Stirling Moss Automobile Racing Team (SMART) 288, 296
Stirling Moss Ltd 133, 134, 137, 154, 248, 269, 271, 274, 275, 282, 285, 306, 307
Straight, Whitney 51, 89, 92, 175
Strudwick, Ann 256
Studio Tecnica Meccanica 278
Suez crisis (October 1956) 170
Sunday Sun 335
Surtees, John 237

Targa Florio 161
Taruffi, Piero 55, 59
Tavoni, Romolo 187, 188
Taylor, David 312
Taylor, Geoffrey 42, 59, 73
Taylor, Henry 227, 229, 233, 237, 244
Taylor, Mike 230-1
Taylor, Trevor 232, 284
Thinwall Special 169
This is Your Life (1959) 52
Thomson Regional Newspapers 335-6
Thornton, Robert 171, 195, 197, 225, 238, 239-40, 275, 276
Tiger Moth (flying lessons) 23
Tilling, James 255
Titterington, Desmond 159, 160
Tojeiro 42
Tresilian, Stuart 201
Trintignant, Maurice 114, 183, 199, 254, 267
Tshombe, Moise 312, 313
Turle, Bryan (Shell Mex & BP competitions manager) 128, 175

two-way radio 178
Tyrrell, Ann (to become Mrs Ken Gregory) 167, 238

UDT-Laystall 246, 247, 250, 266, 267, 272, 273
Uhlenhaut, Rudolf 78, 80, 129, 130, 131, 134, 135, 158
United Dominions Trust 196, 205, 206, 207, 242
United Racing Stable 206

Vandervell, G.A. 'Tony' 126, 169, 170, 179, 192, 193, 202, 205
Vanwall (Park Royal) 42, 138, 168, 169, 176, 177, 178, 185, 191, 193, 197, 213
Villoresi, Luigi 59, 87, 102, 114, 119, 121
von Trips, Count Wolfgang 'Taffy' 116, 159, 160, 208, 232, 243, 247

Walker Cooper-BRM 200
Walker, Peter 56, 62
Walker, Rob 168, 180, 183, 197, 199, 204, 216, 229, 247, 248, 250, 252, 265, 267, 269, 338
Walker-Cooper 180
Wells, Gardner Darton 318-20, 332
Westhampnett aerodrome 25-6
Wharton, Ken 115
White Cloud Farm (Tring) 57, 176, 179
White, Gordon 311, 312
Whitehead, Peter 59, 73
Wicken, George 197, 198
Wickens, David 315
Wiles Group (later Hanson Trust) 311, 320
Wisdom, Anne 50, 57
Wisdom, Tommy (*Daily Herald*) 50
Woodward, George 293
Wyer, John 161

Yeoman Credit 196, 206, 207, 211, 212, 215, 225, 226, 238-40, 241, 245, 275-6
Yorke, David 168

MANAGING A LEGEND